Ego Intelligence

Ego Intelligence

The Architecture of Defense

Glenn Short

ISBN: 979-8-9950238-0-7   Paperback Edition

ISBN: 979-8-9950238-1-4   Hardcover Edition

ISBN: 979-8-9950238-2-1   Digital Online

To Lisa, Skyler, and Taylor

**You amplify everything that is good in this
world and I love you.**

Acknowledgements

To all my students who have enrolled in my Emotional Intelligence courses over the years — you have validated much of the original work in this book, and I appreciate our lengthy discussions.

To Dr. Barbara Tucker, for allowing me to develop the Emotional Intelligence course at SRSU that inspired much of this work.

To Dr. Juan Pedro Martínez Ramón at the University of Murcia, Spain, for offering support during my work.

To Dr. Chuck Coker, for your guidance and support to me and the students at SRSU over the years.

To Dr. Gary Low and Dr. Richard Hammett, for your ongoing support and guidance.

To my wife Lisa, for supporting me patiently and loving me graciously.

Contents

Part I: Foundations

Part II: The Three Faces of Ego

Preface

From a Lecture Hall to Ego Intelligence
The 17-Year Journey of Discovery

The Catalyst (2007)

In 2007, I was a newly licensed professional counselor in private practice, searching for something I couldn't quite name. I knew there was an element in my therapeutic approach that created awareness in clients, but I lacked the language to describe it. That changed when I attended a lecture by Dr. Gary Low and Dr. Darwin Nelson on their Transformative Emotional Intelligence model.

Sitting in that lecture hall, something clicked. As a cognitive behavioral therapist, I'd been working with thoughts and behaviors, but emotional intelligence provided the missing link—the systematic understanding of how emotional skills could be developed. More importantly, it gave me a framework to begin investigating what I'd been sensing: that people possessed capabilities they couldn't consistently access.

The Laboratory Begins (2008-2009)

The real work began in 2008 when I started collaborating with Brian Humphries, who was providing assessments for displaced workers with disabling conditions. Working with the Texas Rehabilitation Commission (later renamed the Department of Assistive and Rehabilitative Services), Brian and I would spend hours debriefing assessment results with my clients, helping them understand their individual potential.

Those debriefing sessions became my laboratory. We weren't just reviewing scores—we were witnessing patterns. The assessments—TTI Driving Forces, DISC, Hartman Value

Profile, Quality of Motivation—were revealing something profound about why people with high potential and intelligence still struggled to access their capabilities.

While my journey with emotional intelligence began in 2007, it was in 2009 when Brian and I began our systematic assessment reviews that the intensive pattern recognition work started—the 15 years of focused observation that would eventually reveal Ego Intelligence.

The Pattern Recognition Years (2009-2015)

Over the next six years, Brian and I reviewed hundreds of assessments together. I began to notice marked trends that deserved closer investigation. Without realizing it, I was conducting informal research—gathering similar assessment results, grouping them, and asking additional questions during debriefing. What I didn't know was that I was collecting external validation data. What I did know was that these assessments were capturing something that needed a different vantage point to fully understand.

The patterns were unmistakable:

- Brilliant people who couldn't access their intelligence when threatened
- High EQ individuals whose emotional skills disappeared in certain situations
- Talented professionals who sabotaged themselves repeatedly despite insight

Simultaneously, I'd begun teaching emotional intelligence at Sul Ross State University, using these same assessments with students. The classroom became another laboratory, confirming the patterns I was seeing in clinical practice.

The Missing Piece (2015-2017)

In 2015, Mike Drinkard, Director of the Crisis Center in West Texas, recommended Don Miguel Ruiz's "The Four Agreements." This book introduced me to Ruiz's conception of the ego through two voices: the Judge and the Victim.

I immediately applied this concept to the assessment patterns I'd been tracking for six years. It explained much, but not everything. There was a third pattern Ruiz hadn't described—those who used knowledge and expertise as their primary defense. I called it "The Expert."

The three faces of ego were born:

The Expert uses knowledge as armor, **the Judge** uses criticism as control, and **the Victim** uses helplessness as protection.

While I'd been observing these patterns since 2009, I finally had names for them.

Integration and Loss (2017-2021)

In 2017, I updated my emotional intelligence lectures to include this theory of ego faces as an element of self-management. Students began recognizing these patterns immediately. The concept resonated in ways that pure emotional intelligence theory hadn't.

Brian and I continued our collaboration, refining our understanding of how these patterns showed up across different assessment tools. We were building something significant, though we didn't fully know what yet.

Then in 2021, Brian passed away. His death was not just a personal loss but threatened the continuation of this work we'd built together over thirteen years.

The Work Continues (2021-Present)

After Brian's passing, I began working with his mentor, Dr. Chuck Coker, who provided updated training on the assessment instruments and continues to support our students at SRSU. This new collaboration brought fresh perspectives to the patterns Brian and I had been tracking.

With Dr. Coker's expertise in assessment interpretation and my years of pattern recognition, the full picture finally emerged. The ego patterns weren't separate from emotional intelligence—they were what blocked access to it. They weren't character flaws—they were defensive architectures that could be mapped and understood.

The Discovery of Ego Intelligence

The breakthrough came when I realized I hadn't been discovering new patterns—I'd been documenting a meta-capacity: the ability to see one's own defensive architecture operating. This wasn't just another form of intelligence to add to IQ and EQ. This was the intelligence that determined whether you could access your other intelligences when you needed them most.

Ego Intelligence emerged not as a theory but as an observed phenomenon:

- The capacity to recognize when defensive patterns activate
- The ability to understand what they're protecting
- The choice to engage or not engage the defense
- The skill to maintain access to other capabilities despite threat

Why This Book Now

After seventeen years since that first emotional intelligence lecture, and fifteen years of intensive pattern observation since

2009, the patterns are undeniable. The ego operates through three primary narratives—Expert, Judge, Victim—that can hijack our emotional intelligence, corrupt our thinking, and sabotage our lives.

But more importantly, we can develop intelligence to see these patterns operating. We can learn to recognize our own defensive architecture. We can choose conscious responses rather than unconscious reactions.

This book is dedicated to Brian Humphries, whose curiosity and dedication made this discovery possible, and to the hundreds of clients and students who trusted me with their assessment results and their stories. Every concept in these pages comes from patterns you helped me see.

The question isn't whether you have these patterns—we all do. The question is whether you can develop the intelligence to see them, understand them, and choose when they serve you and when they don't.

That capacity, Ego Intelligence, can be developed. This book will show you how, using the same journey of discovery that took seventeen years to unfold, with fifteen years of intensive pattern recognition at its core, distilled into principles you can apply immediately.

Welcome to the architecture of human defense, and more importantly, to the intelligence that sets us free from it.

Ego Intelligence

The Architecture of Defense

Glenn Short

Chapter 1: What Is Ego Intelligence?

>> What You'll Learn in This Chapter

- Why traditional intelligence isn't enough to prevent self-sabotage
- How Gardner's Multiple Intelligence theory paves the way for understanding Ego Intelligence
- The three defensive patterns that hijack our best intentions
- The four intensity levels that determine how deeply patterns control us
- Why Ego Intelligence deserves recognition as a distinct intelligence
- How to begin recognizing your own patterns and their intensity

Reading Time: ~25 minutes

"The greatest enemy of knowledge is not ignorance, it is the illusion of knowledge." - Stephen Hawking

Sarah sits in the conference room, presenting her analysis of the new database architecture when Tom, a junior developer, raises his hand. "Actually, Sarah, I think there might be an issue with your connection pooling calculation. If we're expecting 500 concurrent users, wouldn't we need more than the 50 connections you've allocated?"

Sarah feels her chest tighten. Tom is right—she made an error in her math, transposing numbers in her spreadsheet. She knows it but hearing the correction from someone with half her experience triggers something deeper. Instead of acknowledging the mistake, she doubled down.

"Tom, connection pooling is more complex than you realize. The 50 connections account for connection reuse patterns that aren't immediately obvious to someone

without enterprise-level experience. Let me explain the advanced concepts you're missing..."

For the next ten minutes, Sarah creates an elaborate justification for her error, weaving together technical jargon and condescending explanations. She watches Tom's face flush and sees her other colleagues shift uncomfortably. Deep down, she knows she's wrong, but she can't seem to stop herself from proving she's right.

Later, walking to her car, Sarah feels a familiar knot in her stomach. She's technically brilliant, respected for her expertise, but increasingly isolated from her team. She's experiencing something millions of us face daily: being unconsciously driven by defensive patterns that prioritize psychological safety over truth, relationships, or effectiveness. She has traditional intelligence in abundance, but she lacks what we might call "Ego Intelligence", the capacity to recognize and consciously work with the defensive patterns that unconsciously drive our behavior.

What Sarah couldn't see in that moment was that she was trapped in a defensive pattern so deeply ingrained that being right had become necessary for her self-worth. Her considerable intelligence and emotional awareness were hijacked by an automatic response that made her prioritize protecting her expert identity over acknowledging a simple error.

Expanding Our Understanding of Intelligence - Gardner's Framework

To understand Ego Intelligence, we must first expand our conception of what intelligence means. For much of the twentieth century, intelligence was viewed through a narrow lens—primarily as the ability to solve logical problems, manipulate abstract symbols, and perform well on standardized tests. This view gave us the familiar IQ score, a single number meant to capture the essence of human cognitive ability.

This perspective began to shift dramatically with the groundbreaking work of Harvard psychologist Howard Gardner. In his revolutionary theory of Multiple Intelligences (1983), Gardner challenged the notion that intelligence could be captured by a single metric. Instead, he proposed that human beings possess several distinct types of intelligence, each representing different ways of processing information and solving problems.

What makes Gardner's framework so powerful is its recognition that intelligence isn't just about raw cognitive horsepower—it's about how we apply our mental capacities to real-world challenges. Each type of intelligence represents a different lens through which we can understand and interact with our environment.

For those who want to understand the scientific basis for Ego Intelligence as a legitimate intelligence, Gardner established eight criteria any new intelligence must meet. These eight criteria provide a scientific framework for evaluating whether proposed intelligence represents a genuine, distinct human capacity:

1. Potential of Isolation by Brain Damage

Gardner argues that if a specific intelligence exists, damage to brain regions should be able to impair that intelligence while leaving other intelligences relatively intact. This neurological criterion suggests that different intelligences have distinct neural substrates, so localized brain injury should create selective deficits rather than general cognitive decline.

2. Evolutionary History and Evolutionary Plausibility

A legitimate intelligence should have deep evolutionary roots and serve adaptive functions that contribute to human survival and reproduction. Gardner looks for evidence that the cognitive capacity existed in ancestral species and provided evolutionary advantages, demonstrating that the intelligence emerged through natural selection processes.

3. Identifiable Core Operations or Set of Operations

Each intelligence must have specific, identifiable mental processes or operations that are central to its functioning. These core operations should be distinct from other intelligences and represent the fundamental cognitive mechanisms that drive that particular form of intelligent behavior.

4. Susceptibility to Encoding in a Symbol System

Gardner believes that true intelligences can be captured and expressed through symbol systems, whether linguistic, mathematical, musical notation, visual representations, or other symbolic forms. Intelligences should be capable of being represented, communicated, and transmitted through culturally developed symbolic means.

5. Distinct Developmental History and Definable Set of Expert "End State" Performances

Each intelligence should follow a recognizable developmental trajectory from early emergence through expert-level performance. There should be clear stages of development and identifiable "end states" where individuals demonstrate mastery—such as becoming a master musician, mathematician, or athlete—that represent the pinnacle of that intelligence.

6. Existence of Savants, Prodigies, and Other Exceptional People

Gardner looks for individuals who show extraordinary ability in one intelligence while being average or impaired in others. The existence of savants (exceptional ability despite overall cognitive limitations) and prodigies (exceptional early development) suggests that intelligences can operate independently and be selectively enhanced.

7. Support from Experimental Psychology Tasks

The intelligence should be measurable and observable through controlled psychological experiments. There should be research evidence demonstrating the distinct cognitive processes, showing how this intelligence operates differently from others, and validating its unique characteristics through empirical study.

8. Support from Psychometric Findings

Traditional psychometric testing should provide evidence for the intelligence's distinctness. This includes factor analysis showing that abilities cluster together in meaningful ways, correlational studies demonstrating how this intelligence relates to (but differs from) other cognitive abilities, and standardized assessments that can reliably measure the intelligence.

These criteria work together to establish whether a proposed intelligence represents a genuine, distinct form of human cognitive capacity rather than simply a subset of general intelligence or a combination of existing intelligences.

Using these criteria, Gardner identified eight primary intelligences that met his classification model and became the foundation of Multiple Intelligence theory:

1. **Linguistic Intelligence**
2. **Logical-Mathematical Intelligence**
3. **Spatial Intelligence**
4. **Musical Intelligence**
5. **Bodily-Kinesthetic Intelligence**
6. **Interpersonal Intelligence**
7. **Intrapersonal Intelligence**
8. **Naturalistic Intelligence**

The Evolution of Emotional Intelligence

Building particularly on Gardner's interpersonal and intrapersonal intelligences, researchers have developed increasingly sophisticated models of what we now call Emotional Intelligence (EQ), a term coined by Salovey and Mayer in 1990. Most models define emotional intelligence as the ability to recognize, understand, and effectively work with emotions in ourselves and others.

Modern emotional intelligence frameworks identify several core domains that expand our understanding of how intelligent behavior operates in the emotional and social realm. These emotional intelligence capabilities represent sophisticated forms of applied intelligence that are essential for navigating our complex social and professional world. They demonstrate that truly effective human functioning requires not just cognitive ability, but also the intelligence to work skillfully with the emotional and relational dimensions of experience.

If you're a counselor, therapist, or someone committed to personal development, you've likely encountered many approaches to emotional intelligence from Salovey and Mayer, Daniel Goleman, or other authors. However, Transformative Emotional Intelligence (TEI) offers something uniquely practical and comprehensive. Developed by researchers Gary Low, Darwin Nelson, and Richard Hammett, TEI is based on a simple but powerful premise: emotional intelligence is "the learned ability to think constructively and act wisely." What sets TEI apart is that it treats emotional intelligence not as a fixed trait you either have or don't have, but as a collection of specific, learnable skills that anyone can develop with practice and intention.

The TEI framework organizes these skills into four essential life domains that work together to create personal effectiveness and well-being.

The first domain, **Intrapersonal Skills**, focuses on your relationship with yourself and includes Self-Esteem (viewing yourself as competent and valuable), Stress Management (effectively handling life's pressures), and Positive Change (knowing how and when to adapt and grow).

The second domain, **Interpersonal Skills**, centers on how you communicate and connect with others through Assertion (expressing yourself clearly and honestly), Anger Management (handling conflict constructively), and Anxiety Management (communicating confidently even when feeling nervous or uncertain).

The third domain, **Leadership Skills**, develops your ability to understand and positively influence others through Social Awareness (reading social situations and building rapport), Empathy (accurately understanding others' feelings and perspectives), Decision Making (solving problems systematically), and Positive Influence (inspiring and motivating others in healthy ways).

Finally, **Self-Management Skills** help you direct your life purposefully through Drive Strength (setting and achieving meaningful goals), Time Management (organizing your responsibilities effectively), and Commitment Ethic (following through on your promises and completing what you start).

What makes TEI especially valuable is its integration of both logical thinking and emotional wisdom—recognizing that our best decisions come when we use both our rational mind and our emotional intelligence together. The approach emphasizes "constructive thinking," which means learning to interpret and respond to life's challenges in ways that promote growth rather than getting stuck in reactive patterns. For counselors and individuals seeking change, TEI provides both assessment tools to identify current strengths and growth areas, plus a systematic five-step learning process that moves from self-exploration to real-world application. Rather than focusing on what's wrong or broken, TEI builds from existing strengths while systematically developing the specific skills needed for healthier relationships, better stress management, more effective communication, and greater life satisfaction. The ultimate goal is helping people become more aware and invested in how they navigate both their inner world and their relationships with others.

However, there's a critical challenge that undermines all these emotional intelligence domains: the seemingly unconscious influence of ego-driven defensive patterns. When we're operating from ego protection rather than authentic self-expression, our capacity for genuine self-insight becomes clouded by self-deception. Our self-regulation efforts become rigid control mechanisms rather than flexible and genuine responses. Our interpersonal perception gets filtered through defensive assumptions about others' motives. Our relationship cultivation becomes manipulative rather than genuinely connective. Even our visionary guidance becomes about maintaining our image rather than serving genuine purpose.

The ego's fundamental drive is to separate us from our authentic self—to create a protective false identity that prioritizes psychological safety over truth, genuine connection, or effective action.

When Sarah doubled down on her wrong calculation in that conference room, every aspect of her considerable emotional intelligence was hijacked by her ego's need to maintain her expert identity. She knew she was wrong (compromised self-insight), couldn't regulate her defensive reaction (impaired self-regulation), misread the room's dynamics (distorted interpersonal perception), damaged relationships through condescension (failed relationship cultivation), and abandoned her leadership role in favor of self-protection (corrupted visionary guidance).

This is why ego management deserves recognition as a distinct and foundational form of intelligence. While it could theoretically be considered another element of emotional intelligence, the ego's pervasive influence and the daily struggle it presents in every aspect of human functioning warrants its own category. The ego doesn't just interfere with one domain of intelligence—it has the power to corrupt them all by inserting a layer of self-deception between our genuine self and our conscious awareness. Even within Gardner's model of multiple intelligences, ego patterns can distort and inhibit access to functioning genuinely within these domains.

---

*Key Insight

Ego Intelligence addresses capacity ACCESS, not capacity DEVELOPMENT

You can have high emotional intelligence but be unable to use it when defensive patterns create automatic interference. It's not about what you know, it's about what you can access when triggered.

Understanding why Ego Intelligence deserves recognition as a separate intelligence requires examining how it relates to Gardner's existing framework regarding his criteria for intelligence and subsequent developments in emotional intelligence. As stated, Gardner's **Interpersonal Intelligence** (understanding others) and **Intrapersonal Intelligence** (understanding oneself) established the foundation for what later became practical applications like Transformative Emotional Intelligence (TEI), which provides training frameworks for developing these capacities through "thinking constructively and acting wisely."

However, both Gardner's original intelligences and subsequent emotional intelligence frameworks assume that people can access their interpersonal and intrapersonal capabilities when needed. They don't address why highly intelligent, emotionally aware individuals often cannot access these capacities when it matters most. The missing piece is the automatic defensive interference that hijacks our other intelligences—what I call Ego Intelligence.

This creates a crucial distinction: **Gardner's Intelligences and TEI focus on capacity development, while Ego Intelligence addresses capacity access.** You can have high interpersonal intelligence but be unable to use it when your Expert pattern creates automatic interference. You can understand constructive thinking but be blocked from applying it when your Judge pattern's habitual responses activate. Ego Intelligence represents the meta-cognitive ability to recognize and work with these preconscious automatic interferences that operate as learned responses.

To establish the legitimacy of Ego Intelligence as a distinct form of intelligence, I have systematically evaluated it against Gardner's established criteria for identifying authentic intelligences:

Potential of isolation by brain damage: Individuals on the autism spectrum often demonstrate remarkable authenticity and struggle with the social facades that typical ego patterns create, suggesting that automatic defensive interference patterns are neurologically distinct and isolatable. Research shows differences in social brain networks (medial prefrontal cortex, temporal-parietal junction) that are heavily involved in self-concept and learned social responses—the very systems that generate habitual ego defensive patterns. This neurological distinctiveness demonstrates that Ego Intelligence operates through specific brain networks that can be selectively impaired, meeting Gardner's first criterion while showing the pattern recognition capabilities that underline all forms of intelligence.

Evolutionary history and evolutionary plausibility: The three ego patterns I will define in later chapters (Expert, Judge, Victim) evolved as automatic survival responses distinct from general interpersonal/intrapersonal abilities. These learned mechanisms for knowledge/competence (Expert), threat evaluation (Judge), and strategic helplessness (Victim) served specific adaptive functions that became habitual response patterns, different from the broader social and self-awareness capacities Gardner identified. This evolutionary foundation demonstrates the adaptive problem-solving nature of these patterns while explaining why they persist even when no longer appropriate to current contexts.

Identifiable core operations or set of operations: Ego Intelligence demonstrates operations that are fundamentally different from interpersonal/intrapersonal intelligence: automatic pattern recognition (identifying when defensive patterns activate), preconscious interference detection (recognizing when patterns block authentic response), habitual response interruption (creating conscious choice points), contextual evaluation (determining when patterns are helpful versus limiting), and authentic response translation (choosing more effective responses). These operations specifically target the learned automatic interference patterns that block access to other intelligences, demonstrating the metacognitive self-regulation that characterizes sophisticated cognitive functioning.

Susceptibility to encoding in a symbol system: The EJV assessment framework and attachment theory provide symbolic encoding that measures not general emotional or social capacity, but specifically the degree of automatic defensive interference and habitual pattern attachment. This represents a qualitatively different measurement than traditional interpersonal/intrapersonal assessments, with specific symbols and scoring systems that capture the unique operations of Ego Intelligence, demonstrating the learning and memory integration necessary for systematic development.

Distinct developmental history and definable set of expert "end state" performances: The Pattern Intensity framework I utilize provides a developmental framework that moves from automatic defensive responses toward conscious choice, representing a reverse-hierarchical development where mastery involves reducing intensity rather than increasing capacity. Expert end state involves operating at conscious choice rather than automatic habitual reaction, representing mastery over learned interference rather than skill development. This demonstrates the contextual application that allows experts to choose when defensive patterns serve them versus when authentic response is more appropriate.

Existence of savants, prodigies, and other exceptional people: Zen masters and contemplatives like the Dalai Lama demonstrate extraordinary ego intelligence—not just high interpersonal/intrapersonal intelligence, but specifically the ability to interrupt automatic defensive responses under extreme conditions. Humanitarian savants like Mother Teresa showed exceptional capacity to transcend habitual ego patterns. Even ordinary parents demonstrate ego intelligence when they consistently interrupt their automatic Expert (being right), Judge (criticism), and Victim (helplessness) responses for their children's wellbeing, something that requires specific ego management skills beyond general emotional intelligence. These individuals show exceptional pattern recognition and adaptive problem-solving specifically in the domain of defensive pattern management.

Support from experimental psychological tasks: Clinical observations, therapeutic outcomes, and the EJV assessment framework provide empirical support for measuring automatic pattern interference as distinct from general emotional/social capabilities. The framework predicts when people with high traditional intelligence will fail to access their capabilities due to preconscious defensive activation, demonstrating the learning and memory integration that allows for prediction and intervention in defensive pattern cycles.

Support from psychometric findings: The EJV assessment demonstrates reliable measurement of individual differences in automatic pattern recognition and management that are independent of general interpersonal/intrapersonal intelligence scores. People can score high on traditional EI measures while scoring low on ego intelligence, and vice versa, indicating distinct cognitive capacities with the emotional integration necessary for balanced human functioning.

The Logic Chain for Distinct Intelligence:

1. **Gardner established** interpersonal/intrapersonal intelligence as fundamental capacities
2. **TEI and other frameworks** created practical applications for developing these capacities
3. **Both assume** people can access these capacities when needed
4. **Clinical observation reveals** that automatic defensive patterns systematically interfere with access to these capacities

5. **Ego Intelligence addresses** the specific meta-cognitive ability to recognize and work with this preconscious automatic interference
6. **This represents** a fundamentally different cognitive operation—managing learned interference rather than developing conscious capabilities
7. **Therefore,** Ego Intelligence qualifies as a distinct intelligence that enables conscious access to other intelligences

Remarkably, Ego Intelligence meets all eight of Gardner's criteria while demonstrating the core elements that constitute any form of intelligence: sophisticated pattern recognition of defensive activation, adaptive problem-solving when patterns interfere with effectiveness, learning and memory integration that builds defensive awareness over time, contextual application that determines when patterns serve versus limit us, metacognitive self-regulation that creates conscious choice points, and emotional integration that maintains authentic connection even when triggered. Most importantly, it addresses a critical gap that neither Gardner's original framework nor subsequent emotional intelligence models adequately address—the automatic defensive patterns that prevent us from accessing our other cognitive and emotional capabilities when we need them most.

Introducing Ego Intelligence

Building on this foundation, we can now define a new form of intelligence that has profound implications for human functioning: **Ego Intelligence**.

Ego Intelligence is the capacity to recognize, understand, and consciously work with our psychological defense patterns rather than being preconsciously and habitually driven by them. It represents a specific type of intrapersonal intelligence focused on the defensive aspects of the psyche—those automatic, often unconscious patterns we've developed to protect ourselves from perceived threats to our identity, worth, or safety.

Understanding Ego Intelligence requires recognizing that our defensive patterns exist on a spectrum of intensity. The Ego Pattern Intensity scale was inspired by Don Miguel Ruiz Jr.'s Five Levels of Attachment, which brilliantly mapped how humans become progressively identified with their beliefs. While Ruiz's framework addresses attachment to any belief or knowledge, I recognized that his levels perfectly described what I was seeing clinically with the three ego patterns. The Pattern Intensity scale adapts his universal principles specifically for measuring defensive pattern integration, creating a clinical tool that honors spiritual wisdom while providing practical assessment and intervention strategies.

The depth of pattern intensity is fundamentally shaped by neuroplasticity and habit formation—the more we repeat a defensive pattern, the stronger its neural pathways become, making it increasingly automatic and unconscious. At the lowest intensity, we maintain conscious choice about when to engage these patterns. At moderate intensity, these patterns begin to define our identity through repeated reinforcement. At the highest intensity, these patterns become our entire identity, having been etched into our neural architecture through countless repetitions.

Each time we respond to a perceived threat by engaging Expert, Judge, or Victim strategies, we strengthen those neural networks while simultaneously weakening pathways associated with authentic response. This process explains why moving from higher to lower intensity levels becomes increasingly difficult— we're not just changing thoughts or behaviors; we're literally restructuring deeply grooved neural patterns that have become our default operating system.

The Ego Pattern Intensity Scale

The Ego Pattern Intensity Scale provides a crucial framework for understanding how deeply we've integrated these defensive patterns:

Intensity 1: Pattern as Option represents conscious flexibility where patterns are temporarily activated only when genuinely useful. We maintain strong awareness of our true self beyond any single pattern. We can observe and choose patterns without losing self-awareness, and experience moments of pure being without needing defensive strategies. The neural networks remain flexible, allowing authentic response to each situation without automatic defensive activation.

Intensity 2: Pattern as Refuge occurs when patterns become our go-to response for perceived threats, providing temporary relief but creating beginning identity attachment. We maintain intermittent awareness of our authentic self and can still recognize "I am not my pattern," though we increasingly forget this during stress. The pattern creates a thin veil over authentic expression as pathways for defensive responses begin to strengthen through repeated use.

Intensity 3: Pattern as Necessity represents the critical threshold where patterns become required for self-worth. Strong identity fusion occurs—we believe "I am my pattern"—with difficulty functioning without it. We experience only rare glimpses of authentic self, usually in safe, non-triggering moments. The pattern has become the primary filter through which life is experienced, with defensive neural networks now dominating our response system.

Intensity 4: Pattern as Identity occurs when the pattern becomes our entire identity. We cannot conceive alternatives and demand others enable our pattern. Any threat to the pattern feels like a threat to existence itself. We live entirely in what Ruiz calls the "smoke" that obscures true self, with complete disconnection from authentic self. The defensive pattern's neural network has become so dominant that it overrides all other considerations and becomes the standard.

This neurological understanding reveals why traditional therapeutic approaches often struggle with deeply entrenched defensive patterns. Simply gaining insight into these patterns isn't sufficient when they're supported by years or decades of neural reinforcement. Effective intervention requires not just awareness but deliberate, sustained practice of new response patterns to gradually strengthen alternative neural pathways while allowing defensive patterns to weaken through disuse.

The journey back to authentic self involves progressively reconnecting at each intensity level: creating tiny moments of non-pattern identity (from Intensity 4→3), expanding windows of authentic self-awareness (from Intensity 3→2), strengthening ability to choose rather than react (from Intensity 2→1), and ultimately maintaining connection while engaging patterns consciously. This framework shows that ego patterns aren't inherently problematic—they become destructive when they obscure our awareness of who we truly are beneath the defensive strategies.

Remember Sarah from our opening story? We can now understand precisely what was happening: she was operating at Intensity Level 3—Pattern as Necessity—where her Expert pattern had become required for her self-worth.

The telling detail? That knot in her stomach as she walked to her car. This discomfort reveals she hasn't reached Intensity Level 4, where the pattern becomes her entire identity. At Level 4, there would be no remorse, no uncomfortable feeling afterward—she would feel completely justified, even righteous about her behavior. Someone at Level 4 might even feel energized by 'putting Tom in his place' and share the story proudly with others.

But Sarah's knot of discomfort shows she still has some awareness that her response was problematic. She's caught between her authentic self (which knows she was wrong) and her Level 3 Expert pattern (which needed to be right for her self-worth). This internal conflict is a hopeful sign. It means she's not fully lost to the pattern. There's still enough conscious awareness to feel the disconnect between who she really is and how she behaved.

But what exactly are these defensive patterns that Ego Intelligence helps us recognize and manage? Through extensive clinical observation, three primary patterns emerged that account for the vast majority of ego-defensive behaviors: the Expert, the Judge, and the Victim.

The Three Faces of Ego Defense

These patterns (faces) exist on a spectrum of intensity—from conscious tools we can choose to use, to unconscious identities that completely drive our behavior. Understanding both the patterns and their intensity levels is crucial for developing Ego Intelligence.

Through extensive research and clinical observation, building on the foundational work of spiritual teacher Don Miguel Ruiz in "The Four Agreements," I have identified three primary patterns that characterize how the ego defends itself against perceived threats. Ruiz originally identified two internal voices that create human suffering: the Judge and the Victim.

The Judge, in Ruiz's framework, uses our "Book of Laws", our belief system—to evaluate everything, creating guilt, shame, and punishment when we don't meet our own or others' standards.

The Judge relentlessly evaluates both self and others, creating a cycle where judgment leads to condemnation.

The Victim receives the Judge's condemnation, carrying blame, guilt, and shame while repeatedly saying "Poor me, I'm not good enough, I'm not worthy of love." The cycle becomes: Judge decrees → Victim suffers → Repeat thousands of times for the same "mistake."

Over several years in clinical practice and teaching, my observations revealed that many individuals didn't fit neatly into this Judge/Victim dynamic but were trapped in intellectual superiority patterns, using knowledge as their primary defense mechanism. This led to the identification of a third ego pattern: the Expert.

The Expert seeks safety through knowledge and intellectual superiority. When feeling threatened or inadequate, the Expert responds by demonstrating competence, correcting others, or retreating into areas of proven expertise. The underlying fear is being exposed as ignorant, incompetent, or foolish. The Expert's intellect and competence must be right to maintain self-worth and dismisses others' perspectives to protect identity.

The Judge finds security through evaluation and control, creating rigid standards and constantly assessing whether situations, people, and outcomes meet these standards. When threatened, the Judge becomes critical, perfectionistic, or controlling. The core fear is being wrong, making mistakes, or losing control.

The Victim seeks protection through helplessness and external blame, positioning itself as powerless in the face of circumstances and others' actions. When threatened, the Victim becomes passive, complaining, or seeks rescue from others. The fundamental fear is taking responsibility and potentially failing.

These aren't personality types or permanent categories. Rather, they are dynamic patterns that we all move between depending on the situation, our stress level, what feels threatened in any given moment, and our current level of attachment to these defensive strategies. A single person might operate as an Expert in their professional life, a Judge in their parenting, and a Victim in their romantic relationship, with each pattern potentially existing at different levels of attachment and triggered by the situation and perceived threat.

* The Three Ego Patterns at a Glance

Pattern	Core Drive	Primary Fear	Defense Strategy
Expert	Safety through knowledge	Being exposed as incompetent	Intellectualization, correction, superiority
Judge	Security through control	Being wrong or losing control	Criticism, evaluation, rigid standards
Victim	Protection through helplessness	Taking responsibility and failing	Blame, passivity, seeking rescue

Remember: These are not fixed personality types—we all move between these patterns depending on circumstances and stress levels.

The intensity of these patterns varies dramatically based on our level of pattern integration:

At Intensity 2-3 (Pattern as Refuge/Necessity), Expert patterns manifest as an authority on the issue while dismissing others but maintaining relationships. Judge patterns involve having rigid standards and being critical but still being able to be reasoned with. Victim patterns include feeling powerless and blaming others but still seeking solutions.

At Intensity 4 (Pattern as Identity), Expert patterns become so intense that knowledge becomes more important than people, and individuals will destroy relationships to be "right." Judge patterns escalate to where standards become more important than humanity, and the person cannot tolerate imperfection in anyone. Victim patterns intensify to where helplessness becomes the core identity, and individuals may harm themselves or others to prove their victimization.

*** Pattern Intensity Scale**

INTENSITY 1: *Pattern as Option*

└─ Conscious choice — Flexible use — Authentic-self intact

    INTENSITY 2: *Pattern as Refuge*

    └─ Go-to response — Temporary relief — Some self-awareness

        INTENSITY 3: *Pattern as Necessity* **NOTE:**

        └─ Required for worth — Identity fusion — Rare authentic moments

            INTENSITY 4: *Pattern as Identity* !

            └─ Complete identification — No alternatives — Total disconnection

The Evolutionary Origins of Defensive Patterns

To understand why these patterns exist and why they're so persistent, we need to consider them through the lens of evolutionary psychology. Our brains didn't evolve in boardrooms and coffee shops—they evolved over millions of years in environments where survival depended on quickly identifying and responding to threats.

In our ancestral environment, the threats were often immediate and physical: predators, hostile tribes, natural disasters, or social exclusion from the group (which could mean death). Our nervous systems developed sophisticated threat-detection mechanisms that could activate protective responses in milliseconds.

The Expert pattern likely evolved from the survival advantage of knowledge and skill. Those who could understand their environment, predict dangers, and solve complex problems were more likely to survive and reproduce. The desire to be knowledgeable and competent served our ancestors well when their lives depended on their ability to find food, avoid predators, and navigate social hierarchies. In genuinely dangerous environments, having accurate knowledge and demonstrating competence could literally mean the difference between life and death.

The Judge pattern emerged from the need to quickly evaluate threats and opportunities. In a dangerous world, the ability to rapidly categorize situations as safe or dangerous, people as allies or enemies, and behaviors as acceptable or unacceptable was literally a matter of life and death. The tendency toward black-and-white thinking, while problematic in our complex modern world, served our ancestors by enabling rapid decision-making under pressure. Quick evaluation and the establishment of clear standards helped groups survive by maintaining social cohesion and identifying threats.

The Victim pattern developed as a response to overwhelming threat—when fight or flight weren't viable options. Playing dead, appearing helpless, or eliciting care from others could sometimes mean the difference between survival and death. The capacity to shut down, seek help, or deflect responsibility wasn't weakness—it was an adaptive response to genuinely powerless situations where other survival strategies had failed.

The problem arises when we become attached to these patterns at higher intensity levels, making them our default responses even when survival isn't actually at stake. An Intensity 2 Expert might use their knowledge appropriately when genuine expertise is needed. However, at higher intensity levels the Expert pattern becomes so attached to being right that they'll destroy relationships and ignore truth to maintain their intellectual superiority.

How Ego Patterns Serve Survival Functions

Even in our modern world, these patterns continue to serve important functions. They're not "bad" or "wrong", they're sophisticated psychological strategies that helped our species survive and continue to protect us today when used consciously and appropriately.

The Expert pattern helps us build competence, develop expertise, and contribute valuable knowledge to our communities. In moderation and at lower levels of intensity, the drive to learn, understand, and share knowledge creates teachers, researchers, innovators, and skilled professionals who advance human knowledge and capability. When someone's house is on fire, we want the firefighter to operate from genuine expertise, not false humility.

The Judge pattern helps us maintain standards, create order, and make necessary evaluations. Healthy discernment, quality control, and the ability to distinguish between effective and ineffective approaches are essential for everything from parenting to professional excellence. When performed at appropriate levels of intensity, evaluation and standard setting create safety, quality, and progress.

The Victim pattern helps us recognize when we're genuinely overwhelmed, seek appropriate help, and acknowledge our limitations. The capacity to admit powerlessness, ask for support, and recognize when we need assistance prevents us from taking on more than we can handle and helps us build supportive relationships. In situations of actual powerlessness, acknowledging limitations and seeking help is not only appropriate but necessary.

The problems arise not when these patterns exist, but when they become our default, habitual responses to situations that don't actually threaten our survival, and especially when we become attached to them at higher levels. When the Expert pattern activates at Intensity 4 in a brainstorming session, it can kill creativity. When the Judge pattern dominates parenting at high intensity levels, it can damage children's self-esteem. When the Victim pattern takes over in professional settings at intense levels, it can undermine leadership and personal agency.

The Cost of Chronic Defensive Living

While these patterns served us well in our evolutionary past and continue to have appropriate applications today, chronic reliance on them—especially at higher intensity levels—comes at a significant cost. When we're unconsciously driven by defensive patterns, particularly at Intensity 3 and 4, we lose access to our full range of human capabilities and authentic ways of being.

Relationship Costs: Perhaps the most significant cost of chronic defensive living is its impact on our relationships. Each ego pattern, while protective, creates distance between us and others, with this distance increasing dramatically as intensity levels rise.

The Expert pattern at moderate intensity levels can make others feel diminished, ignorant, or inadequate. When we constantly need to be right, correct others, or demonstrate our superior knowledge, we inadvertently communicate that others' perspectives aren't valuable. At Intensity 4, Expert patterns become so extreme that the person will destroy relationships entirely rather than admit being wrong, choosing knowledge superiority over human connection.

The Judge pattern at higher intensity levels creates an atmosphere of evaluation and criticism that makes others feel constantly assessed and found wanting. When we operate from rigid standards and frequent criticism, others learn to hide their authentic selves, leading to superficial relationships based on performance rather than genuine connection. At Intensity 4, Judge patterns become impossible to satisfy, creating environments where no one can ever be good enough.

The Victim pattern, while eliciting sympathy initially, eventually exhausts others and creates one-sided relationships where we're always receiving support but rarely offering it. At higher intensity levels, chronic helplessness can push away even the most caring people. At Intensity 4, Victim patterns become so demanding and consuming that relationships become entirely about caretaking the victim's helplessness.

Professional Costs: In our work lives, unconscious defensive patterns can significantly limit our effectiveness and career advancement, with these limitations becoming more severe as intensity levels increase.

Expert patterns at moderate levels can make us difficult collaborators, resistant to input, and unable to delegate effectively. While expertise is valuable, the need to always be the smartest person in the room can prevent us from learning, growing, and building effective teams. At Intensity 4, Expert patterns become so rigid that the person cannot function on teams at all, becoming completely unable to collaborate or learn from others.

Judge patterns at higher intensity levels can create hostile work environments, stifle innovation, and prevent the psychological safety necessary for high-performance teams. When criticism and perfectionism dominate, people become risk-averse and less creative. At Intensity 4, Judge patterns create such harsh environments that productivity and innovation become impossible.

Victim patterns at moderate intensity can undermine leadership, prevent us from taking initiative, and make us unreliable team members. When we consistently position ourselves as powerless, others stop trusting us with important responsibilities. At Intensity 4, Victim patterns make professional functioning nearly impossible, as the person becomes completely unable to take responsibility or initiative.

Personal Costs: Perhaps most tragically, chronic defensive living at higher intensity levels prevents us from accessing our own authentic capabilities and experiencing genuine fulfillment.

When we're always defending, we're not truly living. We miss opportunities for real learning (because the Expert already knows), genuine connection (because the Judge is too busy evaluating), and personal empowerment (because the Victim is too busy being helpless). At higher intensity levels, these costs become extreme, with individuals losing access to their authentic self entirely.

Defensive patterns also create internal stress and conflict. The constant vigilance required to maintain our defensive postures is exhausting. We may achieve external success while feeling empty inside, disconnected from our true selves and genuine desires. At Intensity 3 and 4, this internal conflict becomes severe, often leading to anxiety, depression, and a sense of living a false life.

Creative and Innovative Costs: Defensive patterns are particularly costly when it comes to creativity and innovation. Creative thinking requires openness to uncertainty, willingness to make mistakes, and the ability to play with ideas without immediately evaluating them.

The Expert pattern's need for certainty can prevent the exploration necessary for innovation. The Judge pattern's immediate evaluation can kill creative ideas before they have a chance to develop. The Victim pattern's learned helplessness can prevent us from believing we have anything valuable to contribute. At higher intensity levels, these patterns completely shut down creative capacity, making innovation and original thinking nearly impossible.

The Promise of Ego Intelligence

The good news is that these patterns, while deeply ingrained, are not permanent or unchangeable. This is where Ego Intelligence comes in. By developing our capacity to recognize these patterns, understand their function, identify our current pattern intensity, and choose more conscious responses, we can maintain the benefits of our defensive strategies while reducing their costs.

Ego Intelligence doesn't mean eliminating these patterns—that would be neither possible nor desirable. Instead, it means developing a conscious relationship with them and learning to operate at lower intensity levels. We can learn to recognize when the Expert, Judge, or Victim is driving our behavior, identify what intensity level we're experiencing, and make conscious choices about when these responses are helpful and when they're limiting us.

A person with high Ego Intelligence might recognize their Expert pattern activating at Intensity 4 (Pattern as Identity) in a meeting and consciously choose to ask questions instead of making statements, moving themselves to Intensity 1 (Pattern as Option) where they can use their expertise as a tool rather than an identity. They might notice their Judge pattern evaluating their child's performance at Intensity 3 (Pattern as Necessity) and choose to offer encouragement instead of criticism, shifting to Intensity 1 authentic response. They might catch their Victim pattern blaming circumstances for a problem at Intensity 3 and choose to focus on what actions they can take, moving to Intensity 2 (Pattern as Refuge) where they can acknowledge genuine limitations while taking appropriate responsibility.

The Pattern Intensity framework provides a roadmap for this transformation. The goal isn't to eliminate defensive patterns but to reduce their intensity, moving from unconscious reaction at higher intensities to conscious choice at lower intensities. Someone operating at Intensity 4 might first work to move to Intensity 3, then Intensity 2, gradually developing the capacity for more conscious, flexible responses.

This conscious choice—the space between trigger and response—is where true freedom lies. It's where we move from being unconsciously driven by ancient survival patterns to consciously choosing responses that serve our actual current circumstances and goals.

The Journey Ahead

In the chapters that follow, we'll explore each of these patterns in detail, learning to recognize their manifestations, understand their triggers, identify intensity levels, and develop strategies for working with them consciously. We'll discover how these patterns interact with each other, how they evolve under different conditions, and how to build our capacity for authentic response while moving to lower levels of intensity.

Most importantly, we'll develop the practical skills of Ego Intelligence, which is the ability to catch ourselves in defensive patterns, assess our intensity level, and choose more effective, authentic ways of being. This isn't about becoming perfect or eliminating all defensive behavior. It's about becoming conscious, choice-full participants in our own lives rather than unconscious prisoners of ancient survival strategies operating at high intensity levels.

The development of Ego Intelligence represents one of the most important frontiers in human development. As our external world becomes increasingly complex and interconnected, our ability to work consciously with our internal defensive patterns becomes not just personally beneficial but collectively essential. The idea of living authentically and forging a genuine self seems impossible as we navigate this complex world where competition sets the pace of the game. Understanding ego patterns and the intensity level of each face explains why some people can't implement transformational practices: their pattern intensity is too high for the practices to penetrate the ego defenses.

The journey toward Ego Intelligence begins with a simple but profound shift: from unconscious reaction to conscious response. From being driven by our patterns to choosing how we engage with them. From defending against life to authentically participating in it. From high-level intensity that controls us to low-level intensity that serves us.

Let's begin that journey together.

Key Concepts:

- Ego Intelligence: The capacity to recognize and work with defensive patterns
- Three Faces: Expert (knowledge), Judge (control), Victim (helplessness)

- Four Intensity Levels: From conscious choice to complete identity
- The Promise: Moving from unconscious reaction to conscious response

In the next chapter, we'll dive deep into the Expert pattern—the drive for intellectual superiority that Sarah experienced—exploring its manifestations, triggers, and the journey from unconscious reaction to conscious choice.

>> Chapter 1 Key Takeaways

1. **Ego Intelligence is distinct** from emotional intelligence—it's about access, not development
2. **Three patterns** dominate our defensive responses: Expert, Judge, and Victim
3. **Four intensity levels** determine how much patterns control us
4. **Meeting Gardner's criteria** establishes Ego Intelligence as a legitimate intelligence
5. **The journey ahead** moves us from unconscious reaction to conscious response

Coming Next: Chapter 2 explores the architecture of defense in detail by exploring the truth formula, bias, defense mechanisms, values and cognitive distortions that align with each face of ego.

Chapter 2: The Architecture of Defense

>> What You'll Learn in This Chapter

- How lies act as "lubricant" for defensive patterns
- The Truth Formula: Why context matters more than content
- How defense mechanisms cluster into Expert, Judge, and Victim patterns
- The role of values in determining your dominant ego pattern
- Why cognitive distortions amplify defensive behaviors
- The complete architecture: VALUES → **PERSONAL DOMAIN** → LIES ↔ BIAS → DEFENSES → DISTORTIONS → EGO FACES

Reading Time: ~20 minutes

I'm sitting at my desk at 2 AM, surrounded by dozens of psychology journals, defense mechanism charts, and three empty coffee cups, trying to write this exact chapter you're now reading. My screen shows five different drafts, each one attempting to explain how our ego patterns maintain themselves through sophisticated self-deception. And I'm stuck.

Not because I don't understand the concepts—I've been teaching emotional intelligence and developing these ideas about ego patterns for over fifteen years. Not because I lack examples; I have hundreds from clinical practice and thousands of hours working with students and clients alike. I'm stuck because my own defensive patterns are running wild, and I'm watching it happen in real-time.

"This book could elevate your standing at the university," my Expert pattern whispers. "Finally, they'll have to recognize your contributions to the field, even without that terminal degree."

Then reality creeps in: "Who are you kidding? This probably won't be the breakthrough you're hoping for. You'll be lucky if your colleagues don't laugh at the concept behind your back." "Someone else has already discovered this and probably done a better job explaining it"

My Judge pattern activates next: "The writing needs more academic citations. Real scholars, the ones with PhDs, will tear this apart. You're trying to stand alongside Gardner and Goleman without their credentials." "You're just an LPC without a terminal degree."

Finally, my Victim pattern delivers the killing blow: "You have no choice but to make this academically bulletproof. Without a doctorate, you have to work twice as hard for half the recognition. That's just reality. If this concept falls flat, I can always blame it on not having the credentials -Ph.D."

I lean back in my chair, caught between two competing narratives that both feel completely true. Maybe this book becomes a bestseller that changes how we understand emotional intelligence and ego patterns. Maybe it sinks without a trace, becoming just another self-published academic attempt that colleagues politely ignore at faculty meetings. Most likely? Something in between, respected by some, dismissed by others, helpful to those who need it, invisible to those who don't.

"Well," I tell myself, "At least I tried."

But that resignation is just another defensive pattern, isn't it? A pre-emptive Victim stance to protect against potential failure.

The truth? I'm terrified. And I'm hopeful. And I'm probably delusional. All at once.

I'm terrified that fifteen focused years of developing this framework won't matter without those three letters after my name. I am hopeful that my clinical expertise and experience count for something. Delusional, perhaps, to think I can contribute something meaningful to a field dominated by terminal degrees and peer-reviewed journals.

Am I an authority or a dreamer? The Expert in me claims authority based on years of practice and teaching. The Judge in me dismisses this as inadequate without academic pedigree. The Victim in me says I had no choice but to write this book because these patterns need to be understood, credentials be damned.

So here I sit, intellectualizing my insecurity about credentials, projecting my fears onto imaginary academic critics, and denying my own agency by claiming I "have to" prove myself. I'm doing exactly what this chapter describes: using technically true statements to construct an elaborate defensive structure.

Yes, credentials matter in academia. Yes, this book might not breakthrough. Yes, colleagues might dismiss it. All true content. But the context—the meaning I'm assigning to these facts—is the lie. I'm not protecting academic integrity; I'm protecting my ego from the vulnerability of offering something meaningful without the traditional armor of a doctorate.

Then something shifts. I remember my client, an MD, who was unable to recognize the judge aspects that were leading him to a failed marriage. I remember the CEO, also a client, who said understanding his Expert pattern saved his company as he made intentional interpersonal adjustments. I remember the thousands of students over fifteen years who have said these concepts changed their lives.

Authority doesn't come from degrees. Maybe it comes from seeing clearly, speaking truthfully, and being willing to share what you've learned even when your Expert pattern insists you need more credentials, your Judge pattern says you're not good enough, and your Victim pattern claims you have no choice but to stay safe and silent. The biases, the distortion of truth and the vulnerability of my values through defenses were all represented in this internal dialogue that consumed me.

I rewrite all drafts and start fresh, this time from a different place—not from my defensive patterns, not from my academic insecurities, but from the simple truth that I've seen these patterns operate in thousands of people, including myself. I've watched them destroy relationships, careers, and lives. I've also witnessed people break free from them to salvage the relationship that may have remained with others. And more importantly they were able to salvage the relationship with themselves as I did here to push through and put my concepts on paper.

What you're about to read isn't just theory, it's fifteen years of pattern recognition distilled into something I hope is useful. It's the system I'm dismantling in myself as I write these words. The beautiful irony is that understanding these patterns doesn't make us immune to them—here I am, writing about defenses while defending—but it does give us choice. And choice, even the choice to write a book that might fail, changes everything.

Let me show you how the lies, these defenses, these distortions we tell ourselves, those subtle distortions of context that keep our defenses smooth and operational, create the invisible prison we mistake for personality. Whether I am an authority or a dreamer does not matter nearly as much as whether this helps you see your own patterns more clearly.

Welcome to the architecture of defense. I have been mapping it for fifteen years, living in it for longer, and I am still finding new rooms. But I have learned enough to share the blueprints. Let us explore them together, Ph.D. or not. Now, let me share what I have discovered about how these patterns maintain themselves, beginning with a century of research that laid the groundwork. We will begin by incrementally introducing the elements of the architecture of defense section by section, culminating in the entire chain by chapter's end.

Universal Challenge

The systematic study of psychological defense mechanisms began with Sigmund Freud's groundbreaking work in the early 20th century, when he first proposed that the human psyche develops automatic strategies to protect itself from anxiety-producing thoughts and feelings. His daughter, Anna Freud, significantly expanded this work in her definitive 1936 text "The Ego and the Mechanisms of Defence," where she catalogued ten core defense mechanisms that appear throughout human psychological functioning and established the foundation for modern understanding of these protective strategies.

Over the past century, psychology has continuously refined our understanding of these defensive patterns. During the classical period (1900-1950s), Freud identified core mechanisms like repression, projection, and displacement, while Anna Freud systematized the field with comprehensive categorization. The modern development phase (1960s-1990s) saw George Vaillant develop hierarchical classifications from adaptive to pathological levels, Otto Kernberg connect primitive defenses to personality organization, and Robert Plutchik linked defense mechanisms to basic emotions and diagnostic structures. Contemporary integration (2000s-Present) has brought empirical measurement through tools like the Defense Mechanism Rating Scale (DMRS), integration with neuroscience revealing the biological basis of defensive patterns, and recognition of cultural and developmental factors in defense formation.

According to this evolving theoretical framework, defense mechanisms serve as psychological processes that protect the self from internal conflicts and external stressors. These patterns often become habitual responses that activate automatically. They work by either distorting uncomfortable realities into more acceptable forms or blocking awareness of them entirely, allowing individuals to maintain a "false sense of stability." The most common means of distorting reality is simply the act of lying. But how exactly does lying enable defense mechanisms to operate so smoothly and automatically? The common lie serves as a very interesting catalyst to the evolution of ego patterns.

The Central Discovery - Truth Formula

Truth emerges from the intersection of two essential elements: **content** and **context**. Content represents the factual substance - the what, who, when, and where of any situation. Context provides the circumstances, conditions, and background that give meaning to that content—the why, how, and under what conditions. When both elements are present and accurate, truth becomes accessible. When either element is distorted or omitted, truth becomes impossible to discern.

This content + context = truth formula reveals the precise mechanics of how lying functions as the lubricant in defensive systems. Rather than creating entirely fabricated realities, most defensive dishonesty operates through the strategic manipulation of content, context, or both. This manipulation reduces the cognitive friction that would otherwise expose the defensive pattern's operation. Again, lies then become the "lubricant" by which content/context distortions allow for the ego to thrive in its varied forms.

Content lies or distortions involve exaggerating, minimizing, or selectively presenting information to support the defensive narrative. These distortions focus on the measurable, observable elements of a situation. Context lies or distortions involve omitting, misrepresenting, or selectively framing the circumstances that give meaning to content. These distortions focus on the environmental, relational, and situational factors that shape how content should be interpreted. Without accurate content AND context, the friction that would expose the defensive pattern's operation is eliminated. The Expert can maintain their superiority narrative, the Judge can sustain their criticism, and the Victim can preserve their helplessness—all because the complete truth (content + context) never fully emerges. The lubricant function of content and context distortion does more than simply enable defensive patterns—it systematically generates bias that becomes increasingly automatic and unconscious. This progression from deliberate lubrication to unconscious bias formation represents one of the most troubling aspects of how ego patterns entrench themselves over time.

Truth isn't just about what we say, it's equally about the circumstances surrounding our words. When either element gets distorted, we edge toward deception. Often, it's the context that gets quietly omitted or twisted, creating a technically accurate statement that nonetheless misleads.

A Brief Detour: Truth on the Golf Course

Let me step away from the clinical and academic world for a moment to illustrate this concept through something more lighthearted - though equally revealing about how we manipulate truth.

I play in a weekly men's golf group, and our format of choice is Shamble—a game where everyone tees off, we select the best drive, and then each player completes the hole with their own ball from that optimal position.

Here's where context becomes everything: Last week, I could tell you I shot a 74. That number is real—I did mark down those strokes on my scorecard. But without mentioning I was playing Shamble, I'd be painting an incomplete picture. That 74 came with an asterisk: I benefited from my playing partners' superior drives on several holes. In stroke play, where you're on your own from tee to green, my score would have been considerably higher.

The content—"I shot 74"—remains factually correct. But stripped of its context, it transforms from an honest account into something that, while not quite a lie, certainly isn't the full truth. This is how misinformation often travels: not through outright fabrication, but through the selective editing of circumstances that give facts their proper meaning. This is one of many examples that we live with daily. The capacity for both truth and distortion exist within each of us. We all possess the ability to see clearly AND the ability to deceive ourselves. This internal territory – where our values, beliefs, experiences, and patterns reside – becomes the setting for cognitive dissonance where two opposing beliefs, values or attitudes collide.

This territory is what I call our personal domain, and within it lies the mechanism that determines whether we respond to life with clarity or distortion. The lies we explored aren't inevitable features of this domain but rather tempting tools available when we feel threatened. The question isn't whether we have the capacity for distortion – we all do – but rather which filter within our domain we allow to dominate our perception.

Understanding this personal domain and its dual nature is essential, because it's here that our automatic responses – our biases – are born.

---

* The Truth Formula

CONTENT + CONTEXT = TRUTH

  ↓   ↓

What   Why/How = What is real!

Facts   Meaning

When either element is distorted:

X Content Lies: Altering facts

X Context Lies: Changing meaning

= No access to truth

= Defensive patterns thrive

Key Insight: Most defensive dishonesty operates through context manipulation rather than outright factual lies.

The Personal Domain: Where Bias Lives

Before we can understand how biases operate, we must understand where they originate. Each of us carries what I call a personal domain — the complete internal architecture of our values, beliefs, experiences, behavioral patterns, quality of motivation, and identity standards that define who we are. Think of it like a hula hoop that surrounds us, with ourselves at the center. Inside that hoop lives everything we hold dear — the specific values, experiences, and beliefs that are uniquely ours. They are the sum total of who we are — or more precisely, who we think we are, a distinction that will matter deeply as we explore how ego patterns distort that definition.

Within this personal domain, two additional sub-filters operate simultaneously:

- **The Authentic Filter** recognizes genuine worth, actual achievements, and real growth potential, which is typically tied to reality and truth.
- **The Egoic Filter** measures everything against internalized and exaggerated standards, often perfectionist or unattainable, creating threat even in success. This filter adheres to distorted reality and exaggerated perception.

These filters generate both positive and negative biases – determining not just what we notice, but how we interpret it and which defensive patterns activate in response.

The Intensity Principle

The strength of our bias-response directly correlates with how foreign or aligned something is with our personal domain. When an idea, person, or experience closely aligns with our domain's existing architecture – matching our values, beliefs, and past experiences – our authentic filter generates strong positive bias, creating immediate receptivity and acceptance. Conversely, when something feels foreign or threatening to our domain, the egoic filter produces intense defensive bias, triggering immediate resistance and ego pattern activation.

This intensity principle explains why minor disagreements with strangers feel manageable while similar disagreements with family members can trigger explosive responses – family challenges hit closer to our personal domain's core. It's why feedback about peripheral skills barely registers, but criticism of our core competencies (especially those tied to our values) activates full defensive patterns. The more central something is to our personal domain, the more intense our bias response becomes.

This principle directly parallels the four intensity levels of ego patterns we'll explore in detail later – from low-level conscious choice to high-level complete identification. When something strikes at the heart of our personal domain, it doesn't just trigger bias; it activates our ego patterns at their highest intensity levels, where the pattern becomes indistinguishable from our identity itself. Understanding this connection helps explain why some triggers barely ripple our defenses while others unleash the full force of our Expert, Judge, or Victim patterns.

Pre-Emotion Bias: The Domain's Response System

Pre-emotion bias represents the automatic responses that occur before emotional awareness emerges. Within the ego intelligence model, pre-emotion bias can originate from either filter within our personal domain.

When generated by the **egoic filter**, it serves as a rapid deployment system – instantly activating the appropriate defensive pattern (Expert, Judge, or Victim) when threat is detected. This operates through what Anna Freud termed "signal anxiety" – the ego's anticipatory response to perceived threats that triggers defensive mechanisms before the actual emotional experience registers consciously.

When generated by the **authentic filter**, pre-emotion bias creates positive anticipatory responses – hope, excitement, and openness – that also occur before conscious emotional processing. For instance, a parent whose children are visiting from college may experience positive pre-emotion bias (excitement, planning, anticipation) even when rationally knowing the visit will be brief as the children spend most of their time with friends.

Both types of pre-emotion bias happen instantaneously, shaping our experience before we're even aware of it.

The Perfectionism Paradox

Consider someone who scores 94 on an exam. Their authentic filter correctly recognizes this achievement – an A, goal met, genuine success. Simultaneously, their egoic filter notes it wasn't the highest score in class. This gap between "successful" and "perfect" registers as domain threat, triggering negative pre-emotion bias despite objective achievement. This explains why assessment tools can detect negative self-view patterns in people who claim high self-esteem – they're revealing the egoic filter's perpetual measurement against unattainable standards while the authentic filter maintains genuine self-worth.

How Pre-Emotion Bias Maintains Patterns

In the ego intelligence framework, pre-emotion bias represents the mechanism through which defensive patterns maintain their grip. The Expert's intellectualization, the Judge's projection, and the Victim's denial all activate through pre-emotion bias – creating defensive responses before authentic emotional experience can emerge.

This understanding is crucial because it explains why simply becoming aware of our patterns isn't enough; we must recognize and interrupt the pre-emotion bias that triggers these patterns before conscious awareness can intervene. More precisely, we must understand how our personal domain's dual filters create competing biases – one toward growth and authenticity, another toward protection and defense.

Key Characteristics of Pre-Emotion Bias:

- Operates below conscious awareness initially
- Learned through repetition and conditioning
- Creates automatic responses that bypass deliberate processing
- Can be identified and modified through conscious awareness and practice
- Serves both protective and connective functions
- Originates from either the authentic or egoic filter within our personal domain

The Path to Intervention

By understanding pre-emotion bias as the automatic activation within our personal domain, we can develop more precise interventions that target the moment between trigger and response – that critical space where pattern activation occurs but hasn't yet solidified into full defensive engagement. This includes recognizing when our egoic filter is creating threat from success, turning achievements into failures through impossible standards, or when our authentic filter is generating positive expectations that may not match reality.

The key insight is that pre-emotion bias isn't inherently problematic – it's a natural function of our personal domain's filtering system. The challenge arises when the egoic filter dominates, creating defensive patterns that prevent authentic emotional experience and genuine connection.

Note: What psychology broadly terms "implicit bias" – those unconscious attitudes and stereotypes affecting our perceptions – can be more precisely understood through the personal domain framework as pre-emotion bias generated by our dual filtering system. While implicit bias research has traditionally focused on social categories like race, gender, and age, the personal domain model reveals the deeper mechanism: automatic responses emerging from either our authentic or egoic filters before conscious processing occurs.

From Bias to Structure: How Defense Mechanisms Organize

The Expert, Judge, and Victim patterns represent a revolutionary integration of classical defense mechanism theory with contemporary understanding of personality organization and behavioral patterns. Rather than viewing defense mechanisms as isolated responses, the EJV framework recognizes that they cluster together in predictable ways, forming coherent defensive strategies. This integration transforms abstract psychological theory into practical, observable, and measurable behavioral patterns. Where classical defense mechanism theory focused primarily on individual pathology, the EJV framework recognizes these patterns as universal human tendencies that exist on a spectrum from adaptive to maladaptive.

Building on over a century of defense mechanism research, we understand that one of the most challenging aspects of these patterns is their automatic nature. Both classical defense mechanism theory and modern EJV pattern recognition face the same fundamental challenge: these protective strategies typically activate automatically, triggering instantaneous responses that feel completely justified in the moment. The justification is built on the perceived alignment of the response to our values, motivational tendencies and it just feels right.

The Breakthrough Synthesis

The transition from adaptive survival mechanism to limiting ego patterns occurs through several key processes. Context changes transform what was once a genuine threat—such as physical danger, social exile, or resource scarcity—into psychological discomfort from criticism, uncertainty, or responsibility, yet the pattern continues responding as if life were at stake. Overuse creates habituation as repeated activation of the same pattern creates neural pathways that make it the default response, even when inappropriate, causing the pattern to become our identity rather than a tool. Secondary gains emerge when the pattern begins providing benefits like attention, control, or protection from responsibility that we become reluctant to give up, even when we recognize the costs. Finally, awareness decreases as the pattern becomes more automatic, leading us to lose conscious awareness of its activation until we begin to believe that our pattern's perspective is simply "reality." The evolution of specialized biases, as well as habit formation, emerge. All EJV patterns rely on defense mechanisms to carry out the mission. These defense mechanisms typically work in clusters that align with the action of the ego face.

This clustering approach represents a significant advancement in defense mechanism theory by creating a comprehensive framework that connects individual psychological defenses with observable behavioral patterns. When clinicians understand someone's dominant EJV pattern and value structure they can predict not only which defense mechanisms are likely to be active, but also how these defenses reinforce each other to maintain the pattern's stability. For instance, an individual may have a high intellectual value and therefore may use their knowledge to create logical explanations to justify their stance even though they may knowingly be wrong. This enables the justification of the expert pattern, and the very pattern echoes its logic to the value of high intellectual. The element of justification is presented as a circuitous looping of rationale, one building on the other.

 This integrated perspective enables more targeted therapeutic interventions that address entire defensive systems at the values and pattern level rather than the isolated mechanism of rationalization, while simultaneously explaining how personal psychological defenses manifest as interpersonal and intrapersonal relationship dynamics. The framework transforms abstract psychological concepts into practical tools for both assessment and treatment, bridging the gap between classical defense mechanism theory, emotional intelligence, and cognitive behavioral therapy.

These defenses work in concert to maintain the core belief that "knowledge equals safety and worth."

Expert Pattern Defense Cluster - The Expert pattern operates through knowledge-based defenses that maintain safety through perceived intellectual superiority:

- **Intellectualization**: Converting emotional threats into abstract, intellectual problems
- **Rationalization**: Creating logical explanations to justify knowledge-based superiority
- **Compartmentalization**: Separating different areas of knowledge to avoid contradictions

Dr. Harrison, the Tenured Professor

When a young professor suggests interactive learning techniques, Dr. Harrison immediately intellectualizes: "That's pedagogical trendiness that ignores fundamental epistemological foundations." He rationalizes with appeals to "decades of research" supporting traditional lectures. When student evaluations favor the interactive classes, he compartmentalizes: "Satisfaction surveys measure popularity, not rigor—that's an administrative concern, not academic." Through this defensive cluster, Dr. Harrison protects his expert identity from any evidence that might challenge his methods.

Judge Pattern Defense Cluster The Judge pattern utilizes evaluation-based defenses that maintain control through criticism and standards:

- **Projection**: Attributing personal flaws and inadequacies to others
- **Reaction Formation**: Overcompensating by acting opposite to feelings (being overly critical to hide insecurity)
- **Displacement**: Redirecting critical energy toward safer targets than the true source

These defenses support the fundamental belief that "control through criticism equals safety and superiority."

Dr. Patricia, the Department Chair to Adjunct Professor

Dr. Patricia projects her anxiety about department performance onto adjunct professor Sarah, criticizing "inconsistent formatting" and "lack of theoretical depth." She demonstrates reaction formation by creating excessive syllabi requirements while secretly fearing her own performance review. When the dean questions retention rates, she displaces blame toward "unrealistic administrative expectations" rather than examining her management. This Judge pattern cluster ensures criticism always flows away from her leadership.

Victim Pattern Defense Cluster - The Victim pattern employs helplessness-based defenses that maintain protection through powerlessness:

- **Denial**: Refusal to acknowledge personal responsibility or capability
- **Regression**: Reverting to earlier, more dependent developmental stages
- **Repression**: Blocking awareness of personal power and agency

These defenses reinforce the core conviction that "helplessness equals safety and sympathy."

Jake, the Struggling Undergraduate

Jake receives a poor grade and immediately denies responsibility: "There's nothing I could have done—the lectures were confusing." He regresses during study sessions, reminiscing about "when high school was easier" while asking others to explain concepts he could grasp with effort. When offered tutoring, he represses his capability: "I'm just not good at this subject." Through these defenses, Jake maintains his victim identity without facing his potential for growth.

* Defense Mechanism Clusters by Pattern

Expert Pattern Knowledge-Based Defenses	Judge Pattern Control-Based Defenses	Victim Pattern Helplessness-Based Defenses
Intellectualization	Projection	Denial
Rationalization	Reaction Formation	Regression
Compartmentalization	Displacement	Repression
Knowledge = Safety	Control = Safety	Helplessness = Safety

The EJV Defense System

Most defense mechanisms work by **reframing the meaning** of events rather than denying the events themselves. I believe **context lies are more fundamental to defense mechanisms than content lies**.

Understanding the relationship between defense mechanisms and the EJV patterns reveals a sophisticated psychological architecture where defensive strategies serve specific ego structures. Defense mechanisms explain *how* people protect themselves psychologically, while the EJV patterns explain *why* from an ego perspective each pattern is ultimately trying to achieve through its defensive strategies.

This complementary relationship creates a comprehensive framework for understanding human psychological defense. The Expert pattern doesn't randomly use intellectual defenses; it specifically employs intellectualization, rationalization, and compartmentalization because these mechanisms best serve its core mission of maintaining safety through perceived knowledge superiority. Similarly, the Judge pattern gravitates toward projection, reaction formation, and displacement because these defenses effectively support its fundamental belief that control through criticism equals safety. The Victim pattern relies on denial, regression, and repression because these mechanisms most efficiently maintain its conviction that helplessness provides protection.

Defense Mechanism Categories and Pattern Alignment

The defense mechanisms naturally organize into categories that align with the EJV patterns:

Cognitive-Based Defenses (Expert Pattern): Intellectualization and rationalization transform emotional threats into abstract problems that can be "solved" through knowledge, perfectly supporting the Expert's need to maintain intellectual superiority.

Redirection-Based Defenses (Judge Pattern): Projection and displacement redirect critical energy away from the self and toward others, while reaction formation creates the appearance of high standards, all supporting the Judge's need to maintain control through evaluation.

Avoidance-Based Defenses (Victim Pattern): Denial, repression, and regression avoid acknowledging personal responsibility or capability, directly supporting the Victim's need to maintain safety through helplessness.

This integration provides practitioners with both the mechanism (how the defense works) and the structure (what ego need it serves), creating unprecedented clarity for recognition, assessment, and intervention. Rather than treating defense mechanisms as isolated responses, this framework reveals them as coordinated strategies serving specific ego architectures, making both individual patterns and their underlying defensive systems more predictable and addressable.

The Dual Expression System: Interpersonal Manifestation and Intrapersonal Justification

Understanding how EJV patterns maintain themselves requires recognizing that they operate simultaneously on two levels: interpersonal behavioral manifestation and intrapersonal narrative justification. This dual expression system explains why these patterns are so persistent and why simple behavioral change often fails. The interpersonal expression represents the external level—what others observe and experience when we interact with them. For the Expert pattern, this external manifestation appears as lecturing, correcting others, and demonstrating intellectual superiority. The Judge pattern interpersonally shows up as criticizing, evaluating, and setting impossible standards for others to meet. The Victim pattern manifests externally as complaining, seeking rescue from others, and positioning other people as responsible for their circumstances.

Simultaneously operating beneath this interpersonal behavior is the intrapersonal expression, a sophisticated internal rationalization system that justifies external behavior to ourselves. The Expert's intrapersonal narrative typically sounds like "I was just sharing important knowledge they needed to understand" or "Someone had to explain the complexity they were missing." The Judge's internal story becomes "I'm maintaining important standards that others are too lazy or incompetent to uphold" or "If I don't enforce quality, everything will fall apart." The Victim's intrapersonal justification presents as "I had no choice given what they did to me" or "I'm just being realistic about how powerless I am in this situation."

Consider Dr. Amanda, a software architect who interrupts a junior developer's presentation to correct his terminology, then spends ten minutes explaining why his approach won't scale properly (interpersonal Expert behavior). From an intrapersonal perspective, Amanda tells herself "I saved the project from a costly mistake, someone with my experience had to step in before we went down the wrong path. I was helping him by sharing my expertise" (internal justification). What Amanda doesn't recognize is that her external "help" humiliated the developer, damaged team dynamics, and prevented her from learning about potentially innovative approaches. Her intrapersonal narrative prevents her from seeing the interpersonal damage because it frames her behavior as necessary expertise-sharing rather than defensive superiority.

Why the Intrapersonal Cover-up Creates Deeper Damage

Each ego face has its primary defenses - the Expert uses intellectualization and rationalization, the Judge employs projection and reaction formation, the Victim relies on denial and regression. But intentional lying acts as the smooth operator that makes all these defenses work more efficiently. It is the lubricant that oils the cluster of defenses when necessary.

It's not the defense mechanism itself, but rather what allows the defenses to operate without the friction of reality. When the Expert needs to rationalize their mistake, a small lie about the circumstances makes that rationalization slide into place easily. When the Judge projects their fears onto others, selective omissions or distortions lubricate that projection. When the Victim denies their agency, lies about their helplessness keep that denial well-oiled. Without this "lubricant," the defenses would grind against the truth and potentially break down, forcing genuine self-examination.

While interpersonal patterns create external problems that can potentially be addressed through feedback or behavioral modification, the intrapersonal justification system prevents the self-awareness necessary for genuine change. Each internal rationalization strengthens the neural pathways of the defensive pattern, literally rewiring the brain to make the pattern more automatic and unconscious. More insidiously, this intrapersonal narrative system gradually develops what can only be described as psychological conceit—a deep-seated sense of superiority that becomes increasingly disconnected from actual competence or circumstances.

Values-Based Drivers and Ego Pattern Influence

Understanding how an individual's core driving forces influence both their emotional intelligence development and their tendency toward specific ego patterns provides crucial insight into the architecture of psychological defense. The TTI Success Insights 12 Driving Forces framework, based on Eduard Spranger's motivational categories, reveals how our deepest values create predictable pathways toward particular ego pattern manifestations.

The Values-EQ-Ego Connection

Individual driving forces shape emotional intelligence development by determining where people naturally invest their emotional energy and attention. These same value-driven priorities create vulnerabilities that ego patterns exploit for defensive purposes. When our core driving forces are threatened or frustrated, we unconsciously activate the ego pattern that best protects those values while maintaining our sense of competence and safety.

Expert Pattern Value Drivers

Individuals with high **Intellectual** (acquire knowledge, discover truth), **Commanding** (advance status, control destiny), and **Resourceful** (maximize productivity, get returns) driving forces demonstrate strong gravitational pull toward Expert pattern manifestation. The Intellectual drive creates identity fusion with knowledge acquisition, making any challenge to their expertise feel like a threat to their core self. The Commanding drive amplifies this by demanding intellectual superiority as a form of status and control. The Resourceful drive ensures they view knowledge as the most efficient path to desired outcomes.

Example Combination: Dr. Harrison from our earlier scenario likely scores high on Intellectual (driven to discover academic truth), Commanding (needs to control his professional destiny), and Resourceful (seeks maximum return on his educational investment). When his teaching methods are questioned, all three driving forces activate simultaneously—his Intellectual drive feels threatened by suggestions of pedagogical inadequacy, his Commanding drive resists loss of academic authority, and his Resourceful drive dismisses "trendy" methods as inefficient. The Expert pattern's defense cluster (intellectualization, rationalization, compartmentalization) perfectly serves all three value systems.

Judge Pattern Value Drivers

Individuals with high **Structured** (advance a cause through diligent work), **Commanding** (control personal freedom and legacy), and **Objective** (create functionality, remove emotions from decisions) driving forces show strong affinity for Judge pattern activation. The Structured drive creates rigid adherence to established standards and traditions. The Commanding drive demands control through evaluation and criticism. The Objective drive justifies emotional detachment as superior functionality.

Example Combination: Dr. Patricia demonstrates high Structured (believes in academic standards as a worthy cause), Commanding (needs to control department outcomes), and Objective (compartmentalizes emotions from "business" decisions). When adjunct retention becomes problematic, her Structured drive interprets this as a threat to academic standards, her Commanding drive demands control through increased criticism, and her Objective drive justifies emotional detachment from the human impact. The Judge pattern's defense cluster (projection, reaction formation, displacement) serves to maintain all three value systems while redirecting responsibility away from her leadership approach.

Victim Pattern Value Drivers

Individuals with high **Selfless** (complete tasks regardless of time/effort), **Altruistic** (respond to people in need), **Collaborative** (contribute to group success), and **Harmonious** (create balance, embrace experience) driving forces often gravitate toward Victim pattern manifestation. The Selfless drive creates vulnerability to become overwhelmed and exploited. The Altruistic drive prioritizes others' needs over personal agency. The Collaborative drive subordinates' individual power to group dynamics. The Harmonious drive avoids conflict that might disrupt relational balance.

Example Combination: Jake likely scores high on Selfless (wants to complete his degree regardless of difficulty), Altruistic (responds to others' academic needs), and Collaborative (values group study success over individual achievement). When academic challenges arise, his Selfless drive interprets struggle as normal sacrifice, his Altruistic drive focuses on how the professor should help him rather than his own responsibility, and his Collaborative drive seeks group dependency rather than individual action. The Victim pattern's defense cluster (denial, regression, repression) protects all three value systems while maintaining the appearance of good intentions.

Complex Value-Pattern Interactions

High Intellectual + Objective + Structured = Expert-Judge hybrid pattern, manifesting as academic perfectionism with harsh standards for both self and others.

High Commanding + Altruistic + Structured = Judge-Victim hybrid, appearing as martyred leadership where criticism serves as a "higher cause" of helping others improve.

High Resourceful + Collaborative + Selfless = Expert-Victim hybrid, using knowledge and competence to serve others while avoiding personal responsibility for outcomes.

* Which Values Drive Which Patterns?

EXPERT PATTERN ← High Intellectual + Commanding + Resourceful

- *"Knowledge is power and efficiency"*

JUDGE PATTERN ← High Structured + Commanding + Objective

- *"Standards and control create order"*

VICTIM PATTERN ← High Selfless + Altruistic + Collaborative

- *"Sacrifice and harmony over agency"*

Hybrid Patterns emerge from value combinations:

- Expert-Judge: Intellectual + Structured = Academic perfectionism
- Judge-Victim: Commanding + Altruistic = Martyred leadership
- Expert-Victim: Resourceful + Selfless = Competent helplessness

Emotional Intelligence Implications

These value-driven ego pattern tendencies create predictable blind spots in emotional intelligence development:

- **Expert-leaning individuals** often develop interpersonal EQ skills (empathy, social awareness) because their

Intellectual and Commanding drives prioritize competence over connection.

- **Judge-leaning individuals** typically struggle with self-awareness and emotional regulation because their Structured and Objective drives view emotions as inefficient obstacles to proper standards.
- **Victim-leaning individuals** frequently do not develop self-management skills (drive strength, commitment ethic) because their Selfless and Altruistic drives discourage healthy self-advocacy and personal agency.

Understanding these value-driven patterns enables more targeted emotional intelligence development by addressing the underlying motivational conflicts that maintain defensive behaviors. Rather than generic EQ skill building, interventions can focus on helping individuals develop emotional competencies that align with rather than threaten their core driving forces. It's not just having these values, it's when they reinforce each other under stress that patterns become rigid.

The Pattern Traps: When Values Become Prisons

Each ego pattern contains a fundamental trap—a core equation that transforms healthy values into psychological prisons. The Expert operates from the trap that knowledge equals worth, creating a reality where any gap in understanding becomes an existential threat to their identity. Admitting "I don't know" doesn't just mean lacking information; it means being worthless. This trap drives the Expert to intellectualize every emotional experience, rationalize every mistake, and compartmentalize contradictions rather than face the terror of intellectual inadequacy. The Judge falls into the trap that evaluation equals control, constructing a world where constant criticism and standard setting become the only means of maintaining safety and superiority. To stop judging would mean losing control, and losing control means vulnerability—an intolerable state that keeps the Judge perpetually finding flaws, projecting inadequacies, and displacing blame. The Victim's trap—that sacrifice equals goodness—creates perhaps the most insidious prison, where self-care becomes selfishness and personal agency becomes moral failure. Every boundary set feels like betrayal, every act of self-advocacy seems selfish, trapping the Victim in endless cycles of self-abandonment disguised as virtue. These traps explain why simple awareness rarely changes patterns: when someone genuinely believes their worth depends on knowledge, their safety requires control, or their goodness demands sacrifice, the pattern isn't just a defense—it becomes their entire identity architecture. Breaking free requires not just recognizing the trap but fundamentally reimagining what creates worth, safety, and goodness in one's life.

People rarely need to change their values as this is almost impossible, but they can learn to manage them in the direction of individual growth. Simply put, they need to learn to express them in healthy rather than defensive ways. An Expert's intellectual drive can fuel genuine learning rather than superiority. A Judge's structured approach can create helpful systems rather than weapons. A Victim's altruism can inspire conscious service rather than self-abandonment.

Cognitive Distortions: The Amplification System for Ego Patterns

Cognitive distortions serve as the amplification system that intensifies and maintains ego patterns through their bidirectional relationship with defense mechanisms. While defense mechanisms protect the ego from emotional threats and ego patterns provide the behavioral framework for that protection, cognitive distortions corrupt the information processing that feeds both systems. This creates a self-reinforcing cycle where distorted thinking triggers defensive responses, which activate ego patterns, which then generate more distorted thinking to justify the defensive behaviors.

Expert Pattern Cognitive Amplifiers

The Expert pattern gravitates toward distortions that maintain intellectual superiority and knowledge-based identity:

- **All-or-Nothing Thinking**: "Either I know everything about this topic or I'm incompetent"
- **Mind Reading**: "Everyone can see that I don't know what I'm talking about"
- **Labeling**: "I'm the expert" vs. "They're amateurs/naive/inexperienced"
- **Mental Filter**: Focusing exclusively on information that confirms expertise while ignoring contradictory evidence
- **Should Statements**: "I should know this," "Others should recognize my expertise"

Example Cycle: Dr. Harrison experiences All-or-Nothing Thinking ("If these interactive methods work better than my lectures, then my entire teaching approach is worthless"). This triggers intellectualization (defense mechanism) as he converts the emotional threat into abstract pedagogical theory. The Expert pattern then activates to protect his academic identity, generating more cognitive distortions: Mental Filter (focusing only on research supporting traditional lectures) and Labeling (dismissing interactive methods as "entertainment-focused"). These distortions then require more rationalization to maintain consistency, perpetuating the cycle.

Judge Pattern Cognitive Amplifiers

The Judge pattern employs distortions that maintain control through evaluation and criticism:

- **All-or-Nothing Thinking**: "Either standards are maintained perfectly or everything falls apart"
- **Should Statements**: "People should meet these standards," "Things should be done correctly"

- **Overgeneralization**: Drawing broad conclusions about competence from single mistakes
- **Catastrophizing**: "If I don't enforce these standards, everything will collapse"
- **Fortune Telling**: Predicting failure when standards aren't met

Example Cycle: Dr. Patricia uses Should Statements ("Adjunct professors should maintain the same standards as tenured faculty"). When retention problems arise, this triggers projection (defense mechanism) as she attributes the problem to others' inadequacies rather than her management style. The Judge pattern activates to maintain control, generating Overgeneralization ("All adjuncts lack real academic experience") and Catastrophizing ("If we lower standards, the department's reputation will be ruined"). These distortions justify more displacement of blame, intensifying the cycle.

Victim Pattern Cognitive Amplifiers

The Victim pattern relies on distortions that maintain helplessness and external blame:

- **Personalization**: Taking responsibility for negative outcomes while attributing positive outcomes to external factors
- **Fortune Telling**: "Nothing I do will make a difference"
- **Emotional Reasoning**: "I feel overwhelmed, so the situation must be impossible"
- **Catastrophizing**: "This failure means I'll never succeed"
- **Mental Filter**: Focusing exclusively on obstacles while ignoring available resources

Example Cycle: Jake experiences Fortune Telling ("I know I'll fail this exam no matter what I do"). This triggers denial (defense mechanism) as he refuses to acknowledge his own role in academic struggles. The Victim pattern activates in order to maintain safety through helplessness, generating Emotional Reasoning ("I feel hopeless, so the situation must be hopeless") and Mental Filter (focusing only on how difficult the material is while ignoring study resources). These distortions then require more regression to maintain the helpless narrative, deepening the cycle.

The Reinforcement Mechanism

Distortions → Defenses → Patterns

Cognitive distortions create emotional distress that activate defense mechanisms, which then engage ego patterns to maintain psychological safety. For example, Catastrophizing ("If I admit I don't know this, my career is over") creates anxiety that triggers intellectualization, which activates the Expert pattern to maintain competence-based identity.

Patterns → Defenses → Distortions

Ego patterns require defense mechanisms to maintain their narratives, which then generate cognitive distortions to justify the defensive behaviors. The Expert pattern uses rationalization to maintain superiority, creating distorted reasoning that supports intellectual dominance while dismissing contradictory evidence.

Defense Mechanisms as Cognitive Distortion Generators

Each defense mechanism inherently produces specific cognitive distortions:

- **Intellectualization** generates Mental Filter (selecting only analytical information) and Should Statements ("Emotions should be controlled through logic")

- **Projection** creates Mind Reading ("Others are thinking critically about me") and Labeling ("They're the problem")
- **Denial** produces Minimization ("This isn't really a problem") and Fortune Telling ("Things will work out without my intervention")

The Simple Chain

VALUES → **PERSONAL DOMAIN** → LIES ↔ BIAS → DEFENSES → DISTORTIONS → EGO FACES

How It Works

1. VALUES (The Why) What we care about most creates vulnerability

- Intellectual values → Expert patterns

- Structured values → Judge patterns

- Altruistic values → Victim patterns

2. PERSONAL DOMAIN (The Container) The internal architecture where everything happens

- Houses our values, beliefs, experiences, and identity

- Contains dual filters: authentic (reality-based) and egoic (distortion-based)

- Determines which filter dominates our response

3. LIES (The Lubricant) Content + context distortions that smooth over contradictions

- Context lies: "This isn't what it seems"

- Content lies: "The facts aren't what they appear"

- Operate through whichever filter is active

4. BIAS (The Automation) Automatic filtering that happens before we think

- What we notice (input bias)

- How we interpret (processing bias)

- What we conclude (output bias)

- Emerges from either authentic or egoic filter

5. DEFENSES (The Tools) Clustered strategies that protect the ego

- Expert: Intellectualization, rationalization, compartmentalization

- Judge: Projection, reaction formation, displacement

- Victim: Denial, regression, repression

6. DISTORTIONS (The Amplifiers) Thinking errors that make everything feel justified

- All-or-nothing thinking

- Should Statements

- Catastrophizing

- Fortune telling

7. EGO FACES (The Behavior) What others see and experience

- Expert: Lecturing, correcting, demonstrating superiority

- Judge: Criticizing, evaluating, setting impossible standards

- Victim: Complaining, seeking rescue, positioning others as responsible

The Key Insight

Each level enables and reinforces the others.

Values shape our personal domain → Personal domain filters determine which lies feel justified → Lies influence automatic pre-emotion bias → Bias triggers defenses → Defenses generate distortions → Distortions manifest as ego faces.

Breaking the chain at any point can disrupt the whole system, but the lies are the most leverage point because they enable everything else.

>> Chapter 2 Key Takeaways

1. **The personal domain is the architecture where everything begins** — the internal container of values, beliefs, experiences, and identity that determines which filter — authentic or egoic — dominates our responses. Think of it as the hula hoop that surrounds us: what we hold dear lives at its center, and everything entering that space gets filtered through who we think we are.
2. **Lies are the lubricant, not the lie detector** — defensive dishonesty operates primarily through context manipulation rather than outright factual falsehood. Shifting the frame of what something means is far more powerful — and harder to detect — than changing the facts themselves.
3. **Pre-emotion bias fires before we think** — automatic filtering shapes what we notice, how we interpret it, and what we conclude, all before conscious awareness

arrives. The personal domain's two filters determine whether that bias serves authentic perception or egoic protection.

4. **Each ego pattern deploys its own defense cluster** — the Expert uses cognitive-based defenses (intellectualization, rationalization, compartmentalization); the Judge uses redirection-based defenses (projection, displacement, reaction formation); and the Victim uses avoidance-based defenses (denial, regression, repression). These clusters are not random; they are perfectly matched to each pattern's core need.

5. **Values are the origin point, not the obstacle** — Intellectual, Commanding, and Resourceful values drive Expert patterns; Structured, Commanding, and Objective values drive Judge patterns; Selfless, Altruistic, and Collaborative values drive Victim patterns. The same values that generate defensive patterns also contain the seeds of their resolution.

6. **Cognitive distortions amplify what defenses protect** — all-or-nothing thinking, should statements, catastrophizing, and fortune telling are not personality quirks but the thinking system each pattern uses to make defensive behavior feel not just reasonable but necessary. Distortions and defenses form a self-reinforcing cycle that deepens with every activation.

7. **The dual expression system runs simultaneously inside and out** — ego patterns manifest as interpersonal behavior that others observe and intrapersonal narrative that justifies that behavior to us. The internal story is the most damaging of the two because it prevents recognition and makes change feel unnecessary.

8. **The chain has a most vulnerable link** — Values → Personal Domain → Lies → Bias → Defenses → Distortions → Ego Faces. Breaking the chain at any point disrupts the system, but the lies are the highest-leverage intervention point because they enable every stage that follows.

>> Coming Next: Chapter 3 – The Expert: Knowledge as Armor

In the next chapter, we bring the architecture to life through the first of the three faces — the Expert. You'll see how the defense clusters, distortions, and values described in this chapter organize into a living pattern: one that uses knowledge as armor, being right as currency, and intellectual superiority as the primary measure of worth. The Expert pattern is the most socially rewarded of the three faces, which makes it the hardest to see in us, and the most important place to begin.

The architecture is now mapped. Let's meet the first face that lives inside it.

Chapter 3: The Expert – Knowledge as Armor

>> What You'll Learn in This Chapter

- Why being right becomes an existential necessity for Experts

- The three core manifestations: Primacy of Being Right, Intellectual Superiority, and Emotional Bypass

- How Expert patterns destroy workplace collaboration and personal relationships

- The sophisticated defense cluster: Intellectualization, Rationalization, and Compartmentalization

- Four devastating paradoxes that trap Experts in their own expertise

- How to recognize Expert patterns across the four intensity levels

- The path from unconscious expertise to conscious wisdom

Reading Time: ~35 minutes

"The trouble with the world is that the stupid are cocksure and the intelligent are full of doubt." - Bertrand Russell

Dr. Amanda Chen stands at the whiteboard, her back to the conference room filled with her software development team. The junior developer who just presented his innovative approach to their current project sits quietly, his enthusiasm gradually deflating as Amanda systematically dismantles his proposal.

"While I appreciate your... creative thinking," Amanda says, her tone suggesting anything but appreciation, "there are fundamental architectural principles you're overlooking. Let me explain why this approach would fail at scale." She launches into a twenty-minute lecture on distributed systems theory, drawing complex diagrams that showcase her expertise while completely missing the practical elegance of the junior developer's solution.

As her team members exchange glances—some sympathetic toward their colleague, others simply resigned—Amanda remains oblivious to the creative energy draining from the room. In her mind, she's not crushing innovation; she's protecting the project from amateur mistakes. She's not alienating her team; she's educating them. This is the Expert pattern in action: using knowledge not as a tool for collaboration and growth, but as armor against the vulnerability of not knowing, of being wrong, of being merely human.

Core Characteristics and Manifestations

The Expert pattern represents one of the three primary ego defensive strategies, characterized using knowledge, competence, and intellectual superiority as protection against perceived threats to identity and worth. At its core, the Expert pattern stems from a fundamental equation deeply embedded in the psyche: Knowledge = Safety = Worth.

* The Expert's Core Equation

KNOWLEDGE = SAFETY = WORTH

$\downarrow$ $\downarrow$ $\downarrow$

Being Right = Control = Identity

This defensive strategy manifests through several interconnected characteristics that create a self-reinforcing system of intellectual protection.

The Expert's Defensive Architecture

Building on the complete defensive architecture from Chapter 2, the Expert pattern follows this predictable cascade:

VALUES → PERSONAL DOMAIN → LIES ↔ BIAS → DEFENSES → DISTORTIONS → EGO FACE

- **VALUES**: Intellectual growth, learning, competence, understanding (*These positive values create vulnerability when threatened, triggering defensive responses*)
- **PERSONAL DOMAIN**: Identity becomes fused with knowledge; intellectual capacity equals self-worth
- **LIES**: *Context:* "This isn't criticism, it's ignorance I must correct" | *Content:* "I possess superior understanding"
- **BIAS**: Selective attention to intellectual threats, interpreting ambiguity as challenges to expertise
- **DEFENSES**: Intellectualization, rationalization, compartmentalization (detailed in sections below)
- **DISTORTIONS**: Mental filter (seeing only confirming data), should statements ("people should be more logical"), all-or-nothing thinking ("either I know everything or I'm worthless")
- **EGO FACE**: Lecturing, correcting, demonstrating superiority—what Amanda's team experiences in our opening story

Remember from Chapter 2: Breaking this chain at any point can disrupt the entire system, with lies being the highest leverage point for change.

The Primacy of Being Right

For those operating from the Expert pattern, being right isn't simply preferable, it's existentially necessary. The need to be correct transcends normal intellectual confidence and becomes a matter of psychological survival. When challenged, the Expert doesn't merely defend their position; they defend their very sense of self.

This existential need to be right permeates every interaction, transforming even casual conversations into opportunities for correction. The Expert compulsively points out errors in others' statements—a friend's misremembered movie quote, a colleague's imprecise terminology, a partner's minor factual mistake—unable to let even trivial inaccuracies pass unchallenged. Admitting uncertainty becomes physically uncomfortable, triggering genuine distress as if saying "I don't know" might cause their entire identity to crumble. When mistakes do slip through their armor, they're quickly reframed: it wasn't an error but a misunderstanding, not their failure but someone else's unclear communication or the system's inadequacy. They'll argue points long after everyone else has moved on, unable to let go until others acknowledge their correctness. Their walls display degrees and certificates like medieval shields, each credential another layer of armor proving they deserve to be heard, to be right, to exist as an expert.

Intellectual Superiority as Identity

The Expert pattern creates identity fusion with knowledge and competence. Rather than viewing expertise as something they possess, Experts experience it as something they *are*. This fusion fundamentally warps how they see the world and everyone in it. They unconsciously construct mental hierarchies, ranking every person they meet on an intelligence scale—this colleague is "sharp," that friend is "simple," this relative is "ignorant." Those deemed less knowledgeable face immediate dismissal, their ideas discounted before they're fully expressed, their contributions viewed as inherently less valuable. Formal education becomes a religion where PhD means prophet and high school diploma means heathen, where credentials determine not just competence but basic human worth. Knowledge transforms from something to be shared into currency to be hoarded, with Experts carefully guarding their expertise like dragons protecting gold, ensuring others remain dependent on their superior understanding. Even their communication becomes performance art—using unnecessarily complex vocabulary when simple words would do, constructing elaborate theoretical frameworks for straightforward concepts, turning every explanation into a demonstration of intellectual superiority that leaves others feeling stupid rather than enlightened.

NOTE: Warning Signs of Identity Fusion:

- Ranking people by perceived intelligence

- Dismissing those deemed less knowledgeable

- Equating formal education with human worth

- Hoarding knowledge to maintain advantage

- Using unnecessary complexity in communication

The Emotional Bypass

Perhaps most significantly, the Expert pattern serves as a sophisticated mechanism for avoiding emotional vulnerability. By intellectualizing experiences and interactions, the Expert maintains a safe distance from the messy, uncertain realm of feelings. When hurt by a partner's criticism, they don't feel the pain—instead they launch into clinical observations: "I'm not hurt, I'm simply observing that your communication style tends toward the aggressive when you're stressed." A friend's tears trigger not empathy but a recitation of grief stage theory and neurotransmitter explanations. They construct elaborate theoretical frameworks to explain away their own feelings, building complex psychological models for why they feel lonely rather than simply experiencing and processing the loneliness itself. Written communication becomes their fortress—emails and texts allow them to craft perfect responses, edit out emotional reactions, and maintain the controlled, intellectual facade that spontaneous conversation might crack. Ambiguity becomes their nightmare; they'd rather have a wrong answer than no answer, rather force false certainty than sit with the discomfort of not knowing. Every uncertain feeling must be analyzed into submission, categorized and labeled until it's no longer felt but merely understood—a specimen pinned to their mental board rather than a living experience flowing through them.

Workplace Scenarios and Relationship Impacts

The Expert pattern profoundly shapes professional environments and workplace relationships, often in ways that seem productive on the surface while creating deeper dysfunction.

The Meeting Monopolizer

Sarah's story from Chapter 1 exemplifies a common Expert pattern manifestation: the compulsive need to demonstrate knowledge at the expense of collaboration. In meetings, the Expert dominates discussion time with lengthy explanations and interrupts others to correct minor inaccuracies. They shift conversations toward their areas of expertise, provide unsolicited education on tangential topics, and create hostile environments where brainstorming and innovation cannot flourish. The impact of this dynamic ripples through the entire organization. Team members learn to stay quiet rather than risk correction. Innovation stagnates as people become afraid to propose imperfect ideas. Meetings become performances rather than collaborations.

The Reluctant Delegator

Dr. Harrison, our tenured professor from Chapter 2, demonstrates another Expert pattern: the inability to trust others with important tasks. He micromanages under the guise of quality control, compulsively reworks others' contributions to meet his personal standards, and creates bottlenecks by insisting on personally reviewing everything. The mindset is "if you want something done right you have to do it yourself". This prevents his team from learning through their own mistakes, stunting their development while driving himself toward burnout from his inability to share the intellectual load.

The Knowledge Gatekeeper

In many organizations, Experts become gatekeepers of critical information, using their knowledge as a source of power and job security. They deliberately cultivate dependency, ensuring they're the sole keeper of critical systems—the only one who knows the legacy database quirks, the undocumented API workarounds, the client's unwritten preferences. When they do communicate, it's in deliberately obscure jargon and acronyms that require translation, turning simple concepts into mysterious incantations only they can decode. Documentation becomes their enemy; they'll find endless excuses to avoid writing anything down, keeping crucial processes locked in their heads where job security lives. During transitions, they perform a subtle sabotage—training sessions that become overwhelming information dumps designed to confuse rather than educate, critical details are "forgotten" until after the replacement fails, passwords and procedures are shared piecemeal to ensure failure. They construct elaborate information silos, hoarding emails in personal folders, keeping essential contacts in private phones, maintaining shadow systems that only they can navigate. Each piece of protected knowledge becomes another bar in the cage they've built around their position, transforming from employees to irreplaceable oracle whose departure would mean organizational chaos. They've made themselves indispensable not through excellence but through strategic opacity, holding their organization hostage to their willingness to share what should have been common knowledge all along.

Relationship Costs

The Expert pattern's impact extends beyond professional dysfunction into personal relationships:

*** Relationship Impact Assessment**

With Partners:

- X Intellectual sparring replaces emotional intimacy

- X Corrections and lectures damage romantic connection

- X Emotional needs get intellectualized rather than met

- X Partners feel inadequate or stupid

- X Conflict becomes about winning rather than understanding

With Children:

- X Every interaction becomes a teaching moment

- X Children's emotional needs get explained away

- X Academic achievement becomes the primary value metric

- X Children learn to hide struggles to avoid disappointment

- X Natural curiosity gets replaced by performance anxiety

With Friends:

- X Social gatherings become platforms for displaying knowledge

- X Friends feel judged for their choices or interests

- X Emotional support gets replaced with advice and analysis

- X Relationships become competitive rather than supportive

- X Social isolation increases as people tire of being lectured

Defense Mechanisms in Detail

The Expert pattern employs a sophisticated cluster of psychological defense mechanisms that work synergistically to maintain the protective barrier of intellectual superiority. Understanding these mechanisms is crucial for recognizing and ultimately transcending the pattern.

Intellectualization: The Primary Shield

Intellectualization serves as the Expert's primary defense mechanism, transforming threatening emotional experiences into abstract intellectual exercises. This isn't simply thinking about problems, it's a systematic conversion of felt experience into theoretical understanding that maintains emotional distance.

How it works: When faced with emotional threat (criticism, uncertainty, vulnerability), the Expert's psyche automatically shifts into analytical mode. The threatening experience gets reframed as an intellectual puzzle to solve rather than an emotion to feel.

Example in action: When Amanda's team provides feedback that her management style is demoralizing, she doesn't feel the hurt or examine her impact. Instead, she launches into an analysis of management theory, citing studies on feedback mechanisms and organizational psychology. She creates a spreadsheet to track "morale metrics" and develops a theoretical framework for "optimized team emotional states." The original emotional message—that she's hurting her team—never penetrates her intellectual armor.

The cost: While intellectualization can provide temporary relief from emotional pain, it prevents genuine learning and growth. Relationships suffer as others feel unheard and emotionally disconnected. The Expert remains trapped in their head, analyzing life rather than living it.

Rationalization: The Justification Engine

Rationalization works hand-in-hand with intellectualization, creating logical explanations that justify the Expert's behavior while maintaining their superior self-image. This defense mechanism constructs elaborate reasoning that makes ego-protective behavior seem not just acceptable but necessary.

How it works: The Expert's mind automatically generates plausible explanations for any behavior that might threaten their self-image. These explanations always position the Expert as acting from knowledge, wisdom, or necessity rather than from ego defense.

Example in action: Dr. Harrison's resistance to interactive teaching methods gets rationalized as "maintaining academic rigor" and "protecting educational standards." His elaborate arguments about pedagogical philosophy mask the simpler truth: he's afraid of losing control in the classroom and having his expertise challenged by student participation.

The deeper pattern: Rationalization in Experts often follows predictable patterns:

* "I'm not being condescending, I'm being helpful"
* "I'm not rigid, I'm maintaining standards"
* "I'm not avoiding emotion, I'm being logical"
* "I'm not controlling, I'm ensuring quality"

* Common Expert Rationalizations:

What They Do	How They Rationalize It
Being condescending	"I'm being helpful"
Being rigid	"I'm maintaining standards"
Avoiding emotion	"I'm being logical"
Being controlling	"I'm ensuring quality"

Compartmentalization: The Cognitive Divide

Compartmentalization allows the Expert to maintain contradictory beliefs or behaviors by keeping them in separate mental categories that never interact. This defense mechanism is particularly sophisticated in Expert patterns, creating elaborate mental architectures that prevent self-awareness.

How it works: The Expert creates distinct mental compartments for different aspects of their life or knowledge, allowing them to maintain their superior self-image even when evidence contradicts it.

Example in action: A therapist operating from Expert pattern might have deep theoretical knowledge about emotional intelligence while being completely unable to apply it in their own relationships. They compartmentalize "professional knowledge" separately from "personal experience," never allowing the two to inform each other. They can lecture on the importance of vulnerability while maintaining rigid emotional armor in their own life.

The paradox: Compartmentalization creates the peculiar phenomenon of the "Knowledgeable Incompetent"—someone who knows everything about a subject theoretically but cannot embody or practice it. This is why we find relationship experts who can't maintain partnerships, financial advisors in debt, and health experts with unhealthy lifestyles.

NOTE: The Paradox of the "Knowledgeable Incompetent"

A therapist with deep theoretical knowledge about emotional intelligence who cannot apply it in their own relationships. They compartmentalize "professional knowledge" from "personal experience," never allowing them to inform each other.

The Intrapersonal Cover-Up System

As identified in Chapter 2, the Expert pattern operates on two levels simultaneously: the interpersonal (external behavior) and the intrapersonal (internal justification). The intrapersonal system is often more damaging than external behavior because it prevents recognition and change.

The Dual Expression System

Level	Expression	Example
Interpersonal (External)	What others see and experience	Dominating meetings, dismissing ideas
Intrapersonal (Internal)	Self-justifying narrative	"Someone has to maintain standards"

*** Critical Insight:**

The intrapersonal narrative is more damaging than external behavior because it prevents recognition and change.

The Internal Narrative: While Amanda publicly dominates meetings and dismisses others' ideas, her internal narrative runs continuously: "Someone has to maintain standards... These people would be lost without my expertise... I'm helping them learn... If I don't correct these mistakes, the whole project will fail..."

This internal story serves multiple functions:

- **Maintains ego syntonic behavior** (feels natural and justified)
- **Prevents cognitive dissonance** (aligns behavior with self-image)
- **Blocks empathy** (others' pain is reframed as their learning)
- **Creates conceit** (develops genuine belief in superiority)

The Conceit Development Process: Over time, the intrapersonal narrative evolves from defensive justification to genuine belief:

1. **Early stage**: "I need to share my knowledge to help"
2. **Middle stage**: "I usually know more than others"
3. **Advanced stage**: "I am more intelligent than most people"
4. **Entrenched stage**: "Others' opinions have little value compared to mine"

This progression represents the shift from using knowledge as a tool to experiencing knowledge as identity, creating increasingly rigid and isolated ways of being.

The Expertise Trap: When Knowledge Becomes Prison

The ultimate tragedy of the Expert pattern lies in how the very knowledge meant to provide safety and worth becomes a prison that limits growth, connection, and authentic experience. This expertise trap manifests in several paradoxical ways:

The Competence-Rigidity Paradox

As expertise deepens, flexibility often decreases. The Expert becomes so invested in their knowledge framework that they cannot see beyond it:

- **New information gets rejected** if it doesn't fit existing models
- **Beginner's mind becomes impossible** as expertise calcifies
- **Innovation is stifled** by adherence to "proven" methods
- **Learning stops** as the Expert believes they already know

Dr. Harrison exemplifies this paradox. His decades of teaching experience, rather than making him more adaptable, have made him more rigid. His expertise has become a prison preventing him from discovering new ways to connect with students and develop his craft.

The Connection-Isolation Paradox

The Expert pattern creates a cruel irony: the more someone tries to connect through sharing knowledge, the more isolated they become:

- Lecturing replaces conversation
- Teaching replaces learning together
- Correcting replaces connecting
- Being right replaces being real

This isolation often surprises Experts who genuinely believe they're being helpful. They can't understand why others withdraw when they're "just trying to share valuable information."

The Strength-Fragility Paradox

While the Expert pattern appears strong and confident, it creates profound fragility:

- **Identity depends on external validation** of expertise
- **Self-worth crumbles** when knowledge is challenged
- **Rapid technological change** threatens accumulated expertise
- **Imposter syndrome** lurks beneath the confident exterior

The very armor meant to protect becomes a vulnerability. Any situation that challenges the Expert's knowledge base threatens their entire sense of self.

The Growth-Stagnation Paradox

Perhaps most tragically, the Expert pattern that initially drives learning and achievement eventually becomes its greatest obstacle:

- **Fear of not knowing** prevents exploration of new fields
- **Need to appear expert** prevents admitting ignorance
- **Attachment to existing knowledge** prevents updating beliefs
- **Identity fusion with expertise** prevents personal evolution

Expert Pattern Across the Intensity Scale

The Ego Pattern Intensity Scale provides a crucial framework for understanding how the Expert pattern manifests with varying degrees of impact and entrenchment. As intensity increases, the pattern moves from a flexible tool to a rigid prison.

Intensity 1 - Pattern as Option

At Intensity 1, the Expert pattern is temporarily activated without becoming identity:

- **Uses knowledge as a tool** without defining themselves by it
- **Conscious choice** about when to share expertise ("which battles to fight")
- **Learn with joy** rather than to prove worth
- **Share information freely** without need for superiority
- **Admitting ignorance easily** without shame
- **Change positions** when presented with better information
- **Strong awareness** of authentic self beyond any expertise

This represents our natural state before ego patterns develop—curious, open, and undefended in our relationship with knowledge. Someone at Intensity 1 might say, "I know about this topic, but I'm curious to hear your perspective."

Intensity 2 - Pattern as Refuge

At Intensity 2, the Expert pattern becomes a go-to response providing temporary relief:

- **Pattern provides temporary relief** from perceived intellectual threats
- **Beginning identity attachment** - more situations feel like they require expertise
- **Enjoy being competent** without requiring constant validation
- **Share expertise helpfully** without condescension
- **Acknowledge others' knowledge** without feeling threatened
- **Making mistakes** without identity crisis
- **Some rigidity** in specific professional contexts
- **Intermittent awareness** of authentic self beyond the pattern

Someone at Intensity 2 might notice themselves defaulting to Expert mode in meetings but can still pull back and engage differently when aware.

Intensity 3 - Pattern as Necessity

At Intensity 3, the Expert pattern becomes required for self-worth:

- **"I am an expert"** becomes a core self-definition
- **Knowledge becomes primary source** of self-worth
- **All perceived threats** to expertise must be extinguished
- **Challenges to expertise** feel like personal attacks

- **Social interactions** become opportunities to display knowledge
- **Career choices** driven by need to be recognized as expert
- **Difficulty functioning** without intellectual superiority
- **Rare glimpses** of authentic self, usually only in safe moments

Dr. Amanda operates primarily at Intensity 3. Her identity as "the software architecture expert" drives her behavior, creating significant life impairment but still allows some professional function.

Intensity 4 - Pattern as Identity

At Intensity 4, the Expert pattern becomes the entire identity:

- **Cannot conceive alternatives** to being the smartest person in the room
- **Any threats to exaggerated intellectual self** must be overcome
- **Demands others enable** their need to be right
- **Severe anxiety emerges** when expertise is questioned
- **Relationships are sacrificed** to maintain expert image
- **Learning becomes threatening** rather than exciting
- **Depression develops** from impossible standards
- **Complete disconnection** from authentic self

Dr. Harrison has reached Intensity 4. His internalized rules about "proper" teaching methods have become so rigid that any challenge creates existential threat. He cannot adapt because change would mean admitting his expertise is incomplete. He lives entirely in the "smoke" of his Expert pattern, unable to access his authentic self.

Case Example - Intensity 4: Dr. Marcus, a renowned physicist, spent forty years developing a theory later disproven by new evidence. Rather than adapting, his Intensity 4 Expert pattern led him to:

- Sabotage the careers of researchers who challenged him
- Fabricate data to support his position
- Alienate his entire family defending his theory
- Experience complete mental breakdown when forced to confront the truth
- Require intensive therapeutic intervention to prevent self-harm

This represents the severe dysfunction possible when the Expert pattern completely obscures authentic identity—when being right becomes more important than relationships, truth, or even personal wellbeing.

Moving Down Intensity Levels: The Path of Recovery

The journey of Ego Intelligence involves consciously moving down intensity levels. For the Expert pattern, this means:

From Intensity 4 to 3:

- Crisis intervention is often required
- Creating tiny moments of non-Expert identity
- Professional therapy to address severe dysfunction
- Gradual separation of self-worth from knowledge

From Intensity 3 to 2:

- Expanding windows of authentic self-awareness
- Developing other sources of identity beyond expertise
- Learning to hold expertise lightly
- Practicing genuine curiosity about others' knowledge

From Intensity 2 to 1:

- Strengthening ability to choose rather than react
- Full integration where knowledge serves life rather than ego
- Maintaining connection to authentic self while engaging expertise consciously
- Using knowledge as a gift rather than armor

Each intensity descent requires specific practices and interventions, which will be explored in later chapters.

The Habit Formation of Expert Patterns

Understanding how Expert patterns become entrenched requires recognizing their nature as cognitive habits rather than conscious choices. Through repetition, what begins as deliberate behavior becomes automatic response, operating below the threshold of awareness.

Every time someone operating from the Expert pattern corrects another person, receives validation for their knowledge, or successfully maintains intellectual superiority, the behavior is reinforced. Like learning to drive or type, these responses gradually shift from conscious effort to unconscious reflex. The Expert no longer decides to correct someone's imprecise terminology—they've already launched into explanation before conscious thought engages.

This automaticity explains why Expert patterns feel so natural to those exhibiting them. The behavior has been rehearsed thousands of times across years or decades, becoming as automatic as breathing. The Expert genuinely believes they're "just being helpful" because the pattern has become so deeply ingrained that it feels like their authentic self rather than a learned defensive response.

The Cognitive Load of Maintaining Expertise

This habitual pattern creates tremendous cognitive burden, though Experts rarely recognize the mental exhaustion they experience. Their minds run constant background processes, scanning every conversation for opportunities to demonstrate knowledge, monitoring for threats to their expertise, preparing corrections and counterarguments even during casual interactions. This hypervigilance drains mental resources that could be used for genuine learning, creativity, or connection.

The cognitive demand intensifies when the Expert encounters situations where their knowledge is genuinely challenged or insufficient. Rather than acknowledging limitations, the habituated pattern demands they maintain superiority, forcing increasingly elaborate mental gymnastics to avoid admitting uncertainty. This cognitive overload often manifests as irritability, exhaustion, and the desperate need to retreat to areas of established expertise where the pattern can operate smoothly.

Breaking Cognitive Habits Through Conscious Practice

The same cognitive plasticity that creates entrenched Expert patterns also enables change. Just as the pattern was built through repetition, it can be modified through deliberate practice of new responses. This requires:

- **Conscious interruption** of automatic responses—catching yourself before the correction leaves your mouth

- **Deliberate practice** of uncertainty—saying "I don't know" or "tell me more" when expertise wants to dominate

- **Cognitive reframing**, viewing not-knowing as curiosity rather than threat

- **New habit formation**—repeatedly choosing connection over correction until the new response becomes natural

The challenge isn't understanding the pattern intellectually—most Experts can analyze their behavior brilliantly. The challenge is interrupting cognitive habits that have been strengthened through thousands of repetitions. This is why awareness alone isn't enough; transformation requires patient, persistent practice of new cognitive patterns until they become as automatic as the old ones.

Cultural and Professional Reinforcement

The Expert pattern doesn't develop in a vacuum—it's often actively reinforced by cultural and professional systems that reward knowledge hoarding and intellectual competition.

Our broader culture sends powerful messages that feed Expert patterns. The ubiquitous phrase "knowledge is power" implies that knowledge should be hoarded rather than shared, creating scarcity where abundance could exist. We've constructed intelligence as a hierarchy where people are ranked and compared, fostering constant competition rather than collaboration. Paradoxically, rising anti-intellectualism makes Experts even more defensive, clinging tighter to their superiority as their value feels threatened. In our information economy, knowledge has become a commodity to be traded rather than wisdom to be cultivated, while social media rewards those who appear knowledgeable regardless of actual understanding—incentivizing performance over substance.

Academic Reinforcement

Educational systems inadvertently cultivate Expert patterns from elementary school through graduate programs. Grading systems rank and compare intelligence, teaching children early that their worth correlates with their intellectual performance relative to peers. Competitive environments transform knowledge into a scarce resource where one student's success means another's failure. Teaching methods that reward memorization over understanding create Experts who can recite facts but not apply wisdom. Credential inflation has made degrees necessary for basic worth—a bachelor's degree now merely grants entry where high school once sufficed, driving people to collect certifications like armor. In higher education, publish-or-perish culture prioritizes output over truth, rewarding those who produce volume rather than those who pursue genuine understanding.

Professional Reinforcement

Many professions actively reward Expert pattern behaviors, creating systemic pressure to maintain intellectual superiority. Medicine perpetuates a "doctor as god" culture that punishes admitting uncertainty, where saying "I don't know" can destroy careers despite being honest. The legal system's adversarial structure rewards being right over finding truth, training lawyers to argue positions rather than seek justice. Academia's tenure system entrenches expertise, protecting those who stopped learning decades ago while blocking fresh perspectives. Technology's "genius culture" worships individual brilliance over collaborative innovation, creating toxic environments where only the "smartest" voice matters. Consulting business models depends on maintaining expertise mystique—if clients understood how simple most solutions are, the industry would collapse.

These systemic reinforcements mean that Experts aren't just dealing with personal patterns but swimming against powerful cultural currents that reward the very behaviors that isolate them.

Recognizing these external pressures is crucial for understanding why Expert patterns are so persistent and why individual change, while necessary, isn't sufficient without systemic awareness.

The Path Forward: Seeds of Transformation

While the Expert pattern can create significant suffering, it also contains the seeds of its own transformation. The very intelligence that creates the pattern can be redirected toward conscious growth.

Each ego pattern, when consciously integrated, offers unique gifts. The Expert pattern's shadow contains remarkable treasures waiting to be reclaimed. Their compulsive need to know everything transforms into deep curiosity about the self—the one subject they've avoided studying. The same hunger that drove them to accumulate credentials and certifications can be redirected toward emotional and spiritual growth, approaching their inner world with the scholarly dedication they once reserved for external achievements. Their highly developed analytical ability, previously used to maintain superiority, becomes a powerful tool for recognizing their own patterns and understanding the hidden dynamics in relationships. Communication skills honed through years of lecturing and explaining can learn a new language—vulnerability, uncertainty, and authentic sharing rather than information transfer. Their sophisticated problem-solving capacity, no longer wasted on winning arguments or proving points, can address real human needs: how to connect authentically, how to love without controlling, how to learn without defending. The Expert's greatest gift may be that they already possess all the tools needed for transformation—they simply need to turn their formidable intelligence inward with the same rigor they once applied to the external world.

The Journey Back to Authentic Self

The recovery process at each intensity involves progressively reconnecting with the authentic self:

- **From Intensity 4→3**: Creating tiny moments of non-pattern identity
- **From Intensity 3→2**: Expanding windows of authentic self-awareness
- **From Intensity 2→1**: Strengthening ability to choose rather than react
- **At Intensity 1**: Maintaining connection while engaging patterns consciously

This framework shows that ego patterns aren't inherently problematic—they become destructive when they obscure our awareness of who we truly are beneath the defensive strategies.

The journey from Expert pattern to integrated wisdom isn't about abandoning knowledge or expertise. It's about holding them lightly, using them in service of connection rather than separation, growth rather than defense.

As we'll explore in subsequent chapters, this transformation requires specific practices, considerable courage, and often the support of others who've walked this path. The Expert who can embrace not knowing opens doorways to wisdom far greater than any accumulation of facts could provide.

In the end, the most profound expertise may be the willingness to say, "I don't know, but I'm curious to discover together." This vulnerability, paradoxically, creates more safety and worth than any armor of knowledge ever could.

Reflecting on the Expert Within

As you read this chapter, you might notice your own Expert pattern activating—perhaps critiquing the writing, finding flaws in the logic, or feeling superior to the examples provided. This is natural and even valuable. The Expert pattern helped you develop whatever knowledge and skills you possess. The invitation isn't to destroy it but to recognize it, appreciate its service, and gradually learn when it serves and when it limits.

Consider:

- Where in your life does knowledge feel like armor?
- When do you use expertise to avoid vulnerability?
- How might your relationships change if you valued connection over being right?
- What would it mean to have expertise without attachment?

The journey toward Ego Intelligence begins with honest recognition. In recognizing our patterns, we create the possibility of choice. And in choice lies freedom—the freedom to be both knowledgeable and kind, both expert and learner, both teacher and student in the grand classroom of life.

>> Chapter 3 Key Takeaways

1. **The Expert equation** - Knowledge = Safety = Worth drives all Expert behavior, making being right an existential necessity rather than a preference.

2. **Three core manifestations** define the Expert pattern: The Primacy of Being Right (compulsive correction), Intellectual Superiority as Identity (ranking people by intelligence), and Emotional Bypass (converting feelings into analyses).

3. **The defense trinity** - Intellectualization transforms emotions into abstractions, Rationalization creates

logical justifications, and Compartmentalization
separates contradictory knowledge to maintain
superiority.

4. **The dual expression system** - Expert patterns operate
    simultaneously as interpersonal behavior (what others
    see) and intrapersonal narrative (self-justification), with
    the internal story being more damaging as it prevents
    recognition and change.

5. **Four paradoxes trap Experts** - Competence creates
    rigidity, connection attempts cause isolation, apparent
    strength masks fragility, and initial growth drivers
    become obstacles to learning.

6. **Intensity determines impact** - From Pattern as Option
    (conscious choice) through Pattern as Identity (complete
    fusion), each level represents deeper entrenchment and
    greater life disruption.

7. **Habits, not character** - Expert patterns are cognitive
    habits formed through repetition, not personality traits,
    which means they can be changed through conscious
    practice.

8. **Cultural reinforcement** - Educational systems,
    professional cultures, and social messages actively
    reward Expert behaviors, making individual change
    challenging without systemic awareness.

9. **The gifts within** - When consciously integrated, Expert traits transform compulsive knowing becomes deep curiosity, superiority becomes genuine expertise in service, and the need to be right becomes the courage to say, "I don't know."

10. **Recovery is progressive** - Moving down intensity levels requires patient practice, from creating tiny moments of non-Expert identity to eventually maintaining authentic self while using expertise consciously.

>> Coming Next: Chapter 4 – The Judge: Control Through Criticism

In the next chapter, we'll explore the Judge pattern—the relentless drive to evaluate, criticize, and control through impossible standards. You'll discover how the Judge's perfectionism isn't about quality but about managing anxiety, why their criticism of others is really about their own fears, and how the very standards meant to create order actually generate chaos. Most importantly, you'll learn how the Judge's gift for discernment can be transformed from a weapon into wisdom.

If the Expert needs to be right, the Judge needs to be righteous. Let's explore why—and how to break free.

Chapter 4: The Judge – Control Through Criticism

>> **What You'll Learn in This Chapter**

- Why perfectionism is really about control, not quality, and how it becomes a prison

- The three core manifestations: Rigid Standards, The Should System, and Control Through Criticism

- How the Judge pattern destroys families through comparison, criticism, and moving goalposts

- The sophisticated defense cluster: Projection, Reaction Formation, and Displacement

- Why the Judge's standards are designed to be unattainable—ensuring perpetual justification for criticism

- The devastating paradoxes: how pursuing perfection creates misery, control creates chaos

- How to recognize Judge patterns across the four intensity levels

- The path from destructive criticism to constructive discernment

Reading Time: ~30 minutes

"The way we judge ourselves is the worst judge that ever existed." - Don Miguel Ruiz

Michael sits at the dinner table, his jaw clenched as he watches his teenage son reach for his phone. Before the device even clears the pocket, Michael's voice cuts through the evening air: "You should know better than to check your phone at dinner. I raised you with proper values." His daughter shifts uncomfortably in her seat, already anticipating the lecture that will follow—about respect, about standards, about how things should be done.

The irony is palpable. Michael's phone sits face-up beside his plate, with notifications lighting up every few minutes. But in his mind, that's different. He's monitoring important work emails. He has responsibilities. His children, however, should know better. They should follow the rules. They should meet the standards he's set; standards that shift and change based on his mood, standards that seem to apply to everyone but himself.

This is the Judge pattern in its essence: using evaluation and criticism as a means of control, creating rigid standards that become weapons against others while protecting the Judge from their own deep-seated fear of imperfection. Where the Expert uses knowledge as armor, the Judge uses criticism as both sword and shield, cutting others down while defending against the terrifying possibility of being wrong, imperfect, or out of control.

Perfectionism and Rigid Standards

The Judge pattern represents the second primary ego defensive strategy, characterized by the compulsive need to evaluate, categorize, and control through criticism and impossible standards. At its core, the Judge pattern operates from a fundamental equation: Control = Safety = Worth.

Perfectionism in the Judge pattern goes far beyond high standards or attention to detail. It's a comprehensive worldview that divides all of existence into binary categories: right/wrong, good/bad, acceptable/unacceptable. This black-and-white thinking serves as a crucial defensive function, in a world of absolutes, the Judge can maintain the illusion of control.

Perfectionism manifests through rigid rule systems that transform life into an exhausting performance evaluation. The Judge constructs elaborate codes of conduct that would rival military regulations, except these apply to loading dishwashers, responding to texts, and expressing gratitude. Every interaction gets filtered through intricate hierarchies of the "Shoulds" and "Musts"—you should call your mother every Sunday, you must arrive ten minutes early, children should speak only when spoken to, partners must anticipate needs without being told. These standards possess a particularly cruel feature: they escalate with each achievement. The moment someone meets the Judge's expectations, the bar rises. Yesterday's A+ became today's bare minimum. The child who finally keeps their room clean for a week suddenly hears, "Well, that's just basic responsibility—now let's talk about your study habits." The Judge builds complex evaluation frameworks that turn every situation into a pass/fail test. There's a right way to pack groceries, a correct tone for apologizing, an acceptable timeframe for grief. Meanwhile, their mind maintains detailed scorecards of everyone's failures—your spouse's forgotten anniversary from 2019, your teenager's lie about homework last month, your colleague's three-minute tardiness to last Tuesday's meeting—all filed away as ammunition for future arguments, evidence in the case they're constantly building about why the world consistently fails to meet their standards.

The Judge's standards are particularly insidious because they're designed to be unattainable through what might be called the "moving goalpost phenomenon." As soon as someone (including themselves) approaches meeting a standard, the Judge unconsciously moves it higher. This ensures perpetual justification for criticism and maintains their superior position as the keeper of standards. By keeping satisfaction forever out of reach, they avoid the vulnerability that comes with contentment and protect themselves from the terrifying possibility of having nothing left to improve—which would leave them without their primary identity and defense mechanism.

The Judge pattern creates an exhausting mental process of constant comparison that never stops running. They compulsively pit siblings against each other, measure current performance against an idealized past that never quite existed, and hold real achievements up against imagined potential that could never be reached. They compare others at their worst moments against themselves at their best, while measuring present reality against a perfect fantasy that exists only in their mind. This comparison engine ensures that nothing and no one ever measures up, perpetuating the cycle of disappointment and criticism that defines the Judge's worldview.

The Judge's Defensive Architecture

Building on the complete defensive architecture from Chapter 2, the Judge pattern follows this predictable cascade:

VALUES → PERSONAL DOMAIN → LIES ↔ BIAS → DEFENSES → DISTORTIONS → EGO FACE

- **VALUES**: Order, justice, excellence, integrity, fairness (*These positive values create vulnerability when threatened, triggering defensive responses*)
- **PERSONAL DOMAIN**: Identity becomes fused with being the standard-keeper; worth equals maintaining control through evaluation
- **LIES**: *Context:* "This isn't criticism, it's necessary correction" | *Content:* "My standards protect everyone from chaos"
- **BIAS**: Selective attention to imperfections, interpreting neutral behaviors as violations of standards
- **DEFENSES**: Projection, reaction formation, displacement (detailed in sections below)

- **DISTORTIONS**: All-or-nothing thinking ("it's either perfect or worthless"), should statements ("everyone should follow the rules"), catastrophizing ("if standards slip, everything falls apart")
- **EGO FACE**: Criticizing, evaluating, correcting—what Michael's family experiences at the dinner table

Remember from Chapter 2: Breaking this chain at any point can disrupt the entire system, with lies being the highest leverage point for change.

The Should System

Don Miguel Ruiz identified the Judge as one of two primary voices that create human suffering (along with the Victim). The Judge operates through what might be called the "Should System"—an internalized book of laws that governs every aspect of existence.

Categories of Shoulds:

Behavioral Shoulds

- "People should arrive on time"
- "Children should respect their elders"
- "Employees should give 110%"
- "Partners should anticipate needs"
- "Everyone should follow the rules"

Emotional Shoulds

- "I should be happy with my success"
- "They shouldn't feel that way"
- "I should be over this by now"
- "People shouldn't be so sensitive"
- "Everyone should control their emotions"

Performance Shoulds

- "Anything less than perfect is failure"
- "Mistakes should never be repeated"
- "Success should come from hard work"
- "Achievement should be recognized"
- "Excellence should be the minimum standard"

Moral Shoulds

- "Good people should never have bad thoughts"
- "Everyone should share my values"
- "Right and wrong should be obvious"
- "People should know better"
- "Society should function properly"

The Should System creates a psychological prison where the Judge becomes both warden and prisoner, constantly evaluating everything against impossible standards while living in perpetual disappointment.

Family and Personal Relationship Examples

The Judge pattern wreaks havoc in intimate relationships where emotional safety and unconditional acceptance are essential for healthy connection.

The Parental Judge

Michael's dinner table scenario exemplifies how the Judge pattern manifests in parenting through three particularly destructive dynamics that poison family relationships.

The double standard dynamic reveals itself the moment Michael's voice cuts through dinner: "You should know better than to check your phone at dinner."

The bitter irony hangs in the air—his own phone sits face-up beside his plate, notifications lighting up every few minutes, which he regularly checks while claiming to monitor "important work emails." His children see this double standard clearly, though they dare not point it out. This creates a maze of confusion where rules seem to shift based on Michael's mood and status. The message becomes clear: rules are for the powerless, standards apply to everyone except the standard-setter. His children learn not morality but manipulation, not values but judgment. They watch him exempting himself while demanding their perfection, eroding his credibility with each correction until his words carry no weight beyond the threat of his disapproval.

The achievement trap springs whenever grades arrive. Michael's son's B+ in mathematics—representing hours of study, genuine understanding, and solid performance—gets twisted into evidence of moral failure. "If you're not getting straight A's, you're clearly not trying hard enough," Michael declares, as if effort and outcome exist in perfect correlation, as if his son's worth can be calculated by grade point average. This creates children who could win Nobel Prizes and still hear their father's voice whispering "not good enough." The "achievement anxiety" becomes so intense it actually impairs the performance Michael demands—his children freeze during tests, terrified that anything less than perfection means they're lazy, stupid, worthless. Their identity fuses with external validation until they cannot separate who they are from what they achieve, losing any intrinsic joy in learning because it's all been poisoned by the need to meet impossible standards.

The comparison weapon gets deployed with surgical precision: "Your sister manages to get her homework done before dinner, so it's only fair that you do the same." Never mind that his daughter is two years older, that she has different teachers with different homework loads, that she processes information differently. Michael weaponizes her compliance against his son's struggle, creating a rivalry where there should be solidarity. The siblings learn to celebrate each other's failures because it means momentary relief from comparison. They define themselves in opposition—if she's the "responsible one," he becomes the "rebel." If he's the "smart one," she becomes the "social one." The competition replaces what could have been collaboration, support, and genuine sibling bond. Decades later, they'll sit in therapy trying to understand why they can't be in the same room without feeling like they're twelve years old again, competing for their father's approval that never quite comes.

The Intimate Partner Judge

In romantic relationships, the Judge pattern creates a particularly toxic dynamic that erodes love through constant evaluation. Dr. Patricia, whom we met in Chapter 2, exemplifies how the criticism cycle operates in intimate partnerships. She criticizes her partner's cooking while refusing to cook herself, points out physical imperfections while demanding acceptance of her own, and evaluates emotional expressions as either "appropriate" or "excessive." She maintains mental catalogs of every mistake and disappointment, weaponizing past failures in present conflicts— that forgotten anniversary from three years ago becomes ammunition in today's argument about taking out the trash.

The Judge pattern systematically destroys intimacy by making vulnerability feel dangerous—any revelation will be evaluated and likely found wanting. This creates performance anxiety in all aspects of the relationship, from conversation to sex, as partners feel perpetually on stage being scored. Acceptance gets replaced with evaluation, love becomes conditional on meeting ever-shifting standards, and partners learn to hide their true selves to avoid judgment. The withholding pattern emerges as Judges use affection as currency for control. "I'll say 'I love you' when you deserve it," they declare, as if love were a salary to be earned. They refuse to compliment expected behaviors and insist that appreciation breeds complacency, while maintaining that their criticism somehow helps their partner improve.

The Social Judge

In broader social relationships, the Judge pattern creates isolation through relentless criticism that pushes others away. As the social evaluator, the Judge mentally critiques everyone at gatherings—their clothing choices, career decisions, parenting styles, and conversation topics all get silently scored. They gossip about others' failures and shortcomings, creating hierarchies of whom it's acceptable to associate with based on arbitrary standards. They bond with other Judges through shared criticism, forming toxic alliances built on mutual superiority while alienating potential friends who grow tired of the constant evaluation.

The Judge also positions themselves as the moral superior, self-appointed arbiter of right and wrong in every situation. They lecture others on proper behavior, from how to raise children to how to maintain friendships, taking secret satisfaction when others experience moral failures that prove the Judge's superiority. This righteousness creates an impenetrable barrier to genuine connection, as people sense the judgment radiating from them and keep their distance. Most tragically, the Judge mistakes their judgment for wisdom, believing their criticism comes from insight rather than insecurity.

Defense Mechanisms in Detail

The Judge pattern employs a sophisticated cluster of defense mechanisms designed to maintain control while avoiding awareness of their own imperfections and vulnerabilities.

Projection: The External Judgment Screen

Projection serves as the Judge's primary defense mechanism, allowing them to see in others what they cannot tolerate in themselves. This isn't simple blame-shifting—it's a complex psychological process that maintains the Judge's self-image while providing outlets for their harsh internal criticism.

How Projection Works in the Judge Pattern:

The Judge's internal critical voice is relentless: "You're not good enough, you're making mistakes, you're failing to meet standards." This creates unbearable psychological pressure. To cope, the psyche projects these judgments outward: "They're not good enough, they're making mistakes, they're failing to meet standards."

Michael's Projection in Action: When Michael screams, "Everyone at school must think we're a dysfunctional family because you can't follow simple rules," he's projecting his own deep fear of being judged as a failed parent. His terror of others' evaluation gets displaced onto his children's behavior. He doesn't recognize that his harsh criticism is creating the very dysfunction he fears others will see.

The Projection-Judgment Cycle:

1. **Internal criticism**: "I'm not a good enough parent"

2. **Unbearable feeling**: Shame, inadequacy, fear
3. **Projection**: "My children aren't good enough"
4. **Judgment**: Criticizing children's behavior
5. **Temporary relief**: "The problem is them, not me"
6. **Consequences**: Damaged relationships, rebellious children
7. **Reinforcement**: "See, they really are the problem"

Sophisticated Projection Patterns:

- **Competence projection**: Judging others as incompetent to avoid acknowledging own limitations
- **Moral projection**: Condemning others' ethical failures while blind to own moral compromises
- **Emotional projection**: Criticizing others' emotional expressions while denying own feelings
- **Effort projection**: Judging others as lazy while avoiding examination of own effort
- **Intelligence projection**: Calling others stupid to avoid confronting own areas of ignorance

Reaction Formation: The Opposite Defense

Reaction formation represents one of the Judge's most complex defenses—acting in ways directly opposite to their unconscious feelings or desires. This creates the peculiar phenomenon of Judges who are harshest in areas where they feel most vulnerable.

When the Judge experiences unacceptable feelings or impulses, the psyche doesn't just repress them—it creates an elaborate opposite response. The more intense the hidden feeling, the more extreme the opposite behavior.

Dr. Patricia's Reaction Formation: Dr. Patricia's excessive focus on creating detailed syllabi requirements and grading rubrics appears to be about maintaining academic excellence.

It's reaction formation against her deep insecurity about her own performance as department chair. Her secret worry about her upcoming dean review transforms into obsessive control over documentation and standards. The more frightened she feels, the more controlling she becomes.

Common Reaction Formation Patterns in Judges:

Common reaction formation patterns in Judges reveal the tragic irony of how we become harshest precisely where we're most wounded, creating elaborate opposite behaviors to mask our deepest fears and desires.

The Moral Crusader wages holy war against the very temptations that torment them in private. Struggling with their own moral impulses—perhaps attraction to someone forbidden, desires that conflict with their stated values, or thoughts they consider sinful—they become excessively moralistic and punitive toward others. The senator who campaigns against homosexuality while hiding same-sex attractions, the minister who preaches against lust while battling pornography addiction, the parent who viciously condemns their teenager's sexuality while suppressing memories of their own youth. They attack others' moral failures with a viciousness proportional to their own internal struggle, as if punishing others might finally silence their own forbidden desires. The more intense their hidden battle, the more brutal their public crusade becomes.

The Neat Freak transforms internal chaos into external tyranny. Inside, they're drowning, because thoughts are scattered, emotions are overwhelming, and life feels utterly out of control. Unable to organize their inner world, they become obsessed with controlling the outer one. Every book must be alphabetized, every surface sanitized, every schedule followed to the minute.

They cannot tolerate even minor deviations—a crooked picture frame causes genuine distress, an unexpected change in plans triggers panic. Their home becomes a museum of rigid perfection that no one can comfortably inhabit, including themselves. The more chaotic they feel internally, the more controlling they become about external order, as if perfect organization might finally bring peace to their churning inner world.

The Brutal Critic weaponizes their own self-hatred against others. Consumed by shame and self-loathing they cannot consciously acknowledge, they become excessively critical of everyone around them. But watch carefully—their harsh criticism targets others displaying the exact traits they despise in themselves. The judge who hates their own sensitivity attacks others for being "too emotional." The one who feels stupid criticizes everyone else's intelligence. The one terrified of their own weakness mocks any display of vulnerability. They're not really talking to others; they're talking to the parts of themselves they cannot accept, attacking others what they're desperate to destroy in themselves.

The Workaholic Perfectionist runs themselves to death trying to outrun inadequacy. Terrified that someone will discover they're not as competent as they appear, they work excessive hours creating elaborate proof of their worth. Eighty-hour weeks become normal, vacation days go unused, family events get missed—all sacrificed on the altar of flawless performance. They volunteer for every committee, accept every project, triple-check every detail, because one mistake might reveal the truth, they're desperate to hide: that they're human, fallible, perhaps even ordinary. Their health deteriorates—stress-related illness, exhaustion, relationship breakdown—but they cannot stop because stopping would mean confronting the terrifying possibility that they're already enough, that all this performance has been unnecessary, that they've been running from a threat that existed only in their mind.

Displacement: The Safe Target System

Displacement allows the Judge to redirect their critical energy toward safer targets when the true source of frustration is too threatening to confront directly.

How Displacement Functions:

When Judges encounter situations where they cannot express criticism toward the actual source (a boss, a powerful person, their own limitations), they unconsciously redirect that critical energy toward safer targets—typically those with less power or those who won't retaliate.

Dr. Patricia's Displacement Chain: When the dean questions the department's adjunct retention rates (the real threat), Patricia cannot safely criticize the dean. Instead, she:

1. **Redirects criticism toward adjuncts**: "They lack real academic experience"
2. **Blames abstract systems**: "Budget constraints make quality impossible"
3. **Attacks institutional policies**: "Unrealistic expectations from administration"
4. **Criticizes broader trends**: "The decline of academic standards nationwide"

Never does she examine her own management approach—the one thing under her control.

The Family Displacement Pattern: Michael provides a classic example of workplace-to-home displacement:

- Humiliated by his boss at work (unsafe to criticize)
- Comes home primed with unexpressed judgment
- Children's minor infractions become major violations
- Partner's small mistakes trigger disproportionate criticism
- Family bears the brunt of workplace frustration

Displacement Hierarchies: Judges often create unconscious hierarchies of "safe" criticism targets:

1. **Children** (least power, most dependent)
2. **Service workers** (paid to tolerate criticism)
3. **Subordinates** (organizational power differential)
4. **Partners** (emotional dependence creates safety)
5. **Peers** (when no power differential exists)
6. **Rarely: Superiors** (only when extremely triggered)

The Intrapersonal Cover-Up System

Like the Expert pattern, the Judge operates simultaneously on interpersonal and intrapersonal levels, with the internal justification system often more damaging than the external behavior.

The Internal Prosecution

While Michael criticizes his family's behavior at dinner, his internal narrative runs continuously: "Someone has to maintain standards in this house... If I don't correct these behaviors, they'll grow up to be failures... I'm doing this for their own good... They'll thank me someday for having high standards..."

This internal story serves crucial psychological functions:

- **Maintains Ego syntonic behavior**: The criticism feels natural and necessary
- **Prevents empathy**: Others' pain is reframed as necessary for their growth

- **Blocks self-awareness**: The Judge never has to examine their own failures
- **Creates superiority**: Positions the Judge as the standard-keeper

The Righteousness Development Process:

Over time, the Judge's internal narrative evolves from defensive justification to genuine belief in their righteousness:

1. **Early stage**: "Someone needs to point out problems"
2. **Middle stage**: "I see things others miss"
3. **Advanced stage**: "My standards are what keep things from falling apart"
4. **Entrenched stage**: "Without my judgment, everyone would fail"

This progression represents the shift from using criticism as a tool to experiencing criticism as identity, creating increasingly rigid and isolated ways of being.

The Judgment Trap: When Standards Become Isolation

The ultimate tragedy of the Judge pattern lies in how the very standards meant to create safety and worth become a prison that ensures loneliness, disconnection, and perpetual dissatisfaction.

Michael's family dinner exemplifies this paradox. His intention is to create a perfect family meal—a time of connection and proper behavior. Instead, his criticism creates tension, rebellion, and emotional distance. The very standards meant to ensure a good family life destroy the possibility of authentic family connection.

The Connection- Isolation Issue

The Judge's pursuit of perfection creates its opposite in a cruel paradox that ensures misery. Their standards ensure failure because nothing ever measures up, and each achievement simply raises the bar higher, making satisfaction impossible. Their criticism prevents the very improvement they claim to seek, as people shut down defensively rather than open to grow. Their need for control creates chaos as rigidity breeds rebellion, especially in children and partners who eventually explode against the constraints. Their constant evaluation prevents appreciation, as they become so focused on finding flaws that they lose the ability to see beauty, joy, or simple goodness in anything. Michael's family dinner exemplifies this paradox perfectly: his intention to create a perfect family meal—a time of connection and proper behavior—instead creates tension, rebellion, and emotional distance. The very standards meant to ensure a good family life destroy the possibility of authentic family connection.

The Judge pattern creates profound loneliness through the connection-isolation paradox. Criticism replaces connection as every interaction becomes an evaluation rather than an exchange. Evaluation replaces acceptance, making others feel perpetually assessed rather than appreciated. Standards replace spontaneity, turning natural moments into performances that must meet criteria. Judgment replaces joy, as the simple pleasure of being together gets lost in constant assessment. The Judge often feels bewildered by their isolation, thinking "I'm only trying to help people improve," unable to see how their criticism creates emotional walls that no one wants to breach.

While the Judge pattern appears strong and authoritative, the strength-brittleness paradox reveals extreme fragility beneath the facade. Their identity depends entirely on being right, their self-worth crumbles when standards aren't met, and any imperfection threatens their entire self-concept. Most tellingly, the Judge who dishes out constant criticism often cannot handle even gentle feedback about their own behavior—the very armor of standards meant to protect becomes their greatest vulnerability.

Perhaps most tragically, the growth-stagnation paradox shows how the Judge pattern that initially drives improvement eventually becomes its greatest obstacle. Fear of judgment prevents risk-taking, as the possibility of failure becomes too threatening. Perfectionism paralyzes action—better to do nothing than to do something imperfectly. Criticism kills creativity before ideas can bloom, and rigid standards prevent the experimentation essential for growth. The very force that once pushed toward excellence now locks the Judge in a prison of their own making.

Judge Pattern Across the Intensity Scale

The Ego Pattern Intensity Scale reveals how the Judge pattern intensifies from a useful discernment tool to a destructive force that can destroy lives and relationships.

Intensity 1 - Pattern as Option

At Intensity 1, the Judge pattern is temporarily activated without becoming identity. People at this level:

- **Use discernment without judgment**

- **Maintain standards without rigidity**

- **Offer feedback without criticism**

- **Accept imperfection as human**

- **Appreciate growth over perfection**

- **Strong awareness** of authentic self beyond any evaluation

This represents our natural state before the Judge pattern develops—able to evaluate without condemning, to have preferences without requirements. Someone at Intensity 1 might say, "I prefer things done this way, but I understand there are many valid approaches."

Intensity 2 - Pattern as Refuge

At Intensity 2, the Judge pattern becomes a go-to response providing temporary relief from perceived chaos or imperfection:

- **Pattern provides temporary relief** from anxiety about disorder

- **Beginning identity attachment** - more situations feel like they require evaluation

- **Appreciate excellence without demanding perfection**

- **Offer constructive feedback without harsh criticism**

- **Maintain personal standards without imposing them**

- **Accept others' different approaches** with some discomfort

- **Some rigidity** in specific contexts

- **Intermittent awareness** of authentic self beyond the pattern

Someone at Intensity 2 might notice themselves defaulting to Judge mode during stress but can still pull back and engage differently when aware.

Intensity 3 - Pattern as Necessity

At Intensity 3, the Judge pattern becomes required for self-worth:

- **"I am someone with high standards"** becomes core self-definition

- **Criticism becomes primary mode of interaction**

- **All perceived imperfections** must be corrected

- **Others' mistakes feel like personal affronts**

- **Social interactions** become opportunities to evaluate

- **Career choices** driven by need to maintain control through standards

- **Difficulty functioning** without constant evaluation

- **Rare glimpses** of authentic self, usually only in safe moments

Michael operates primarily at Intensity 3. His identity as "the father who maintains standards" drives his behavior, creating significant family tension but still allowing some relationship function.

Intensity 4 - Pattern as Identity

At Intensity 4, the Judge pattern becomes the entire identity:

- **Cannot conceive alternatives** to maintaining rigid standards

- **Any deviation from perfection** must be eliminated

- **Demands others enable** their need for control

- **Severe anxiety emerges** when standards aren't met

- **Relationships are sacrificed** to maintain righteousness

- **Joy becomes impossible** due to perpetual evaluation

- **Depression develops** from constant disappointment

- **Complete disconnection** from authentic self

Dr. Patricia has reached Intensity 4. Her internalized rules about academic standards have become so rigid that any flexibility creates existential threat. She cannot adapt because change would mean admitting her standards might be wrong. She lives entirely in the "smoke" of her Judge pattern, unable to access her authentic self.

Case Example - Intensity 4: Judge Catherine, a renowned federal judge, maintained such rigid standards for her family that her daughter attempted suicide after getting a B in college, her son cut off all contact after being criticized for his career choice, and her husband left after 30 years of relentless criticism. She died alone, maintaining to the end that her standards were correct. This represents the severe dysfunction possible when the Judge pattern completely obscures authentic identity—when being right becomes more important than being loved, connected, or even alive.

Moving Down Intensity Levels: The Path of Recovery

The journey of Ego Intelligence involves consciously moving down intensity levels. For the Judge pattern, this means:

From Intensity 4 to 3:

- Crisis intervention is often required

- Creating tiny moments of non-Judge identity

- Professional therapy to address severe dysfunction

- Gradual separation of self-worth from perfect standards

From Intensity 3 to 2:

- Expanding windows of authentic self-awareness

- Developing other sources of identity beyond standards

- Learning to hold evaluation lightly

- Practicing genuine acceptance of imperfection

From Intensity 2 to 1:

- Strengthening ability to choose rather than react

- Full integration where discernment serves life rather than ego

- Maintaining connection to authentic self while using standards consciously

- Using evaluation as a tool rather than identity

Each intensity descent requires specific practices and interventions, which will be explored in later chapters.

Cultural and Professional Reinforcement

The Judge pattern doesn't develop in isolation—it's actively reinforced by cultural and professional systems that reward criticism and perfectionism. Many cultures cultivate Judge patterns through "tough love" parenting philosophies that equate criticism with care, educational systems that rank and compare students from kindergarten through graduate school, and religious frameworks that emphasize sin, judgment, and moral failure. Media profits from judgment and criticism, while social media algorithms specifically reward outrage and condemnation with greater reach and engagement.

Certain professions actively reward Judge behaviors by design. Law's adversarial system trains lawyers to find flaws and attack opposing arguments. Academia's peer review process is built on criticism, where careers advance by tearing down others' work. Medicine's "morbidity and mortality" conferences focus exclusively on mistakes and failures. Military advancement depends on passing increasingly stringent inspections. Quality control professionals are literally paid to find problems. These aren't corruptions of these systems—they're features.

Modern society has created entire economies based on judgment. Review culture has turned everyone into critics, from restaurant meals to delivery drivers. Comment sections are designed to facilitate judgment, with engagement metrics rewarding the most inflammatory criticisms. Reality TV monetizes judgment, creating shows where people compete to avoid criticism or judge others most harshly. Political systems have devolved into attack machines where defeating opponents matters more than governing. News media profits from outrage, knowing that anger drives more clicks than appreciation. The Judge pattern isn't just personal psychology—it's economically incentivized behavior.

The Path Forward: Seeds of Transformation

While the Judge pattern creates significant suffering, it contains within it the seeds of its own transformation. The very discernment that creates judgment can be redirected toward wisdom and compassion.

Each ego pattern, when consciously integrated, offers unique gifts. The Judge pattern's shadow contains valuable abilities waiting to be transformed. Their compulsive criticism can become discernment that recognizes truth without condemnation—the ability to see clearly without needing to attack what they see. Their rigid standards can inspire rather than crush when held with flexibility and compassion. Their evaluation skills, freed from the need to criticize, can support genuine growth by identifying areas for development without shame. Their attention to detail, no longer scanning for flaws, can appreciate beauty and excellence that others might miss. Their desire for improvement, released from perfectionism's grip, can be channeled constructively into genuine progress rather than perpetual dissatisfaction.

Learning to recognize the Judge pattern as it activates is crucial for transformation. The body provides early warning signals: jaw tension from clenched teeth, a furrowed brow creating that familiar crease between the eyebrows, and rigid posture as the whole body tightens in disapproval. Emotional cues include the rising irritation when things aren't "right," disgust at others' choices, and that intoxicating feeling of righteousness that comes with knowing the correct way. Thought patterns reveal themselves through constant "should" statements, endless comparisons between what is and what ought to be, and automatic evaluations of everything encountered. Behavioral flags include compulsive correcting, unsolicited lecturing, and that telltale sign of disapproval that escapes before words form. Most telling are the relational indicators—watch how others respond: they become defensive, start withdrawing, make excuses to leave early, or simply stop sharing anything real.

The Invitation to Acceptance

The journey from Judge pattern to integrated wisdom isn't about abandoning discernment or standards. It's about holding them with compassion, using them in service of growth rather than control.

As we'll explore in subsequent chapters, this transformation requires specific practices, considerable humility, and often the support of others who can offer the acceptance the Judge cannot give themselves. The Judge who can embrace imperfection—their own and others'—opens doorways to connection and joy that no amount of perfection could provide.

In the end, the most profound judgment may be the decision to stop judging—to accept the messy, imperfect, beautiful reality of human existence. This acceptance, paradoxically, creates more positive change than any criticism ever could.

Reflecting on the Judge Within

As you read this chapter, you might notice your own Judge pattern activating—perhaps criticizing the writing style, finding flaws in the arguments, or judging the examples as too extreme or not extreme enough. You might even be judging yourself for having Judge patterns. This is natural and even valuable. The Judge pattern helped you develop whatever standards and discernment you possess. The invitation isn't to destroy it but to recognize it, appreciate its service, and gradually learn when it serves and when it imprisons.

Consider:

- Where in your life do standards feel like prison bars?
- When do you use criticism to avoid vulnerability?
- How might your relationships change if you value acceptance over improvement?
- What would it mean to have discernment without judgment?

The journey toward Ego Intelligence begins with honest recognition. In recognizing our patterns, we create the possibility of choice. And in choice lies freedom—the freedom to be both discerning and kind, both principled and flexible, both committed to growth and accepting of what is.

>> Chapter 4 Key Takeaways

1. **The Judge equation** - Control = Safety = Worth drives all Judge behavior, making criticism and standards essential for psychological survival.
2. **Three core manifestations** define the Judge pattern: Rigid Standards (escalating goalposts), The Should System (internalized laws for everything), and Control Through Criticism (evaluation as weapon and shield).
3. **The defense trinity** - Projection attributes internal criticism to others, Reaction Formation creates opposite behaviors to hidden feelings, and Displacement redirects judgment toward safer targets.
4. **Four paradoxes trap Judges** - Pursuing perfection creates misery, control generates chaos, strength masks brittleness, and standards meant to drive growth create stagnation.
5. **Family destruction patterns** - Double standards erode credibility, achievement-traps poison success, comparison weapons create lifelong sibling rivalry, and criticism cycles destroy intimacy.
6. **Intensity determines impact** - From Pattern as Option (flexible discernment) through Pattern as Identity (rigid righteousness), each level represents deeper entrenchment and relationship destruction.
7. **Cultural reinforcement** - educational ranking systems, "tough love" philosophies, and the criticism economy actively reward and create Judge patterns.
8. **The withholding weapon** - Judges use affection, approval, and appreciation as currency for control, believing love must be earned through meeting standards.
9. **The gifts within** - When transformed, the Judge's criticism becomes discernment, standards become

inspiration, and the desire for improvement becomes
constructive change.
10. **Recovery is possible** - Moving down intensity levels
requires recognizing that acceptance creates more
positive change than criticism ever could.

>> Coming Next: Chapter 5 – The Victim: Safety in Helplessness

In the next chapter, we'll explore the Victim pattern—the
paradoxical strategy of seeking protection through
powerlessness. You'll discover how learned helplessness
becomes identity, why the Victim's suffering is real even when
self-created, and how external blame becomes an elaborate
shield against the terror of personal responsibility. Most
importantly, you'll learn how the Victim's sensitivity and
awareness of suffering can transform into genuine empathy and
powerful agency.

*If the Expert needs to be right and the Judge needs to be
righteous, the Victim needs to be rescued. Let's explore why—
and how to reclaim the power they never lose.*

Chapter 5: The Victim – Safety in Helplessness

>> **What You'll Learn in This Chapter**

- Why helplessness becomes a fortress protecting against responsibility's terror

- The three core manifestations: Externalization Engine, Impossibility Framework, and Sympathy Economy

- How the Victim pattern creates power through powerlessness—controlling through need

- The sophisticated defense cluster: Denial, Regression, and Repression

- Why the Victim's suffering is real even when self-created

- The devastating paradoxes: seeking protection creates paralysis, sympathy creates isolation

- How to recognize Victim patterns across the four intensity levels

- The path from learned helplessness to genuine empowerment

Reading Time: ~30 minutes

"Poor me, I'm not good enough, I'm not worthy of love." - Don Miguel Ruiz

Jake stares at the red "F" on his midterm exam, his stomach churning with a familiar mixture of anxiety and resignation. "There's nothing I could have done differently," he tells his roommate later, slumping into his desk chair. "The professor's lectures are confusing, the textbook is poorly written, and nobody told me this material would be on the test."

His roommate suggests joining a study group, but Jake waves him off. "What's the point? I'm just not good at this subject. I never learned how to study properly in high school." He pulls out his phone, scrolling through social media instead of opening his textbook, already crafting the story he'll tell his parents about how unfair the professor is, how impossible the class is, how he's doing his best, but the system is against him.

This is the Victim pattern in action: using helplessness as both weapon and shield, creating an elaborate narrative of powerlessness that protects against the terrifying possibility of taking responsibility. Where the Expert uses knowledge as armor and the Judge uses criticism as control, the Victim uses helplessness as a fortress—impenetrable walls built from "I can't," "It's not my fault," and "What's the point?"

Powerlessness and External Blame Patterns

The Victim pattern represents the third primary ego defensive strategy, characterized by the systematic cultivation of helplessness and the attribution of all control to external forces. At its core, the Victim pattern operates from a fundamental equation: Helplessness = Safety = Sympathy.

The Architecture of Powerlessness

The Victim pattern is perhaps the most paradoxical of the three ego defenses because it derives power from powerlessness. This isn't mere passivity or genuine limitation—it's an active, though often unconscious, strategy of learned helplessness that serves crucial protective functions.

The architecture of powerlessness manifests through:

The Externalization Engine

- Every problem has an external cause
- Every failure has someone else to blame
- Every limitation is imposed by circumstances
- Every struggle is someone else's responsibility to fix
- Every solution is beyond personal reach

The Impossibility Framework - The Victim creates elaborate mental structures that prove why change is impossible:

- "I can't because of my past"
- "I can't because of my circumstances"
- "I can't because others won't let me"
- "I can't because I don't know how"
- "I can't because it's too hard"

Each "I can't" adds another bar to the prison of helplessness, creating an increasingly elaborate cage that feels both protective and permanent.

The Sympathy Economy - The Victim pattern operates on a unique emotional currency system:

- Helplessness generates sympathy
- Sympathy provides connection (however superficial)
- Connection validates the "helpless" identity
- Validation reinforces the pattern
- The cycle continues, requiring ever greater displays of helplessness

The Victim's Defensive Architecture

Building on the complete defensive architecture from Chapter 2, the Victim pattern follows this predictable cascade:

VALUES → PERSONAL DOMAIN → LIES ↔ BIAS → DEFENSES → DISTORTIONS → EGO FACE

- **VALUES**: Connection, support, understanding, compassion, care (*These positive values create vulnerability when threatened, triggering defensive responses*)
- **PERSONAL DOMAIN**: Identity becomes fused with helplessness; worth equals receiving care and sympathy from others
- **LIES**: *Context:* "This isn't avoidance, it's genuinely impossible" | *Content:* "I have no power to change my circumstances"
- **BIAS**: Selective attention to obstacles and barriers, interpreting neutral situations as evidence of persecution or impossibility
- **DEFENSES**: Denial, regression, repression (detailed in sections below)
- **DISTORTIONS**: Catastrophizing ("everything is impossible"), personalization ("bad things always happen to me"), fortune telling ("nothing will ever work out"), emotional reasoning ("I feel helpless, therefore I am helpless")
- **EGO FACE**: Complaining, seeking rescue, positioning others as responsible—what Jake's roommate experiences in their dorm room

Remember from Chapter 2: Breaking this chain at any point can disrupt the entire system, with lies being the highest leverage point for change.

The Blame Distribution System

Don Miguel Ruiz identified the Victim as the recipient of the Judge's criticism, carrying blame, guilt, and shame while repeatedly reinforcing unworthiness. But the Victim pattern goes beyond merely receiving judgment, actively redistributes responsibility to maintain its helpless position.

The Victim's blame distribution system operates as a sophisticated psychological defense network, assigning responsibility across four comprehensive categories that ensure accountability never touches their shoulders.

Historical blame anchors helplessness firmly in an unchangeable past. "My parents didn't prepare me" becomes the explanation for every adult struggle, as if parental perfection were a prerequisite for personal capability. "My childhood was too difficult" transforms early challenges into permanent disabilities, treating resilience as impossible rather than developed. "My education was inadequate" explains away every knowledge gap, ignoring that learning continues throughout life. "My past relationships damaged me" turns previous pain into present paralysis, as if healing were fantasy rather than possibility. "My early experiences made this impossible" creates a deterministic universe where the past dictates the future with no room for growth, change, or choice. Each historical blame adds another link to chains that exist only in memory but feel as real as iron.

Circumstantial blame shifts responsibility to current conditions that feel equally immutable. "The economy is against me" personalizes global forces, as if economic systems specifically target them for failure. "The system is rigged" contains enough truth to feel completely true—yes, systemic inequalities exist, but the Victim uses this reality to justify complete surrender rather than strategic navigation. "My job doesn't pay enough" becomes the reason for every limitation, though others with similar incomes manage differently. "My location limits opportunities" ignores both local possibilities and the option of relocation. "My schedule makes it impossible" treats time as an external force rather than a series of choices, forgetting that everyone has the same twenty-four hours. These circumstances become prison walls that feel impossible to scale, though others in identical situations find ways through, around, or over.

Interpersonal blame creates a universe where everyone else holds the keys to their life. "My boss is unreasonable" may be true but it becomes the excuse for never developing skills that would create options. "My partner doesn't support me" transforms relationships into one-way support systems where their needs matter but their own agency doesn't exist. "My friends don't understand" creates isolation while blaming others for the distance. "My family holds me back" may reflect real dysfunction, but the Victim extends family influence far beyond its actual reach, giving others power they don't possess. "Nobody helps me enough" becomes a bottomless pit—no amount of help is sufficient because help without personal action changes nothing. Each person in their life becomes responsible for the Victim's outcomes while the Victim themselves remains curiously absent from their own story.

Cosmic blame elevates helplessness to spiritual dimensions. "I'm just unlucky" transforms random events into personal persecution, as if the universe keeps a ledger of their suffering. "The universe is against me" creates a paranoid cosmology where unseen forces conspire toward their failure. "This is my fate" invokes destiny to explain what's often simply consequence, treating patterns as predetermination rather than choices compounded. "Some people have it easy" focuses on others' advantages while blind to their struggles, creating false comparisons that justify giving up. "Life isn't fair to people like me" creates a special category of victimhood, as if they're uniquely cursed while others sail through charmed existences.

This cosmic framework transforms helplessness from a psychological pattern into a metaphysical reality, making change not just difficult but cosmically impossible.

This comprehensive blame system creates an impenetrable fortress where every avenue of personal responsibility is sealed off. Past, present, and future; people, circumstances, and cosmos—all become co-conspirators in their helplessness. The system is so complete that even suggesting personal agency feels like an attack on their reality. They've built a prison of explanations so elaborate that they can't see the door has no lock—they're holding it closed from the inside, but that truth is too terrifying to acknowledge. The fortress of helplessness feels safer than the vast, open territory of personal responsibility, even as it slowly suffocates the life it was meant to protect.

* The Powerful Victim Paradox

The Victim wields surprising control through strategic helplessness:

- **Controls through GUILT** → "Look what you've done to me"
- **Dominates through NEED** → "I can't do this without you"
- **Manipulates through WEAKNESS** → "I'm too fragile to handle that"
- **Punishes through SUFFERING** → "See how much pain I'm in because of you"
-

Result: Others become hostages to the Victim's helplessness, unable to set boundaries without appearing cruel

Social and Professional Manifestations

The Victim pattern creates particularly complex dynamics in social and professional settings where initiative and responsibility are expected.

Lisa's friend group scenario exemplifies how the Victim pattern manifests socially through three destructive dynamics. The personalization spiral transforms every neutral interaction into rejection—a friend being busy means "they're avoiding me," a quiet group chat means "nobody wants to talk to me," low social media interaction means "everyone thinks I'm annoying," and changed plans mean "they don't want me there." This creates a self-fulfilling prophecy where her negative assumptions lead to withdrawn behavior, which creates actual distance, confirming her beliefs. Her catastrophic social framework turns minor situations into existential threats—one missed party means total social exile, one disagreement means friendship over forever, one awkward moment means permanent humiliation, one unreturned text means complete rejection. Rather than addressing issues directly, Lisa engages in passive-aggressive communication: posting vague, sad updates hoping others will ask what's wrong, making comments designed to elicit reassurance, withdrawing suddenly to test if others will pursue, using guilt as her primary communication tool, and creating drama to generate attention and sympathy.

In workplace settings, the professional Victim creates unique challenges through systematic avoidance of competence and responsibility. They claim "I've never been trained properly" while avoiding training opportunities, insist "nobody explains things clearly" while never asking questions, complain "the tools don't work right" while not learning to use them, declare "deadlines are unrealistic" while procrastinating, and maintain "expectations are unfair" while consistently underperforming. Initiative paralysis sets in as they wait for explicit instructions for every task, require constant reassurance and validation, avoid decision-making by claiming inadequate authority, deflect opportunities by claiming inadequate preparation, and maintain plausible deniability for all outcomes. They unconsciously become workplace drama generators, procrastinating until crisis validates their "overwhelmed" story, avoiding clarification to maintain "nobody tells me anything," resisting help to preserve "nobody supports me," sabotaging success to confirm "nothing ever works out," and creating conflicts to prove "everyone is against me."

Jake's undergraduate scenario provides a perfect example of academic victim patterns. While claiming the material is impossible, he doesn't attend office hours, avoids study groups, doesn't read the textbook, skips optional review sessions, and ignores available resources—his energy goes into explaining why success is impossible rather than attempting it. Every element becomes part of the conspiracy against him: "the professor can't teach," "the textbook is poorly written," "the tests are unfair," "the material is irrelevant," "the grading is arbitrary." The educational system becomes the enemy rather than the resource.

Defense Mechanisms in Detail

The Victim pattern employs a sophisticated cluster of defense mechanisms designed to maintain helplessness while avoiding awareness of personal agency and capability.

Denial: The Agency Elimination System

Denial serves as the Victim's primary defense mechanism, but it operates differently than simple refusal to acknowledge reality. For the Victim, denial specifically targets personal agency, power, and capability.

The Victim's denial is selective and strategic. They can clearly see external problems, others' failures, and systemic issues. What they cannot see—what gets systematically denied—is their own role in creating or maintaining their circumstances.

The denial operates through five protective layers. First comes capability denial: "I don't have the ability," as if abilities were fixed at birth rather than developed through practice. Next, opportunity denial: "I don't have the chance," blind to the opportunities they actively avoid or dismiss. Then resource denial: "I don't have what I need," ignoring available resources or the possibility of acquiring them. Knowledge denial follows: "I don't know how," while refusing to learn or ask for guidance. Finally, impact denial: "Nothing I do matters anyway," a preemptive surrender that justifies complete inaction. Each layer adds another wall of protection against the terrifying possibility of personal responsibility.

Sophisticated denial patterns reveal the complexity of this defense. Selective competence allows them to be highly capable in areas that don't threaten their Victim identity—expertly navigating social media while claiming complete inability to learn work software, mastering complex video games while insisting they can't understand basic math. Strategic forgetfulness erases instances of personal success or agency from memory, genuinely unable to recall times they solved problems independently. Exception elimination treats any success as a fluke rather than evidence of capability—that promotion was luck, that good grade was an easy test, that problem they solved was coincidence. Help rejection denies that offered assistance could make any difference: "That won't work for me," "My situation is different," "You don't understand." Most remarkably, solution blindness renders them literally unable to see obvious solutions, their minds automatically filtering out possibilities that would require personal action.

Jake's Denial in Action: When Jake insists "there's nothing I could have done differently," he's not lying consciously. His psyche has literally blocked awareness of:

- The study sessions he skipped
- The homework he didn't complete
- The questions he didn't ask
- The help he didn't seek
- The effort he didn't make

This isn't simple laziness—it's a sophisticated psychological process that protects him from the anxiety of responsibility.

Regression: The Retreat to Dependence

Regression represents one of the Victim's most powerful defenses—retreating to earlier developmental stages where others were responsible for solving problems and meeting needs. When faced with adult challenges, the Victim's psyche retreats to childlike states where helplessness was appropriate and caretaking was guaranteed. This isn't conscious manipulation—it's an automatic return to a developmental stage that feels safer.

Common regression patterns reveal how comprehensively this defense operates. The Emotional Child emerges through tantrums when frustrated, pouting when disappointed, whining instead of asking directly, tears as primary communication, and expecting others to guess needs rather than stating them. The Helpless Student appears in learning situations with "I don't understand" before trying, "This is too hard" before attempting, "Show me how" repeatedly for the same task, "I can't do it alone" for basic tasks, and "It's not fair" when challenged to grow. The Dependent Employee manifests through needing constant supervision, requiring step-by-step instructions for routine tasks, inability to handle any ambiguity, avoiding independent decisions, and seeking parental figures in bosses who become surrogate caretakers. The Needy Partner surfaces in intimate relationships through requiring constant reassurance, inability to self-soothe, making partners responsible for emotional regulation, using baby talk or childlike behavior, and expecting mind-reading and caretaking rather than adult communication.

Lisa's Regression in Action: When Lisa calls her parents crying after minor social disappointments, she's not just seeking comfort. She's psychologically returning to a time when:

- Parents solved social problems
- Tears brought immediate comfort
- Responsibility wasn't expected
- Protection was guaranteed
- Solutions came from others

Repression: The Capability Burial System

Repression in the Victim pattern specifically targets memories and awareness of personal power, success, and capability. This creates the genuine feeling of helplessness by burying evidence to the contrary.

How Repression Functions:

The Victim's psyche actively represses:

- Memories of past successes
- Evidence of personal capability
- Instances of effective action
- Moments of independence
- Examples of problem-solving

This repression is so complete that Victims often genuinely cannot remember times when they were capable and effective.

The Repression Process:

1. **Success occurs** (problem solved, goal achieved)
2. **Anxiety arises** (responsibility implied)
3. **Repression activates** (memory fades)
4. **Narrative adjusts** ("That wasn't really me" or "That was luck")
5. **Identity maintains** (helpless self-concept preserved)

What Gets Repressed:

- Academic achievements that require effort
- Professional successes that demonstrated capability
- Relationships where they showed agency
- Problems they solved independently
- Times they helped others (reversing victim role)

The Intrapersonal Cover-Up System

Like the Expert and Judge patterns, the Victim operates on both interpersonal and intrapersonal levels, with the internal narrative often more damaging than the external behavior.

The Internal Helplessness Narrative

While Jake complains to others about unfair professors and impossible material, his internal narrative runs deeper: "I'm just not smart enough... I'll never be good at this... Why do I even try... Everyone else gets it but me... I'm destined to fail..."

This internal story serves crucial functions:

- **Maintains ego syntonic behavior**: Helplessness feels natural and true
- **Prevents anxiety**: No responsibility means no pressure
- **Blocks growth**: Can't fail if you never really try
- **Creates identity**: "I am someone who can't"

The Learned Helplessness Development Process:

Over time, the Victim's internal narrative evolves from defensive strategy to core belief:

1. **Early stage**: "This is too hard for me"
2. **Middle stage**: "Most things are too hard for me"
3. **Advanced stage**: "I'm not capable of handling life"
4. **Entrenched stage**: "I am fundamentally helpless"

This progression represents the shift from using helplessness as a tool to experiencing helplessness as identity, creating increasingly limited and dependent ways of being.

The Victim Trap: When Helplessness Becomes Identity

The ultimate tragedy of the Victim pattern lies in how the very helplessness meant to provide safety and sympathy becomes a prison that ensures stagnation, dependency, and unfulfilled potential. The Victim pattern creates four devastating paradoxes that transform protective strategies into prisons of limitation.

The protection-paralysis paradox reveals how the Victim's helplessness initially protects but ultimately paralyzes. Safety creates stagnation as avoiding risk prevents any possibility of growth. Sympathy creates superficiality because relationships based on pity can never develop real depth or mutual respect. Excuses create emptiness as avoiding responsibility prevents any genuine achievement or satisfaction. Dependency creates desperation as the need for others becomes all-consuming, a bottomless pit that no amount of help can fill. Jake's academic situation exemplifies this perfectly—his helplessness protects him from the anxiety of trying and potentially failing, but it absolutely ensures actual failure. The very mechanism meant to provide safety guarantees the outcome he fears most.

The connection-isolation paradox creates cruel irony in relationships. Sympathy replaces genuine connection, creating interactions based on pity rather than mutual respect. Need replaces mutual exchange, turning relationships into one-way rescue operations. Drama replaces authentic sharing as crisis becomes the primary way to engage others. Dependency replaces healthy interdependence, creating relationships where one person is always the giver, the other always the taker. Victims often feel deeply lonely despite constant efforts to elicit care from others, unable to understand why the connections formed through helplessness feel inherently unequal and ultimately unsatisfying.

The power-powerlessness paradox exposes how appearing powerless grants considerable manipulative control. The Victim controls through guilt, dominates through need, manipulates through helplessness, and punishes through suffering. This creates the phenomenon of the "powerful victim" who controls entire family systems or workplace dynamics through strategic helplessness, wielding their weakness like a weapon that others cannot defend against without appearing cruel.

Perhaps most tragically, the care-exhaustion paradox shows how the pattern that initially elicits care eventually exhausts all sources of support. Helpers burn out from constant, bottomless need. Sympathy transforms into frustration as people realize nothing they do makes a lasting difference. Support becomes enabling as help prevents growth rather than facilitating it. Eventually, caregivers withdraw for self-preservation, leaving the Victim more alone than ever, confirmed in their belief that no one really cares.

Victim Pattern Across the Intensity Scale

The Ego Pattern Intensity Scale reveals how the Victim pattern intensifies from occasional strategic helplessness to complete identity fusion with powerlessness.

Intensity 1 - Pattern as Option

At Intensity 1, the Victim pattern is temporarily activated without becoming identity. People at this level:

- **Acknowledge limitations without identifying with them**
- **Seek help without dependency**
- **Face challenges without predetermined defeat**
- **Take responsibility naturally**

- **Learn from struggles without becoming them**
- **Strong awareness** of authentic self beyond any helplessness

This represents our natural state before the Victim pattern develops—able to experience genuine difficulty without creating identity from it. Someone at Intensity 1 might say, "This is challenging for me, and I could use some help figuring it out."

Intensity 2 - Pattern as Refuge

At Intensity 2, the Victim pattern becomes a go-to response providing temporary relief from overwhelming situations:

- **Pattern provides temporary relief** from anxiety about capability
- **Beginning identity attachment** - more situations feel overwhelming
- **Ask for help when genuinely needed** without creating dependency
- **Express vulnerability without manipulation**
- **Acknowledge difficulties without exaggeration**
- **Accept support** while maintaining some independence
- **Some avoidance** of challenging situations
- **Intermittent awareness** of authentic self beyond the pattern

Someone at Intensity 2 might occasionally retreat into helplessness when stressed but can still recognize this pattern and choose different responses when aware.

Intensity 3 - Pattern as Necessity

At Intensity 3, the Victim pattern becomes required for self-worth and safety:

- **"I am someone who struggles"** becomes core self-definition
- **Helplessness becomes primary source** of connection and sympathy
- **All perceived challenges** must be avoided or delegated
- **Others' independence feels threatening**
- **Success creates anxiety** rather than satisfaction
- **Problems become proof** of victim identity
- **Difficulty functioning** without external support
- **Rare glimpses** of authentic self, usually only in safe moments

Lisa operates primarily at Intensity 3. Her identity as "someone with bad luck in friendships" drives her behavior, creating significant relationship difficulties but still maintaining some connections.

Intensity 4 - Pattern as Identity

At Intensity 4, the Victim pattern becomes the entire identity:

- **Cannot conceive alternatives** to being helpless
- **Any capability requirement** creates existential threat
- **Demands others enable** their helplessness
- **Severe anxiety emerges** when required to show capability
- **Relationships are sacrificed** to maintain helpless position
- **Growth becomes impossible** due to complete avoidance
- **Depression develops** from genuine belief in powerlessness
- **Complete disconnection** from authentic self

Jake has reached Intensity 4. His internalized beliefs about his inability to succeed academically have become so rigid that any suggestion of capability creates panic. He cannot take even basic steps toward improvement because change would mean admitting he has power. He lives entirely in the "smoke" of his Victim pattern, unable to access his authentic self.

Case Example - Intensity 4: Victoria, a 45-year-old woman, maintained such complete victim identity that she sabotaged three job opportunities to prove "nobody will hire her," drove away supportive friends who encouraged capability, created medical crises when faced with any expectation, and attempted suicide when family suggested she had choices, leaving a note blaming everyone but herself. This represents the severe dysfunction possible when the Victim pattern completely obscures authentic identity—when being helpless becomes more important than being alive.

Moving Down Intensity Levels: The Path of Recovery

The journey of Ego Intelligence involves consciously moving down intensity levels. For the Victim pattern, this means:

From Intensity 4 to 3:

- Crisis intervention is often required
- Creating tiny moments of capability and success
- Professional therapy to address severe dysfunction
- Gradual separation of self-worth from helplessness

From Intensity 3 to 2:

- Expanding windows of authentic self-awareness
- Developing other sources of identity beyond struggle
- Learning to hold difficulties lightly
- Practicing genuine resilience without drama

From Intensity 2 to 1:

- Strengthening ability to choose rather than collapse

- Full integration where challenges serve growth rather than identity
- Maintaining connection to authentic self while having trouble
- Using vulnerability as connection rather than manipulation

Each intensity descent requires specific practices and interventions, which will be explored in later chapters.

Cultural and Professional Reinforcement

The Victim pattern doesn't develop in isolation—it's often inadvertently reinforced by cultural and professional systems that, while intending to protect and support, actually enable helplessness.

Modern culture increasingly enables Victim patterns through well-intentioned movements that transform victimhood from a temporary state into permanent identity. Social movements that began by validating real suffering sometimes evolve into spaces where victim status becomes social currency, where the most oppressed voice carries the most weight, creating incentive to amplify rather than overcome struggles. Trauma, once understood as something to process and integrate, becomes a permanent excuse that explains all current difficulties without requiring growth or change. Trigger warnings, designed to help people prepare for difficult content, can reinforce fragility by teaching avoidance rather than resilience. Participation trophies eliminate the valuable lessons that come from failure and genuine achievement. Litigation culture rewards victim positioning with financial settlements, teaching that claiming harm can be more profitable than developing strength.

Educational systems inadvertently cultivate Victim patterns through policies meant to support struggling students. Grade inflation protects students from distress but also from the growth that comes through genuine challenge and occasional failure. Excessive accommodation, while crucial for students with real disabilities, sometimes extends to avoiding all difficulty rather than building capability. Helicopter parenting eliminates struggle before children can develop problem-solving skills, creating young adults who've never learned to navigate challenges independently. Safe spaces, important for processing difficult experiences, sometimes become hiding places from all discomfort rather than temporary refuges. An excuse culture prioritizes comfort over learning, accepting "I couldn't" without exploring "How could you?"

Professional environments increasingly reward Victim patterns through policies designed to prevent lawsuits rather than promote growth. HR policies may overprotect against any challenge or criticism, creating employees who cannot handle feedback or improve performance. Fear of discrimination lawsuits leads to incompetence tolerance, where obviously struggling employees cannot be addressed directly. This creates burden shifting where high performers must compensate for those who've learned that helplessness protects them from expectations. Drama becomes rewarded through attention and accommodation—the squeaky wheel doesn't just get oil; it gets excused from squeaking properly.

Even therapeutic settings can inadvertently reinforce Victim patterns when compassion isn't balanced with challenge. Empathy turns to enabling, and validation without confrontation may feel supportive but prevents genuine growth. Excuse-making gets disguised as understanding when therapists, afraid of seeming harsh, accept all explanations without exploring agency. Dependency creation occurs when ongoing therapy becomes about maintaining relationships rather than building independence. Symptom focus rather than capability building keeps clients stuck in their problems rather than developing solutions. The therapeutic space, meant to heal, can become another arena where helplessness is rewarded with attention and care without expectation of change. These dynamics have been well documented by clinicians across multiple therapeutic traditions.

The Path Forward

While the Victim pattern creates significant limitations, it contains within it the seeds of its own transformation. The very sensitivity that creates victimhood can be redirected toward genuine empathy and connection.

Each ego pattern, when consciously integrated, offers unique gifts. The Victim pattern's shadow contains profound treasures waiting to be reclaimed. Their heightened sensitivity, currently tuned to detecting threats and slights, can develop into deep empathy that truly understands others' pain without drowning in it. Their intimate awareness of struggle, now used to justify helplessness, can transform into genuine compassion for human difficulty without enabling avoidance. Their understanding of limitations, currently experienced as permanent barriers, can teach the humility that comes from knowing we all have genuine constraints while still having choices within them. Their desire for support, now expressed as bottomless need, can build authentic community based on mutual aid rather than one-way rescue. Their knowledge of suffering, accumulated through years of pain both real and self-created, can become wisdom that helps others heal—not by joining them in helplessness but by showing the path through.

Learning to recognize the Victim pattern as it activates is crucial for transformation. The body provides early warning signals: collapsed posture that shrinks them smaller, shallow breathing that maintains low energy, and the distinctive energy drain that makes everything feel impossibly heavy. Emotional cues bubble up as self-pity that says "poor me," hopelessness that insists "nothing will change," and resentment toward those who seem to have it easier. Thought patterns reveal themselves through constant "I can't" statements, "It's not fair" complaints, and "Why me?" questions that don't seek answers but confirmation of victimhood. Behavioral flags include chronic procrastination that ensures failure, endless complaint without action, and withdrawal from opportunities that might challenge the helpless narrative. Most telling are the relational indicators—watch how others respond with visible frustration, compulsive advice-giving, or the exhausted look of someone who's tried to help too many times.

The Invitation to Empowerment

The journey from Victim pattern to integrated strength isn't about denying real difficulties or becoming invulnerable. It's about developing genuine resilience while maintaining appropriate vulnerability, the difference between "I can't handle this alone" and "I won't even try."

As we'll explore in subsequent chapters, this transformation requires specific practices, considerable courage, and often the support of others who can hold space for growth rather than enabling helplessness. The Victim who can embrace their own power—starting with tiny steps—opens doorways to contribution and connection that no amount of sympathy could provide. A single moment of choosing action over excuse, effort over explanation, attempt over avoidance, creates a crack in the fortress of helplessness through which light can enter.

In the end, the most profound transformation may be the shift from "I can't" to "I'll try" - from helplessness to hope, from paralysis to possibility. This shift, however small initially, creates more genuine safety than any fortress of helplessness ever could. When the Victim discovers they can impact their own life, even in small ways, the entire architecture of helplessness begins to crumble, revealing the capable person who was always there, waiting behind the walls of "I can't."

Reflecting on the Victim Within

As you read this chapter, you might notice your own Victim pattern activating—perhaps feeling overwhelmed by the information, thinking "I could never change these patterns," or finding excuses for why this doesn't apply to you. You might even feel victimized by being called a victim. This is natural and even valuable. The Victim pattern helped you survive whatever overwhelming experiences you've faced. The invitation isn't to deny real difficulties but to recognize when you use helplessness beyond its useful purpose.

Consider:

- Where in your life does "I can't" stop you from trying?
- When do you use helplessness to avoid anxiety?
- How might your relationships change if you owned your power?
- What would it mean to ask for help without giving away responsibility?

The journey toward Ego Intelligence begins with honest recognition. In recognizing our patterns, we create the possibility of choice. And in choice lies freedom—the freedom to be both vulnerable and capable, both limited and empowered, both needing support and offering strength in the grand dance of human interdependence.

>> Chapter 5 Key Takeaways

1. **The Victim equation** - Helplessness = Safety = Sympathy drives all Victim behavior, making powerlessness an active strategy for avoiding the terror of personal responsibility.
2. **Three core manifestations** define the Victim pattern: The Externalization Engine (every problem has an external cause), The Impossibility Framework (elaborate proofs why change is impossible), and The Sympathy Economy (trading helplessness for connection).
3. **The blame distribution system** operates across four categories - Historical (past trauma), Circumstantial (current conditions), Interpersonal (others' failures), and Cosmic (fate/universe) - ensuring accountability never touches their shoulders.
4. **The defense trinity** - Denial eliminates awareness of personal agency, Regression retreats to childlike dependence, and Repression buries memories of capability and success.
5. **Four paradoxes trap Victims** - Protection creates paralysis, connection attempts cause isolation, powerlessness becomes manipulative control, and care-seeking eventually exhausts all support.
6. **The powerful victim phenomenon** - Victims control through guilt, dominate through need, and punish through suffering, wielding weakness like a weapon others cannot defend against without appearing cruel.

7. **Learned helplessness progression** - From "This is too hard for me" to "I am fundamentally helpless," the pattern evolves from defensive strategy to core identity.
8. **Intensity determines dysfunction** - From Pattern as Option (acknowledging limitations without identifying) through Pattern as Identity (complete fusion with powerlessness), each level represents deeper entrenchment.
9. **Cultural enablement** - Well-intentioned movements, educational accommodations, HR overprotection, and even therapy can inadvertently reinforce Victim patterns by rewarding helplessness overgrowth.
10. **Recovery requires tiny steps** - Moving down intensity levels starts with microscopic moments of choice - from "I can't" to "I'll try," from paralysis to possibility, each small action creates cracks in the fortress of helplessness.

>> Coming Next: Chapter 6 – Pattern Combinations – When EJV Patterns Merge

In the next chapter, we'll explore what happens when ego patterns don't simply alternate but merge into unified defensive systems more powerful than any single pattern alone. You'll discover the three primary combinations — Expert-Judge, Judge-Victim, and Expert-Victim — and how each creates a unique defensive architecture that's harder to recognize and interrupt than a single pattern operating on its own.

Most importantly, you'll learn about pattern stacking — when all three faces activate simultaneously, creating an impenetrable fortress where one pattern can explain everything, another can criticize everything, and the third can avoid responsibility for anything. Understanding how these combinations reinforce each other is the key to seeing through them.

Chapter 6: Pattern Combinations – When EJV Patterns Merge

- Why ego patterns rarely exist in isolation but combine into complex defensive strategies
- The three primary pattern combinations: Expert-Judge, Judge-Victim, and Expert-Victim
- How intellectual criticism (Expert-Judge) creates impenetrable superiority
- Why self-critical helplessness (Judge-Victim) ensures perpetual suffering
- How intellectual helplessness (Expert-Victim) uses knowledge to avoid action
- How pattern combinations exploit attribution theory to obscure simple behaviors
- The phenomenon of "pattern stacking" - when all three patterns activate simultaneously
- How to recognize your unique pattern combination through assessment indicators
- The path from blended patterns to integrated awareness

Reading Time: ~35 minutes

"The most sophisticated ego defense isn't a single pattern but the intricate dance between multiple patterns, each reinforcing the other's protective illusion." - Integration insight from clinical observation

The Perfect Storm: When Patterns Converge

Dr. Patricia sits in her office, surrounded by academic journals and perfectly organized files. As department chair, she embodies what happens when ego patterns don't just alternate but merge into a unified defensive system. She is simultaneously the Expert who knows everything about academic standards, the Judge who criticizes anyone failing to meet them, and the Victim overwhelmed by the impossibility of maintaining excellence with limited resources.

"The problem," she explains to a colleague, launching into her familiar refrain, "is that I'm the only one who truly understands the complexity of maintaining academic rigor." Here, her Expert pattern provides the knowledge base. "These adjunct instructors simply don't meet professional standards, their syllabi are inadequate, their grading is inconsistent, their pedagogical approaches are outdated." The Judge pattern weaponizes that expertise into criticism. "But what can I do? The administration gives me no budget for proper training, no authority to enforce standards, no support when I try to maintain quality." The Victim pattern shields her from any responsibility for the department's dysfunction.

This isn't pattern cycling, it's pattern fusion. All three defenses operate simultaneously, creating an impenetrable fortress of intellectual superiority (Expert), righteous criticism (Judge), and justified helplessness (Victim). She can explain exactly why everything is wrong, whose fault it is, and why she's powerless to fix it, all while maintaining her position as the most knowledgeable, most discerning, and most put-upon person in the room.

The Evolution of Defensive Complexity

Not everyone operates at Dr. Patricia's level of defensive sophistication. Pattern combinations develop progressively, typically following three distinct stages:

Stage 1: Single Pattern Dominance Most people begin with one primary pattern that handles their defensive needs. The Expert relies on knowledge, the Judge on criticism, or the

Victim on helplessness. Other patterns remain dormant or minimal. Tyler, for instance, started as primarily Expert—using his research about learning styles to avoid homework. At this stage, defenses are simpler and more transparent.

Stage 2: Dual Pattern Activation Under increased stress or when single patterns prove insufficient, a second pattern activates regularly. Two patterns working together create more sophisticated defensive strategies that are harder to recognize and interrupt. Tyler evolved to Expert-Victim: "I understand precisely why my learning style makes success impossible here." These dual combinations—Expert-Judge, Judge-Victim, or Expert-Victim—become stable defensive strategies.

Stage 3: Full Pattern Stacking Under extreme or chronic stress, all three patterns activate simultaneously, creating what Dr. Patricia demonstrates—an impenetrable defensive fortress. The Expert provides knowledge-based justification, the Judge offers critical evaluation, and the Victim supplies helplessness-based excuses. This triple activation creates a closed system where every challenge to one pattern gets deflected by the others.

Understanding Pattern Combinations

The EJV assessment reveals that most people don't operate from a single ego pattern but from combinations that create unique defensive styles. These combinations aren't random; they follow predictable patterns based on which defenses complement and reinforce each other.

When ego patterns combine, they don't just add up—they multiply. Like ingredients in a recipe that create something entirely new when mixed, combined patterns form defensive systems far stronger than any single pattern alone. Think of it like a security system where a single lock can be picked, but multiple locks working together create an impenetrable fortress.

The Three Ways Patterns Strengthen Each Other

Mutual Reinforcement - They Back Each Other Up

Each pattern provides "evidence" for the others in a continuous loop of self-validation. Your expertise proves your criticism is valid, your high standards justify why you feel helpless, and your helplessness explains why you need more knowledge. For example, someone might say, "I know exactly what's wrong because I've studied this extensively, these standards aren't met by anyone, but I can't fix it alone." Each part of this statement reinforces the others, creating a logical-seeming whole that's a defensive structure.

Defensive Depth - Backup Plans for Your Backup Plans

When one defense fails, another immediately activates like a security system with multiple triggers. If someone challenges your expertise, you switch to criticism. If you can't criticize effectively, you become helpless. When helplessness is questioned, you return to expertise. Watching someone whose knowledge is challenged suddenly become critical of the challenger's qualifications. If that doesn't work, they claim they're overwhelmed and can't explain such complex matters to someone who won't understand. Each layer protects against different vulnerabilities.

Blind Spot Amplification - Can't See What You Can't See

Combined patterns create massive blind spots that become invisible to the person experiencing them. The Expert-Judge can't see how their "helpful" criticism destroys others—they genuinely believe they're educating. The Judge-Victim can't see how they create the very problems they complain about through their impossible standards. The Expert-Victim can't see how their extensive knowledge about their problems keeps them stuck in those problems. Consider the person who researches solutions for hours but never acts, then wonders why nothing changes. They're blind to how their expertise has become their excuse.

The Expert-Judge Combination: Intellectual Criticism

The Expert-Judge combination represents the merger of knowledge superiority with critical evaluation, creating what might be called "weaponized expertise." This combination uses intellectual prowess not just to maintain superiority but to actively diminish others.

Core Characteristics

The Perfectionist Scholar embraces the idea that knowledge must be both comprehensive and flawless. Any gap in understanding or error in execution becomes grounds for harsh self-criticism and brutal evaluation of others. The Expert's need to know everything merges with the Judge's need for everything to be perfect, creating impossible standards for intellectual performance.

The Intellectual Enforcer uses expertise to police others' knowledge and performance. Every conversation becomes an opportunity to correct, every interaction a chance to demonstrate superior understanding while highlighting others' inadequacies. Knowledge becomes a measuring stick used primarily for finding others wanting.

The Competitive Educator views teaching as performance of superiority rather than an act of service. The Expert-Judge doesn't share knowledge to empower but to establish dominance. They create hierarchies of understanding where they always occupy the summit, looking down on the intellectually inferior masses.

Principal Marcus Thompson: Expert-Judge Combination

Principal Marcus Thompson sits behind his imposing oak desk, his office walls adorned with three master's degrees, his doctorate in Educational Leadership, and numerous certificates from administrative workshops. Mrs. Chen sits across from him, visibly frustrated, having just learned her son Tyler is failing three classes.

"Mrs. Chen, I completely understand your concerns," Marcus begins, his voice carrying practiced empathy. "As someone who's been in education for twenty-three years and wrote my dissertation on student engagement strategies, I can assure you we take these situations very seriously." The Expert establishes his credentials while appearing supportive.

"I just don't understand," Mrs. Chen says. "Tyler says his teachers don't explain things well, and when he asks for help, they seem irritated."

Marcus leans forward, nodding knowingly. "Unfortunately, this aligns with patterns I've been observing. The research on differentiated instruction is quite clear—every student learns differently, and it's the educator's responsibility to adapt." He pulls out a tablet, scrolling through data. "I've been tracking our faculty's professional development participation, and I have to say, the engagement with best practices is... concerning."

"So, it's not just Tyler?"

"Absolutely not. You're being a wonderful advocate for your son." Marcus's voice shifts to conspiratorial concern. "Between you and me, some of our veteran teachers have become rather... set in their ways. They're not implementing the modern pedagogical approaches that research shows are essential for student success. I've provided them with seventeen different educational journals and twelve online professional development platforms, but..." he sighs heavily, "you can lead a horse to water."

Later that afternoon, Marcus calls Mrs. Rodriguez, Tyler's English teacher, into his office.

"I just finished meeting with Mrs. Chen," he begins before she's even fully seated. "She's quite concerned, and frankly, so am I. Can you explain why Tyler has been struggling in your class?"

Mrs. Rodriguez, exhausted from teaching six periods with thirty-five students each, responds carefully. "I've reached out three times about Tyler's missing assignments and offered after-school help, but…"

"Reaching out isn't teaching," Marcus interrupts, his Expert-Judge combination fully activated. "The current research on adolescent learning clearly indicates that traditional assignment structures don't work for all students. Have you considered project-based learning? Gamification? Flipped classroom models? I sent everyone links to several studies on these approaches last month."

"Marcus, with thirty-five students per class and no aide support".

"That's exactly why you need to be implementing more efficient strategies," he cuts her off. "I managed larger classes when I taught, before I moved into administration where I could actually effect systemic change. It's about working smarter, not harder. The pedagogical literature is quite clear on this."

The Judge-Victim Combination: Self-Critical Helplessness

The Judge-Victim combination creates a particularly painful internal experience where harsh self-criticism leads directly to learned helplessness. This combination turns the Judge's critical eye inward while simultaneously claiming powerlessness to meet the very standards they set.

Core Characteristics

The Judge-Victim combination manifests in three distinct but interrelated ways, each creating its own form of sophisticated suffering.

The Paralyzed Perfectionist sets impossible standards then collapses when unable to meet them. First, the Judge creates the rules—everything must be perfect, deadlines must be met early, work must be flawless. Then the Victim declares these same standards impossible to achieve, creating a state of paralysis through over-analysis. This creates a self-reinforcing cycle where criticism generates helplessness, which generates more criticism for being helpless. They can't win because they've designed a game that's impossible to win, yet they can't stop playing because that would mean abandoning their standards.

The Passive-Aggressive Controller uses criticism and helplessness as dual weapons in their relationships. They judge others harshly while claiming they're too overwhelmed to do better themselves. "You should be more organized," they tell their partner while their own life remains in chaos they claim they're powerless to address. "The kids should know better," they say, while explaining they're too exhausted to enforce consistent rules. This creates a maddening dynamic where they maintain moral superiority through criticism while avoiding accountability through helplessness.

The Martyred Critic suffers loudly while making others suffer quietly. They're simultaneously the harsh judge dispensing criticism and the perpetual victim of circumstance, usually circumstances they've created through their own impossible standards. They'll spend an hour explaining how everyone has failed them while describing in detail their overwhelming burdens. Their suffering becomes a weapon, their criticism a shield, and everyone around them feels both judged and guilty—exactly the combination that keeps others off-balance and the Martyred Critic in control.

Judge-Victim Combination: The Parent's Paradox

Mrs. Chen: The Critical Helplessness Performance

After leaving Principal Marcus Thompson's office, Mrs. Chen sits in her BMW in the school parking lot, texting furiously in the group chat with her wine club friends.

"Just left another useless meeting. These teachers are INCOMPETENT. But what can I do? I'm just one parent against an entire broken system "

The responses come immediately: "You're such a good mom, Lisa!" "Tyler is lucky to have you fighting for him!" "The school system is failing our kids!"

Mrs. Chen drives home, feeling both vindicated and victimized. In Marcus's office, she had played the concerned but overwhelmed parent perfectly. Now, with her social circle, she can unleash the full Judge-Victim combination that defines her relationship with Tyler's education—and Tyler himself.

That evening, at her friend Katherine's house, Mrs. Chen holds court. The other mothers gather around the kitchen island with their Pinot Grigio as Lisa performs her well-rehearsed tragedy.

"Tyler's English teacher is absolutely worthless," she begins, the Judge fully activated. "I mean, how hard is it to teach teenagers to read books? She can't even get him to turn in assignments. When I was in school, teachers knew how to motivate students. They had standards. They commanded respect."

"What does the principal say?" Katherine asks.

Here, Mrs. Chen shifts seamlessly to Victim: "Oh, he tries, but his hands are tied. And I'm drowning here. I work sixty hours a week at the firm, I'm managing the house renovation, I'm on three charity boards—when am I supposed to also teach Tyler English? That's literally what we pay taxes for."

The Expert-Victim Combination: Intellectual Helplessness

The Expert-Victim combination creates a sophisticated form of avoidance where extensive knowledge about problems substitutes for action to solve them. This combination uses expertise to explain and justify helplessness, creating elaborate intellectual frameworks for why change is impossible.

Core Characteristics

The Expert-Victim combination manifests in three distinct ways, each using knowledge as a sophisticated escape from action and responsibility.

The Informed Avoider knows exactly why they can't succeed. They've researched their limitations extensively, can cite studies about their challenges, and have developed comprehensive theories about their inability. Their expertise becomes evidence for their helplessness rather than a tool for growth. They're the people who can explain in detail why their anxiety is treatment-resistant, citing five different studies, but won't try the simple breathing exercises their therapist suggests. They know everything about their problems, the origins, the symptoms, the statistical outcomes—and use this knowledge to prove that change is impossible rather than to create it.

The Analytical Paralytic understands problems deeply but claims inability to solve them. They can provide detailed analysis of their situation, complex explanations for their struggles, and sophisticated frameworks for their failures while maintaining nothing can be done. They'll spend three hours explaining the intricate dynamics of their dysfunctional workplace, complete with organizational charts and psychological profiles of every colleague, then conclude that the situation is too complex to address. Their understanding becomes a substitute for action, their analysis a replacement for attempts at change.

The Scholarly Sufferer uses intellectual understanding to validate victimhood. They're experts in their own trauma, scholars of their own limitations, professors of their own pathology. Knowledge becomes a way to avoid the vulnerable work of actual change. They can lecture for hours about their attachment style, their childhood wounds, their neurological differences, but use this expertise to explain why they can't form relationships rather than risk the messy, imperfect work of connecting with another human being. They've made their dysfunction into a dissertation, their problems into a field of study, ensuring they remain the world's foremost expert on why they can't succeed.

Tyler Chen: Expert-Victim Combination

Tyler sits at his desk, laptop open to an empty essay document. Instead of writing, he's deep in a Reddit thread about "gifted burnout," taking screenshots to show his mom later. His dad is at work—as always—managing his sales territory to maintain their comfortable suburban lifestyle.

His phone buzzes—Mom texting from downstairs: "How did the meeting with Principal Thompson go? Did you explain about your learning style?"

"He understood," Tyler texts back. He doesn't mention he spent most of the meeting agreeing with Marcus that his teachers need better training.

Earlier that day, Tyler had sat in Marcus's office with his mother.

"Tyler's obviously brilliant," Mrs. Chen had started, her Judge-Victim pattern already active. "But these teachers just don't understand how to engage gifted students."

Marcus, in full Expert-Judge mode, had nodded sagely. "The research on gifted underachievement is quite clear. Traditional pedagogical approaches often fail these learners."

Tyler had seized his opening: "Exactly. I've been researching this myself. There's a Stanford study showing that gifted kids need completely different educational approaches. Mrs. Rodriguez just assigns these rigid five-paragraph essays that kill creativity. Einstein would have failed her class."

"Tyler's done so much research," his mom added, shifting to Victim. "We're just overwhelmed trying to navigate this broken system."

Marcus had turned to Tyler. "It's impressive that you understand educational theory so well."

"I've read everything—Ken Robinson, Sal Khan, even some Montessori. The traditional model is based on 19th-century Prussian factory schools. It's designed to create compliant workers, not creative thinkers. That's why I struggle—my brain is wired for innovation, not regurgitation."

Taking Your Eye Off the Ball: How Pattern Combinations Exploit Attribution Theory

Start with the simple truth: Tyler doesn't do his homework.

That's the ball. Clear, observable, measurable. Either Tyler does homework or accepts consequences. But watch this behavior vanish through an elaborate shell game where everyone shifts blame and no one watches the ball.

Understanding the Attribution Game

Attribution theory, developed by psychologist Fritz Heider and later refined by Harold Kelley and Bernard Weiner, examines how we explain behavior—both our own and others. We make internal attributions (personal choice, effort, character) or external attributions (circumstances, other people, systems). In healthy functioning, we use both appropriately: taking credit for success, learning from mistakes, acknowledging real limitations, and maintaining realistic self-esteem.

But ego pattern combinations exploit attribution theory. They systematically distort attributions to protect the ego, making everything external when responsibility threatens, or everything internal when self-punishment serves the pattern. The result? Actual behavior never has to change.

Tyler's Sleight of Hand

He transforms a simple choice (gaming instead of writing) into a systemic critique. The educational system is outdated (external). Teachers don't understand innovation (external). School wasn't designed for minds like his (external).

Tyler provides exactly what each adult needs to hear. With Mom: "These teachers don't understand gifted kids." With Principal: "Traditional pedagogy fails creative learners." With teachers: "Your methods stifle innovation."

Never once does Tyler acknowledge the internal attribution—his choice to game instead of work. By becoming an Expert on why he can't succeed (external factors), he creates a Victim narrative where his behavior isn't even his responsibility.

Mom's Protective Shield

Mrs. Chen can't face what Tyler's behavior might mean about her parenting (internal attribution too painful). So teachers become incompetent (external), the system becomes broken (external), she becomes overwhelmed by work and renovations (external).

She performs both Judge ("These teachers are worthless") and Victim ("I'm drowning here") to avoid one internal attribution: "What if I'm failing as a mother?"

The Principal's Political Theater

Marcus can't challenge parents (would threaten his position) or admit leadership failures (internal attribution). His survival depends on appearing knowledgeable while deflecting responsibility.

So, teachers need more training (external to him). Methods are outdated (systemic external). Faculty resists change (external to leadership).

By making all attributions external, specifically to teachers, Marcus keeps parents happy while never addressing his role in enabling Tyler.

Mrs. Rodriguez: The Only One Watching the Ball

The English teacher sees the truth—Tyler chooses not to work (accurate internal attribution). But she's buried under everyone's "projections".

- Tyler: "Your methods don't suit my learning style" (external)
- Mom: "You don't understand gifted kids" (external)
- Marcus: "You need better pedagogical training" (external)

The one person who accurately attributes behavior to choice gets gaslit into doubting herself.

The Cost of Attribution Manipulation

When pattern combinations weaponize attribution theory:

- **Behaviors never change** - Everyone's so busy debating why something happened that they forget to address what happened
- **Responsibility disappears** - Everything becomes someone else's fault or the system's problem
- **Solutions become impossible** - You can't fix behavior you can't even see through the fog of explanations
- **Patterns strengthen** - Each successful manipulation reinforces the defensive system

- **Systems fail** - Schools, families, relationships break down when simple behaviors can't be addressed directly

Why Pattern Combinations Love Attribution Theory

Each ego pattern has a preferred attribution style that serves its defensive needs:

- **Expert**: "Research shows..." (external attributions with intellectual backing)
- **Judge**: "Standards aren't being met..." (external attributions with moral weight)
- **Victim**: "I can't because..." (external attributions with helpless flavor)

When patterns combine, they create attribution fortresses:

- **Expert-Judge**: "Research proves others are failing" (intellectual authority + moral criticism)
- **Judge-Victim**: "Others are wrong and I'm powerless" (moral superiority + learned helplessness)
- **Expert-Victim**: "I understand exactly why I can't" (knowledge as excuse for inaction)

These combinations don't just deflect responsibility—they make it intellectually and emotionally impossible to even locate responsibility.

The result is that Tyler still hasn't written his essay. The behavior hasn't changed. Everyone's exhausted from attribution battles.

Pattern Stacking: When All Three Merge

Under extreme stress or in highly defended individuals, all three patterns can activate simultaneously, creating what the assessment identifies as "pattern stacking." This represents the ego's maximum defensive deployment.

The Triple Defense

Dr. Patricia embodies complete pattern stacking:

Expert Layer: "I understand the complexities of academic administration better than anyone—the accreditation requirements, the budgetary constraints, the pedagogical theories, the institutional politics."

Judge Layer: "The administration is incompetent, the adjuncts are unprofessional, the students are unprepared, the system is broken."

Victim Layer: "But I'm powerless to fix any of it. I have responsibility without authority, expectations without resources, standards without support."

All three patterns operate simultaneously, creating an impenetrable defensive structure. She can explain everything (Expert), criticize everything (Judge), and take responsibility for nothing (Victim).

Behavioral Signs of Pattern Stacking:

- Exhausting others with defensive complexity
- Creating arguments that can't be countered
- Maintaining problems while appearing to address them
- Generating drama while claiming to want peace
- Being simultaneously superior, critical, and helpless

The Simple Solution No One Can See

Someone needs to say: "Tyler, I don't care why you think you can't do homework. The behavior is simple: you either write the essay tonight or you fail. Your choice. No discussion about systems, creativity, or teaching methods. Just behavior and consequence."

But this requires:

- Seeing through the attribution maze
- Refusing to engage with elaborate explanations
- Focusing solely on behavior
- Accepting you'll be the "bad guy" who "doesn't understand"

How Pattern Stacking Becomes Self-Perpetuating

When all three patterns activate together, they create a self-reinforcing loop where each pattern feeds the others:

The Reinforcement Loop

- **Expert provides knowledge** → Judge uses it as evidence for criticism
- **Judge sets impossible standards** → Victim has proof of helplessness
- **Victim creates helplessness** → Expert must acquire more knowledge to compensate

Each pattern validates the others, creating a closed circuit that feels like sophisticated understanding but is the same defensive loop running repeatedly.

Dr. Patricia's Internal Circuit

Watch how her three patterns reinforce each other:

Expert Voice: "I understand academic complexity better than anyone..." → Validates Judge: "Therefore I can evaluate what's wrong"

Judge Voice: "Everything is failing to meet standards..." →
Validates Victim: "See? The situation is impossible"

Victim Voice: "I'm powerless to fix any of it..." → Validates
Expert: "I need to understand more about why"

The cycle continues, each rotation strengthening all three
patterns.

Why This Becomes Identity

This system is:

- **Self-validating**: Each pattern "proves" the others are
  correct
- **Self-perpetuating**: Each pattern triggers the next in
  sequence
- **Self-reinforcing**: Each successful cycle makes the loop
  more automatic

The person feels they're thinking deeply, but they're running the
same circuit repeatedly. Each repetition strengthens the neural
pathways until the loop becomes identity itself.

Breaking the Loop

Simple behavioral consequences work because they cut through
all three loops simultaneously: "Do your homework or fail. No
explanations needed."

This interrupts the circuit by refusing to engage with:

- The Expert's elaborate theories
- The Judge's impossible standards
- The Victim's helplessness narrative

Just behavior and consequence. But the patterns will fight to rebuild their circuit, which is why pattern combinations are so persistent.

The Ball Remains "Unplayed"

At the end of all this sophisticated psychological maneuvering:

- Tyler still hasn't written his essay
- The behavior hasn't changed
- Everyone's exhausted from attribution battles
- Tyler wins by keeping everyone's eye off the ball

The ego pattern combinations haven't solved anything. They've just created such an elaborate attribution performance that the simple behavior—a teenager avoiding homework—has vanished entirely into a fog of psychological warfare.

And Tyler? He's already researching attribution theory itself, preparing to explain why the tendency to seek behavioral explanations represents outdated behaviorist thinking that doesn't account for complex systemic factors affecting modern learners.

The ball remains "unplayed". Tyler remains unaccountable. The patterns remain unbroken.

Everyone lost sight of the ball. Tyler won the game.

>> Chapter 6 Key Takeaways

1. **Pattern combinations multiply, not add** - When ego patterns merge, they create defensive systems exponentially more powerful than individual patterns, like multiple locks creating an impenetrable fortress.

2. **Three primary combinations dominate** - Expert-Judge (intellectual criticism), Judge-Victim (self-critical helplessness), and Expert-Victim (intellectual helplessness) each create unique forms of sophisticated defense.

3. **Mutual reinforcement locks patterns in place** - Each pattern provides "evidence" for the others: expertise validates criticism, standards justify helplessness, helplessness necessitates more expertise.

4. **Defensive depth ensures protection** - When one pattern fails, another immediately activates—challenged expertise becomes criticism, failed criticism becomes helplessness, questioned helplessness returns to expertise.

5. **Blind spots amplify in combinations** - Expert-Judge can't see their destructive impact, Judge-Victim can't see their self-sabotage, Expert-Victim can't see their avoidance—and none can see that they can't see.

6. **Attribution theory gets weaponized** - Pattern combinations systematically shift all attributions external, making simple behaviors invisible behind elaborate explanations about systems, others, and circumstances.

7. **Taking your eye off the ball** - Everyone gets so lost in attribution debates that the actual behavior (Tyler not doing homework) completely disappears.

8. **Pattern stacking creates maximum defense** - When all three patterns activate simultaneously, the person can explain everything (Expert), criticize everything (Judge), and take responsibility for nothing (Victim). Meta conditioning has one face supporting the other in an uninterrupted circuit.

9. **Simple solutions become impossible** - Pattern combinations make obvious answers seem naive while intellectual understanding of patterns often strengthens them, ensuring problems persist behind sophisticated defenses.

>> Coming Next: Chapter 7 – The Frequency Mechanism of Internal Dialogue

In the next chapter, we'll explore the actual mechanism through which these pattern combinations broadcast themselves into your daily experience—and discover why authentic recovery is always possible. You'll learn about the two frequencies of internal dialogue, the space between thoughts where choice exists, and the restore point that's always available for returning to authentic voice.

Chapter 7: The Frequency Mechanism of Internal Dialogue

>> What You'll Learn in This Chapter

- How internal dialogue acts as a broadcasting system for EJV patterns
- The two primary frequencies: Ego and Authentic Self
- Why Beck's cognitive triad and Meichenbaum's self-talk only work at certain frequencies
- The restore point concept: returning to authentic voice control
- How to recognize which frequency is broadcasting
- Practical tools for frequency recognition and switching
- Why the space between thoughts matters more than the thoughts themselves

Reading Time: ~30 minutes

"The voice in your head is not who you are. You are the one who hears it." - Eckhart Tolle

---

My wife and I are standing at the international departures gate at DFW in Dallas, passport in hand, watching planes taxi outside the window. In 9 hours, I'll be in Madrid, then on to Murcia where the University of Spain has invited me to deliver a keynote on emotional intelligence. They're calling it a fellowship—an honor that should fill me with pride. Instead, my internal dialogue runs on a loop that's been playing for months.

"Is your lecture too elementary? Spanish professors probably have a completely different theoretical framework. You're about to embarrass yourself in front of an international audience. They'll be polite, of course, but they'll know you're out of your depth."

I've revised the presentation seventeen times. Searched for every paper published by their faculty. Practiced my pronunciation of Spanish professors' names. Still, the voice persists: "You're not ready. You'll never be ready. This was a mistake."

My phone buzzes. A text from my daughter: "Dad, I've been in an accident."

My heart stops. Then, in the space of a microsecond, something shifts in my internal frequency. The voice that's been cataloging my inadequacies suddenly changes its tune—but not in the way you'd expect.

"This is it," the voice says, almost triumphant. "You have to cancel. No one could blame you for canceling. Your daughter needs you. Family comes first. The university will understand completely."

I called her immediately, my hands shaking. She answers on the second ring, voice trembling but coherent. She's been T-boned at an intersection as I see the picture she texted me. The car is "totaled" and looks bad, but she's okay - shaken, scared, but physically fine. Her grandparents are already on their way.

"Should I cancel my trip?" I ask.

"Absolutely not," she says firmly. "Dad, you've prepared for months. I'm fine. Go give your lecture."

But the voice had found its opening: "A good father would stay. What if she's minimizing her injuries? What if she needs you and won't say it? This is your sign—the universe giving you an out

from potential humiliation of being a bad father and a bad
lecturer."

I recognize this voice now. It's not paternal concern—that voice
would sound different, would be focused solely on my
daughter's wellbeing. This voice is using my love for her as
camouflage for its real mission: protecting me from the
possibility of professional failure. It's weaponizing my deepest
values—being a good father—to serve its defensive agenda.

"You could frame it perfectly," the ego frequency continues,
broadcasting its elaborate escape plan. "No one would question a
father staying for his injured child. You'd be seen as devoted, not
incompetent. Your reputation stays intact."

Standing there in the airport, I experience something I'll later
recognize as crucial to understanding the frequency mechanism:
I can hear the voice, but I am not the voice. I'm the one listening
to it broadcast its fear disguised as virtue.

Another frequency speaks up, quieter but clearer: "Your
daughter is safe. She has support. You've prepared thoroughly
for this opportunity. Both things can be true—you can be a
caring father and a capable professional. The fear you're feeling
isn't about her; it's about you."

I confirm once more that my daughter is okay, that her
grandparents are with her, that she genuinely wants me to go.
Then we board the plane, both frequencies still broadcasting
their competing narratives.

The flight to Madrid becomes a masterclass in frequency
recognition. The ego frequency shifts tactics every hour:

"Your examples are too American-centric." "What if your
research is outdated?" "They invited you by mistake—they

meant to invite someone with a doctorate." "You should have cancelled when you had the perfect excuse."

Each broadcast sounds reasonable, even responsible. That's the insidious nature of the ego frequency—it disguises fear as prudence, self-protection as wisdom.

The authentic frequency responds differently each time, not arguing but simply stating what is:

"You were invited because of your expertise." "Your practical experience adds value to theory." "Different perspectives enrich academic discourse." "You're exactly where you're supposed to be."

In Murcia, standing before an audience of professors and graduate students, I notice both frequencies still broadcasting. The ego voice catalogs every facial expression, interprets every whisper as criticism. The authentic voice reminds me why I'm here—to share knowledge that might help others understand emotional intelligence more deeply.

Halfway through the lecture, something shifts. A professor asks a question that shows she's genuinely engaged with my framework. A graduate student shares how one of my examples clarifies something she's been struggling with. The ego frequency doesn't stop broadcasting—it never completely stops—but I stop tuning in. I find what I'll later call the "restore point," that state where the authentic voice maintains control not through battle but through conscious choice.

The lecture is a success. More than that—it leads to ongoing collaboration with the university, joint research projects, possibly return visits. Everything the ego patterns said would go wrong, went right.

On the flight home, the ego frequency tries one more strategy: "Was it really what they expected? You could have done better. Next time you should..."

But now I recognize this pattern. Success doesn't silence the ego frequency—it just changes its tactics. From "you'll fail" to "you didn't succeed enough." From "they'll reject you" to "they were just being polite." The ego's mission never changes; maintain the defensive identity at all costs, even if that identity is "never quite good enough."

Sitting on that plane home, I finally understood - I spent months believing I was preparing for my lecture when actually I was wrestling with frequencies. The real preparation wasn't in the PowerPoint slides or the research citations—it was in learning to recognize which internal broadcast was running my life.

The Journey Ahead

That trip to Murcia taught me something profound about the mechanism of internal dialogue. We all have these competing frequencies broadcasting inside us, each claiming to be true, each with its own agenda. The ego frequency—born from our earliest wounds and fears—broadcasts defensive messages designed to keep us safe by keeping us small. The authentic frequency speaks from our genuine values and capabilities, inviting us toward growth and connection.

But here's what I discovered: we are neither frequency. We are the consciousness that can observe both broadcasts and choose which one to tune into. This isn't about positive thinking or suppressing negative thoughts. It's about recognizing that thoughts are frequencies we can tune into or away from, not commands we must obey.

The moment my daughter texted about her accident revealed how sophisticated the ego frequency can be—it will use anything, even our most noble feelings, to maintain its protective mission. It took genuine paternal concern and twisted it into an escape route from professional vulnerability. That's ego intelligence at work: strategic, opportunistic, and always disguised as something more acceptable than raw fear. As Mark Twain rightly said, 'Courage is resistance to fear, mastery of fear, not absence of fear.' The ego frequency would have us believe that feeling fear means we shouldn't proceed, but courage exists precisely because fear exists.

This chapter explores how these frequencies operate, why traditional interventions sometimes fail (they're working on the wrong frequency), and how to find that space between broadcasts where real choice exists. We'll discover how childhood experiences install certain frequencies as our default broadcast, why the ego frequency intensifies under stress, and most importantly, how to achieve the restore point—that state where authentic voice naturally maintains control.

The internal dialogue will always be with us. The question isn't whether we'll have self-talk but which frequency we'll allow to dominate our mental airspace. In that choice, a choice that becomes available only through awareness shows our freedom.

Historical Foundations: Mapping the Inner Voice

The recognition that our internal dialogue shapes our reality is not new. Through decades of psychological research and millennia of philosophical inquiry, thinkers have identified this inner voice as a crucial determinant of human experience. Each perspective adds a layer to our understanding of what we'll call the frequency mechanism—the broadcasting system through which our deepest patterns manifest into consciousness.

The Cognitive Revolution: Beck and Meichenbaum

Aaron Beck's cognitive triad revealed how internal dialogue creates totalizing realities. His identification of three channels—negative views of self, world, and future—showed how depression isn't just a mood but a frequency that hijacks all temporal dimensions. When someone's internal dialogue insists "I'm worthless" (self), "Everything is against me" (world), and "It will never get better" (future), they're not experiencing three separate thoughts but one ego frequency broadcasting across all channels simultaneously.

Donald Meichenbaum pioneered the clinical application of internal dialogue modification. His self-instructional training recognized that we literally talk ourselves through every action, and that changing behavior requires changing this self-talk. His three-phase model—self-observation, introducing incompatible thoughts, and developing meta-cognition about change—revealed that awareness must precede alteration. His stress inoculation training exposed a crucial truth: under pressure, our practiced positive self-talk often crumbles, revealing that surface changes don't hold when the underlying frequency remains unchanged.

The Wisdom Traditions: Ruiz and Tolle

Miguel Ruiz's "Four Agreements" describes what he calls the "voice of knowledge" or internal "Book of Law", the inherited agreements that run our mental programming. His concept of "mitote," the chaos of thousands of conflicting voices in our mind, perfectly captures the experience of a hijacked frequency system. He traces how external voices from childhood become internalized as our inner judge, constantly evaluating us against impossible standards. His work reveals that these aren't our authentic thoughts but domesticated programming—what we call EJV patterns broadcasting through internal dialogue.

Eckhart Tolle introduces perhaps the most radical perspective: you are not your thoughts but the awareness that observes them. His concept of the "witnessing presence" reveals a third position beyond both ego and authentic frequencies. The "pain-body" he describes parallels our understanding of EJV patterns—accumulated emotional pain that becomes semi-autonomous, hijacking our internal dialogue to feed on more suffering. Most crucially, Tolle points to the space between thoughts, the gaps in internal dialogue where neither ego nor authentic-self broadcasts—where pure potential exists.

The Integration: Ego Intelligence Framework

The Ego Intelligence framework brings precision to understanding how these frequencies operate. The ego isn't inherently destructive—it's a protective mechanism that becomes problematic when it dominates our internal dialogue to preserve the exaggerated perceived self. This framework helps us understand that the ego frequency broadcasts from a specific mission: maintain the constructed identity at all costs.

When we understand ego intelligence, we see why certain patterns are so persistent. The ego has intelligence—it knows exactly which frequencies to broadcast to maintain its narrative. For the perfectionist, the expert judge broadcasts impossible standards while the victim internalizes the failure to meet them. For the martyr, the expert judge declares the nobility of suffering while the victim accepts it as deserved. For the gifted child grown into a paralyzed adult, the expert judge warns of the danger in any situation that might reveal ordinariness while the victim remains frozen in fear. The ego isn't stupid; it's strategically protecting what it believes keeps us safe, even when that safety has become a prison.

The Broadcasting System Within

With these historical foundations, we can now understand internal dialogue as a frequency mechanism—a broadcasting system through which our psychological patterns manifest into conscious thought and behavior. This isn't metaphorical; it's the actual mechanism through which abstract patterns become lived experience.

Every moment of our waking lives, an internal voice narrates our experience. But this narration isn't neutral—it's always broadcasting from one of two primary frequencies, each with its own signature, purpose, and impact on our lives.

Where Patterns Find Their Voice

Our internal dialogue serves as the carrier wave for our psychological patterns. Just as a radio transmits information through electromagnetic frequencies, our EJV patterns broadcast themselves into consciousness through the channel of self-talk. The frequency isn't just about what we think, but how often these patterns hijack our mental airspace and with what intensity they broadcast their defensive messages.

Consider how defense mechanisms, cognitive distortions, pre-emotion bias, and maladaptive behaviors all require internal dialogue to manifest. We don't simply *have* these patterns—we give them voice through our self-talk. The person who self-defeats talks themselves out of opportunities: "Why try? I'll just fail anyway." The self-saboteur talks themselves into old limiting habits: "One drink won't hurt," "I don't really need to finish this project." The self-punisher maintains an internal dialogue that normalizes taking punches: "I deserve this," "This is what I get for being stupid." The self-martyr has been talked into believing their suffering serves others: "They need me more than I need rest," "Good people always sacrifice."

This frequency operates like malware in a computer system—running background processes that consume our mental resources and redirect normal operations. The patterns insert themselves into our thought stream automatically, often below conscious awareness, running their defensive scripts on repeat. For those who recover from their patterns, this frequency remains minimal, manageable—they've learned to recognize the malware and stop it from running. For others, it becomes a dominant force that enables tri-pattern stacking, where one defensive pattern activates another, creating a resonance that completely hijacks the internal narrative.

Two Frequencies: The Source of the Broadcast

The distinction between destructive and constructive internal dialogue isn't about positive versus negative thinking, it's about the source of the broadcast. Destructive dialogue emerges from EJV patterns operating through ego intelligence, while constructive dialogue flows from the authentic self, aligned with genuine values.

The Ego Frequency

The ego frequency broadcasts from the exaggerated perceived self—the identity constructed for protection. Operating primarily from fear, its singular mission is preserve the constructed identity at all costs.

This isn't random—it's strategic. The ego knows your vulnerabilities, pride points, fears, and dreams, using all of them to maintain its protective narrative.

Pattern-Specific Broadcasts:

The Martyr's Frequency: "Good people always put others first. Your needs don't matter as much. Creating conflict makes you selfish." The ego weaponizes genuine care, creating a perverse loop where self-abandonment becomes virtue.

The Perfectionist's Frequency: "That wasn't good enough. Everyone expects excellence. One mistake and it all falls apart." The ego maintains an impossible paradox: You're superior, therefore you should always be doing better.

The Expert's Frequency: "They need to understand how wrong they are. Your knowledge is what gives you value. If you don't know, you don't matter." The ego conflates worth with knowledge.

Behavioral Outcomes:

- Over-analysis masquerading as thoroughness
- Risk aversion protecting identity, not safety
- Procrastination avoiding potential failure
- Self-sabotage at the threshold of success
- Self-criticism loops maintaining status quo

The Authentic Self Frequency

The authentic self-broadcasts from genuine values integrated with emotional intelligence. This frequency aligns with who we are rather than who we fear we're not.

When internal dialogue comes from the authentic self, it has a different quality entirely. Analysis serves exploration rather than protection. Caution emerges from wisdom rather than terror. Self-reflection occurs without self-attack.

Authentic Frequency Characteristics:

- Integration over splitting
- Expansion over contraction
- Growth over preservation
- Connection over isolation
- Curiosity over judgment
- Values alignment without extremism

The difference is immediately recognizable: The ego frequency contracts and defends. The authentic frequency expands and explores. One speaks from fear disguised as logic. The other speaks from wholeness, even when acknowledging uncertainty.

The Question of Frequency Recognition

Teaching clients to recognize their internal dialogue's frequency becomes remarkably clear when we apply the receipts concept to the entire defensive architecture from Chapter 2. Rather than checking isolated elements, we can trace any internal dialogue backward through the complete chain to reveal its source.

The Diagnostic Chain Method

When internal dialogue activates, you can run it through this systematic check, asking for receipts at each level of the defensive architecture:

Start with the surface: Is this a cognitive distortion? Check if your internal dialogue contains all-or-nothing thinking, catastrophizing, mind reading, or fortune telling. When I thought "Spanish professors will definitely think I'm incompetent," I had no receipts for their actual thoughts—this was mind reading combined with fortune telling. The ego frequency relies heavily on distortions that sound convincing but lack factual receipts. The authentic frequency makes observations based on actual evidence.

Go deeper: Is this a defense mechanism at work? Examine whether you're using intellectualization, projection, denial, or other defenses. My elaborate analysis of why canceling for my daughter would be "the responsible choice" was intellectualization—using logic to avoid facing my fear of professional exposure. When you catch yourself in lengthy internal explanations for why you "have to" do something that conveniently protects you from vulnerability, that's your receipt for active defense. The authentic frequency responds to situations directly without elaborate defensive maneuvers.

Check the emotional foundation: What's the pre-emotion bias? Before conscious thought forms, what emotional assumption is already present? When I saw my daughter's accident text, the ego frequency's bias toward escape was already operating before I consciously processed anything. The bias reveals itself in the speed and direction of the initial reaction—no conscious receipts needed because it precedes thought. The authentic frequency carries biases toward growth and capability that are supported by actual life experience.

Identify the core deception: What lie is being served? The context lie wraps around true content to create a defensive narrative. "I don't have a PhD" (true content) becomes "Therefore I don't belong on that stage" (context lie). Check your receipts: Has anyone actually said you don't belong? Has lack of credentials prevented your contribution before? The ego frequency consistently takes true receipts and assigns false meaning to them. The authentic frequency presents receipts in accurate context without catastrophic interpretation.

Find the root: What personal domain is being protected? This is where identity and worth have become fused with external criteria. My domain had fused professional worth with academic credentials—every piece of internal dialogue ultimately served to protect this fusion. The ego frequency will have excessive receipts here, years of evidence for why this domain must be defended at all costs. The authentic frequency needs no receipts to justify worth because it hasn't fused identity with external criteria.

THE DIAGNOSTIC CHAIN METHOD

1. Check for Distortion (receipts for claims?)

2. Identify Defense (protecting what?)

3. Detect Bias (pre-existing assumption?)

4. Expose Lie (true content, false context?)

5. Find Domain (identity fused with what?)

Reverse Engineering Any Internal Dialogue

Starting with any piece of internal dialogue, you can trace it backward through the chain to reveal which frequency is broadcasting. Take the thought "Everyone will know I'm incompetent" and work backward:

This is fortune telling without receipts (distortion) → protecting through intellectualization that creates elaborate escape plans (defense) → carrying a pre-existing bias toward professional inadequacy (pre-emotion) → serving the lie that equals credentials (false context) → protecting the domain where professional identity requires academic validation (root).

Once you see the complete chain, the frequency becomes unmistakable. The ego frequency shows distortions without receipts, defenses that protect vulnerabilities, biases toward threat, lies about meaning, all desperately protecting a constructed domain. The authentic frequency presents factual observations, genuine responses without defensive elaboration, curious engagement, accurate context, all flowing from wholeness rather than defending a position.

The Power of the Complete Chain

This diagnostic chain transforms frequency recognition from guesswork to systematic inquiry. When internal dialogue feels overwhelming or confusing, start anywhere in the chain and work backward. Spot the distortion, notice the defense, catch the bias, identify the lie, or recognize the domain being protected. Each element leads to the others, eventually revealing whether you're tuned to ego or authentic frequency.

The receipts requirement at each level provides clarity. The ego frequency consistently lacks receipts for its distortions ("Everyone thinks..."), uses receipts selectively for its defenses (remembering only failures), ignores receipts that contradict its biases (dismissing successes), twists receipts to support its lies (true content with false context), and desperately accumulates receipts to justify its domain ("See? I need credentials to matter"). The authentic frequency has actual receipts for its observations, acknowledges all receipts without selection, carries biases supported by genuine experience, presents receipts in accurate context, and needs no receipts to justify inherent worth.

This unified approach explains why traditional cognitive interventions sometimes fail—they often address only the distortion level without tracing back to the domain being protected. Unless you address what's being protected, the ego simply generates new distortions. But when you can trace any thought through the complete chain, you not only identify which frequency is broadcasting but understand exactly what it's protecting and why.

The Ego's Counterattack

Understanding ego intelligence helps us anticipate and navigate the counterattack that comes with frequency recognition. When we begin to recognize these patterns, especially when we successfully trace them through the diagnostic chain—the ego perceives an existential threat. It has built its entire identity structure around these narratives: "the selfless one," "the gifted one," "the perfect one," "the strong one." The moment someone sees these as distortions rather than virtues; the ego launches its counterattack through intensified internal dialogue.

When someone uses the diagnostic chain to expose the ego's defensive structure—tracing from surface distortion back to protected domain—the ego responds by amplifying each level of the chain. Distortions become more catastrophic ("If I'm not perfect, I'm worthless"), defenses more elaborate (creating complex justifications for why change is impossible), biases more entrenched (seeing only evidence that confirms inadequacy), lies more convincing (wrapping more truth in false context), and domain protection more desperate ("Without this identity, I cease to exist").

The ego's intelligence shows how it tailors its attack to each person's specific vulnerabilities. For the martyr who's begun checking receipts, it might say: "They don't understand how caring you are," "You're not like those selfish people," "If you stop helping, you'll become everything you hate." Notice how each statement lacks actual receipts—no one has called them selfish; there's no evidence that boundaries equal cruelty. For the perfectionist applying the diagnostic chain: "Lowering your standards means becoming mediocre," "Everyone will see you're a fraud," "This therapist is trying to make you ordinary." Again, no receipts exist for these catastrophic predictions.

The ego hijacks the internal dialogue with increased intensity, recruiting shame, guilt, fear, even rage to maintain control. It might even recruit internalized voices of others: "What would your mother think?" "Your colleagues expect better," "Everyone depends on you being strong." This is sophisticated ego intelligence at work—it knows exactly which frequencies to broadcast to keep you locked in the pattern. When you ask for receipts at each level of the chain during this counterattack, you'll find the ego's arguments collapse into emotional manipulation without factual foundation.

Programs That Install Frequencies

The origins of these frequencies often trace back to early programming—moments when external voices became internalized as our default broadcast system. These early programs don't just install a frequency; they construct the entire defensive chain that we can now trace with our diagnostic method.

Consider how "gifted and talented" programs can install complete defensive architecture. The label creates the domain (worth equals natural ability), which generates the lie (struggle means not gifted), establishes the bias (toward effortless performance), activates defenses (intellectualization of any difficulty), and produces distortions (catastrophizing any challenge). When a child internalizes "I'm gifted," their internal dialogue starts operating from this fixed chain rather than a growth process.

This creates an impossible bind visible through the diagnostic chain. If you must work hard, you're not really gifted (lie without receipts—many gifted people work intensely). If you struggle, you're exposed as a fraud (distortion—struggle is human, not fraudulent). The internal dialogue becomes: "Gifted people don't need to study" (no receipts—successful gifted people study constantly), "If you can't figure it out immediately, maybe you're not as smart as they said" (false context around true content of momentary confusion), "Everyone expects you to just know" (mind reading without receipts).

These individuals often become adults showing extreme paralysis through over-analysis—brilliant people stuck between their potential and their ego's need to protect the "gifted" narrative. When they apply the diagnostic chain to their paralysis, they can trace it directly back to this original programming. The valedictorian architect who won't take business risks can trace their frozen state: catastrophic predictions about failure (distortion) → intellectualizing why the timing isn't right (defense) → bias toward needing guaranteed success (pre-emotion) → lie that risk equals stupidity (false context) → protecting the domain where worth equals never struggling (root programming).

The diagnostic chain reveals how childhood programming installs not just a belief but an entire defensive structure. Every level of the chain gets programmed simultaneously, creating a self-reinforcing system that maintains itself for decades. Understanding this allows us to see that we're not dealing with a single problematic thought but an entire installed architecture that needs systematic dismantling through conscious recognition at each level.

The Restore Point: Reclaiming Authentic Control

The goal of understanding the frequency mechanism isn't to eliminate internal dialogue or achieve some perfect state of mental quiet. Rather, we're working to achieve what we might call a "restore point", bringing the authentic voice frequency back into control by dismantling the defensive chain that maintains ego dominance.

This restore point concept is crucial because it reframes the entire therapeutic endeavor. We're not trying to create something new or foreign, but rather to restore access to the authentic frequency that's always been there, just buried under layers of defensive architecture. Like a computer's restore point that exists before the system gets corrupted, the authentic voice exists before the EJV patterns construct their defensive chains.

The diagnostic chain method becomes our primary tool for reaching this restore point. By systematically checking receipts at each level—exposing distortions without evidence, defenses without genuine threat, biases without current foundation, lies wrapped in false context, domains requiring no protection gradually dismantle the ego's defensive structure. Each time we trace a piece of internal dialogue back through the chain and recognize it as ego frequency, we weaken its hold.

This understanding removes the pressure of having to "become" something different or better. People aren't broken needing to be fixed, they're just unable to access their authentic frequency through the layers of defensive chains. The restore point reminds us that health and wholeness already exist within. Most interventions try to add more positive thoughts, more coping skills, more strategies. But the restore point concept suggests we need to clear the interference by dismantling the defensive chains, and the authentic voice naturally resurfaces.

Once we restore the authentic frequency to control - living authentically becomes the default state. The authentic frequency doesn't need elaborate defensive chains because it has no constructed identity to protect. It can have receipts without weaponizing them, experience bias without being controlled by it, acknowledge truth without adding defensive context. The restore point isn't a destination but a return to our natural state of being, where our internal dialogue aligns with genuine values rather than protected domains, supports actual goals rather than defensive missions, and speaks from wholeness rather than fragmented chains of protection.

Reverse Engineering: "Everyone will know I'm incompetent"

Chain Level	What to Check	What You Find	Receipts?
Surface	Distortion	Fortune telling: "Everyone will know"	No
↓	Defense	Intellectualizing escape plans	No
↓	Bias	Assuming inadequacy	No
↓	Lie	"No PhD = Incompetent"	No
Root	Domain	Worth requires credentials	No

Result: Ego frequency identified - no receipts at any level

The Space Between Frequencies: Clarity Beyond Choice

Having traced the diagnostic chains, witnessed the ego's counterattacks, understood the programming that installed our frequencies, and worked toward the restore point, we arrive at a crucial recognition: there exists a space beyond both ego and authentic frequencies—a place of pure awareness where true clarity resides.

This isn't merely another concept to understand but the foundation that makes all frequency work possible. As Tolle illuminates, you are not your thoughts but the awareness that observes them. The Taoist proverb captures this: "the usefulness of what is comes from what is not." Like a room where walls define the structure but the space between creates utility, the gaps in our internal dialogue are where real freedom exists.

In this space, the entire defensive architecture becomes visible but not controlling. You can observe the diagnostic chain constructing itself, distortions forming, defenses activating, biases coloring perception, lies being served, domains being protected—without being identified with any level of it. From here, even the distinction between ego and authentic frequencies becomes just another observable phenomenon rather than an identity to claim or reject.

This space of clarity is what enables the restore point. Without this witnessing presence, we might switch from ego frequency to authentic frequency but remain trapped in the game of identification—now identifying as "someone who broadcasts authentically" rather than "someone who protects their domain." The space between reveals that we are neither frequency; we are the consciousness that can observe both and choose which to engage or choose to rest in silence.

When you find this space, you temporarily step outside the entire frequency mechanism. You're not checking receipts, tracing chains, or even choosing between broadcasts, you're simply aware. This is where genuine reflection occurs, where you can ask: "What is being authentic for me?" Not what opposes the ego (which is still ego-defined), not what sounds spiritually correct, but what emerges from this space of pure potential when neither defensive nor authentic frequencies are broadcasting their agendas.

The restore point isn't just about returning control to the authentic frequency, it's about recognizing yourself as the space in which all frequencies arise and fall. From this recognition, authentic living becomes not another performance or correct frequency to maintain, but a natural expression of consciousness that needs no defensive chains, requires no receipts to justify its worth, and speaks from the wholeness that exists in the space between all broadcasts.

This is the ultimate insight of the frequency mechanism: Yes, we can learn to recognize which station is broadcasting. Yes, we can trace defensive chains back to their roots. Yes, we can work toward restore points where authentic voice regains control. But beneath all of this activity lies the space of pure awareness; "the you" that exists before, between, and beyond all internal dialogue. Finding this space isn't the end of the journey but the beginning of true freedom, where choice emerges not from switching between predetermined frequencies but from the creative potential that exists in silence.

The Clinical Application

Understanding the frequency mechanism and working toward this restore point transforms intervention from combat to tuning. Rather than fighting the ego with more ego—using willpower, harsh discipline, or positive thinking to overpower the destructive voice—clients learn to apply the diagnostic chain: "Let me trace this thought backward. What's the distortion? What defense pattern is active? What bias is present? What lie is being served? What domain is being protected?" Once they identify the ego's defensive architecture, they can consciously tune back to the authentic channel.

This understanding explains why traditional cognitive approaches sometimes fall short. Beck's cognitive restructuring and Meichenbaum's self-instructional training can be powerful, but only when applied to the right frequency. If someone's operating from authentic self-frequency, these techniques help refine their internal dialogue. But if the ego has hijacked the frequency, these same techniques might just create a more sophisticated ego defense—teaching the ego to construct better defensive chains while remaining in control.

The ego intelligence framework reveals why this happens: the ego is intelligent enough to co-opt any intervention that doesn't address the complete chain. It will use CBT to rationalize its distortions with better receipts. It will use positive affirmations to strengthen its domain protection. It will even use mindfulness to become a "superior" meditator whose worth depends on meditation prowess. Unless we trace the complete defensive chain, the ego incorporates every intervention into its protective architecture.

This diagnostic chain awareness must come before any other intervention technique. Without tracing internal dialogue through the complete chain, people might:

- Apply values work that strengthens their martyrdom pattern (the ego adding more "receipts" for why self-sacrifice equals virtue)
- Use cognitive restructuring that teaches the ego to build more sophisticated defensive chains
- Practice self-compassion that the ego corrupts into avoiding genuine receipts about harmful patterns
- Attempt behavioral change that the ego sabotages by intensifying every level of the defensive chain

Practical Frequency Recognition

Clients can develop frequency recognition through daily practice, applying the diagnostic chain method to identify not just the content but the complete defensive architecture of their internal dialogue, always working toward that restore point where authentic voice regains control:

Morning Check-In: Upon waking, before the ego fully constructs its defensive chains, notice the quality of internal dialogue. Is there spaciousness or urgency? Run a quick diagnostic: Are there distortions present? Defenses activating? Biases coloring the day ahead? This liminal moment often reveals the authentic frequency before the ego's protective architecture fully assembles.

Decision Points: When facing choices, pause to trace the internal dialogue through the chain. "You must decide now" (urgency without receipts) → protecting through catastrophizing (defense) → bias toward control (pre-emotion) → lie that wrong choices are irreversible (false context) → protecting domain where worth requires perfection (root). The authentic frequency presents actual receipts: "Here are the real factors to consider."

Emotional Triggers: Strong emotions often indicate the defensive chain activating. Trace backward: The attacking thought (distortion) → protecting through projection (defense) → bias toward threat (pre-emotion) → lie about what this means (context) → domain being threatened (root). The authentic frequency can hold emotions without the elaborate defensive architecture.

Success and Failure Moments: Apply the diagnostic chain to inflated or devastating responses. "I'm amazing" or "I'm worthless" both lack balanced receipts. Trace them back: What distortion is this? What's being defended? What bias is operating? What lie is being served? What domain needs this interpretation? The authentic frequency has actual receipts: "This specific thing went well" or "This particular approach didn't work."

Relationship Interactions: Notice how the defensive chain constructs itself around interactions. "They think I'm stupid" (mind reading without receipts) → protecting through withdrawal (defense) → bias toward rejection (pre-emotion) → lie that their opinion defines worth (false context) → protecting domain where value requires universal approval (root). The authentic frequency engages without elaborate pre- and post-processing chains.

Integration and Moving Forward

The frequency mechanism of internal dialogue provides the diagnostic foundation for all change work. It reveals that our suffering doesn't come from having thoughts but from the defensive chains that generate and maintain them. The diagnostic chain method shows us this isn't random suffering—

it's the ego's systematic architecture protecting a constructed identity at each level.

Recovery isn't about achieving perfect internal dialogue or eliminating all critical self-reflection. It's about developing the ability to:

1. Apply the diagnostic chain to any internal dialogue (checking receipts at each level)
2. Trace thoughts backward from distortion to protected domain
3. Recognize when defensive chains are constructing themselves
4. Distinguish between actual receipts and ego fabrications
5. Find the space between thoughts where chains dissolve
6. Work toward the restore point where authentic voice naturally operates without defensive architecture

This understanding transforms the therapeutic process. Rather than fighting individual thoughts, we dismantle entire defensive chains. Rather than adding more techniques, we expose the ego's co-opting of existing techniques. The ego's defensive architecture only maintains power when we don't recognize it as a constructed chain. Once we can trace any thought back through its defensive levels, checking for receipts at each stage, its power diminishes.

The historical perspectives—from Beck's cognitive triad to Tolle's witnessing presence—all point to this same truth: we are not our thoughts, but we can choose which thoughts we tune into. The diagnostic chain method adds the crucial tool for making this choice conscious and systematic.

As we prepare to explore specific interventions in the next chapter, remember: all techniques must build on this fundamental recognition. Without the diagnostic chain method, even the most powerful interventions can be corrupted by the ego into more sophisticated defensive architectures. But with the ability to trace any thought through its complete chain, checking for receipts at each level, every intervention becomes a tool for dismantling defensive structures and returning to authentic broadcast—the voice that needs no elaborate chains, requires no false receipts, and speaks from wholeness rather than fragmentation.

The internal dialogue will always be with us. The question isn't whether we'll have self-talk but whether we'll recognize the defensive chains that generate it. In that recognition, we made systematic through the diagnostic chain method—lies our emotional freedom. The restore point isn't about perfection; it's about operating without defensive architecture, where internal dialogue flows from genuine receipts rather than elaborate protective chains.

>> Chapter 7 Key Takeaways

1. Internal dialogue operates on two frequencies: ego (defensive) and authentic (genuine)

2. The diagnostic chain method traces any thought through five levels to reveal its source

3. Checking for "receipts" at each level exposes whether ego or authentic frequency is broadcasting

4. When the ego frequency lacks receipts—it makes claims without evidence at every level

5. Childhood programming installs entire defensive chains, not just single beliefs

6. The ego's counterattack amplifies when exposed but collapses when receipts are requested

7. The restore point returns control to authentic frequency by dismantling defensive chains

8. The space between frequencies reveals you are the awareness, not the broadcast

9. Traditional interventions fail when applied to wrong frequency—ego co-opts them

10. Freedom comes from recognizing defensive chains, not fighting individual thoughts

---

>> Coming Next: Chapter 8 – Emotional Sovereignty

In the next chapter, we'll explore how pattern amplifiers block access to emotional intelligence skills you already possess. We will explore the Pareto principle and how it guides access to these skills. You'll discover why someone can score high on EQ assessments yet be unable to apply those skills when patterns activate. We'll map specific blocking mechanisms and show how clearing interference through frequency recognition restores natural emotional intelligence.

Chapter 8: Emotional Sovereignty – The 80/20 Rule of Liberation

>> What You'll Learn in This Chapter

- **The Fundamental Question**: How to recognize when emotions are controlling you through ego patterns versus when you're consciously working with emotions as information
- **The 80/20 Liberation Principle**: How identifying and addressing your pattern amplifiers can restore emotional control and resolve most of your life challenges
- **Pattern Amplifiers**: The vital few factors that give ego patterns totalitarian control over your emotional life
- **The Hijacking Mechanism**: How each ego face corrupts emotional intelligence in specific, predictable ways
- **The Liberation Discovery**: Why addressing amplifiers naturally strengthens five key elements that become your recovery foundation

Reading Time: ~20 minutes

Clinical Foundation: Based on therapeutic outcomes using the Pareto Principle for pattern intervention

---

"Between stimulus and response there is a space. In that space is our power to choose our response. In our response lies our growth and our freedom." - Viktor Frankl

The Man Who Couldn't Stand Himself

He sat across from me in my therapy office, a man who couldn't stand himself. His wife was filing for divorce. His children had lost all respect for him. His job hung by a thread. His finances were in ruins. His health was declining rapidly. By every measure, his life was collapsing, yet he couldn't see the common thread weaving through each disaster.

"I don't understand," he said, his hands trembling slightly. "I'm smarter than this. I know what I should be doing. I can tell you exactly what's wrong and exactly what needs to change. But somehow..." He trailed off, the gap between his knowledge and his reality too painful to articulate.

As we explored deeper, a disturbing pattern emerged. When drinking, he became a master of pattern stacking—all three ego faces working in perfect destructive harmony. His Expert face would lecture his family on their failings, demonstrating intellectual superiority while intoxicated. His Judge face would harshly criticize his wife's "inadequacies" and his children's "disappointments," setting impossible standards from his barstool throne. Then his Victim face would emerge, using others' angry responses to his behavior as proof that nobody understood him, that life was unfair, that he had no choice but to drink more.

Each face fed the others in an endless loop. The Expert justified drinking ("I understand alcohol's effects better than these doctors"). The Judge criticized everyone who tried to help ("They don't really care; they just want to control me"). The Victim used the resulting isolation as evidence for why he needed to drink ("With my life, who wouldn't drink?"). All three faces provided the energy to keep the destruction going, each one activating to protect him from seeing what he was doing to himself and others.

His emotions weren't informing his choices; they were controlling him through his ego patterns. Fear drove the Expert's need to be superior. Anger fueled the Judge's criticism. Sadness fed the Victim's helplessness. He had become a passenger in his own life, with his pattern-hijacked emotions at the wheel.

The Fundamental Question of Emotional Intelligence

In all my years of teaching emotional intelligence, one question stands above all others: **Are your emotions controlling you, or are you controlling your emotions?**

This isn't about suppressing emotions or becoming emotionally numb. It's about the difference between emotions as tyrants versus emotions as advisors. When we're emotionally sovereign, we feel everything fully but choose our responses consciously. When we're emotionally hijacked, our patterns use our emotions to control our behavior, destroying our lives while we watch helplessly.

My client exemplified complete emotional hijacking. His fear, anger, and sadness weren't just feelings; they had become his masters, commanding him through his ego patterns. The Expert pattern weaponized his fear of inadequacy. The Judge pattern channeled his anger into criticism. The Victim pattern transformed his sadness into helplessness. Together, they formed a triumvirate of emotional tyranny.

The Space That Disappears

In healthy emotional functioning, there's a space between feeling and action—a moment where we can consider our response. When ego patterns take control, this space disappears. The emotion and the pattern response become fused:

- Fear instantly triggers Expert superiority
- Frustration immediately activates Judge criticism
- Sadness automatically engages Victim helplessness

My client has lost this space entirely. Every emotion triggered its corresponding pattern without pause, without choice, without awareness. He wasn't living his life; his patterns were living it through him.

The Pareto Principle of Liberation

The breakthrough in my client's treatment came through applying an unexpected principle to emotional healing: the Pareto Principle, also known as the 80/20 Rule.

Understanding the Principle

Named after Italian polymath Vilfredo Pareto, who in 1906 observed that 20% of Italy's population owned 80% of the land, this principle reveals a fundamental pattern of imbalance: roughly 80% of consequences come from 20% of causes. Joseph M. Juran later applied this to quality management, discovering that 80% of problems stemmed from 20% of defects.

In emotional healing, the Pareto Principle offers profound hope. While clients may present with dozens of symptoms— relationship problems, work stress, health issues, financial troubles—often 80% of these problems are maintained by 20% of causes. These "pattern amplifiers" act as force multipliers for ego defenses.

The Pattern Amplifier Discovery

Pattern amplifiers are the vital few factors that give ego patterns excessive power over our emotional lives. Without amplifiers, patterns remain manageable quirks. With amplifiers, they become tyrannical forces of destruction.

In my client's case, alcohol was the critical 20%. It wasn't causing all his problems directly, but it was the amplifier giving his pattern intensified control. Remove the amplifier, and suddenly the patterns lose their stranglehold.

Common Pattern Amplifiers

Through clinical observation, certain amplifiers consistently emerge:

Substances (alcohol, drugs) - Lower conscious defenses, allowing patterns free rein

Chronic Stress - Depletes emotional regulation capacity, making pattern activation automatic

Sleep Deprivation - Weakens executive function, reducing ability to interrupt patterns

Toxic Relationships - Continuously trigger defensive responses, keeping patterns hyperactive

Success/Failure Extremes - Threaten or inflate ego, intensifying pattern activation

Social media - Provides endless comparison triggers that activate all three faces

Unprocessed Trauma - Keeps nervous system in defensive mode, lowering pattern activation threshold

To understand how pattern amplifiers create this 80/20 effect in your own life, consider these clinical examples that likely mirror dynamics you've witnessed or experienced.

Real Clinical Examples - The 80/20 in Action

Visual Framework: The Pattern Amplifier Effect

The Vital Few (20%)	The Resulting Many (80%)
Abusive Partner	Depression, anxiety, financial ruin, health decline, lost friendships, career destruction, children's trauma, self-worth collapse
Alcohol/Substances	Marriage failing, lost respect, job jeopardy, financial crisis, health deterioration, isolation, legal problems, pattern stacking
Toxic Workplace	Sunday dread, chronic stress, family tension, health issues, lost confidence, sleep disruption, emotional exhaustion, identity confusion
Unprocessed Trauma	Relationship sabotage, career underachievement, addiction patterns, parenting struggles, chronic health issues, trust inability, emotional dysregulation

Other Case Examples

The Abusive Partner Amplifier Sarah, 42, came to therapy with severe depression, crippling anxiety, and financial ruin. Her unemployed husband criticized her constantly, isolated her from friends, and drained their savings. This one relationship, her 20%, was destroying every aspect of her life. Six months after leaving him, her depression lifted, anxiety became manageable, and she received a promotion at work. Removing one amplifier transformed everything.

The Success Trap David, 38, a CEO, couldn't understand why his life felt empty despite his wealth. His extreme success had hyperactivated his Expert-Judge stack. He criticized everyone, needed to be the smartest person in every room, and had turned all relationships into transactions. Stepping back from the CEO role—addressing his 20%—allowed his patterns to calm and authentic connections to return.

The social media Spiral Emma, 28, spent six hours daily on Instagram, triggering all three patterns simultaneously. This single habit created an eating disorder, $30K in debt, relationship problems, and work issues. A 30-day social media detox followed by strict boundaries transformed her life within months.

Identifying Your Pattern Amplifiers

Finding your 20% requires honest self-examination. Ask yourself:

1. "What triggers my pattern stack most reliably?"
2. "What do I organize my life around avoiding or managing?"
3. "What would others say is my obvious problem?"
4. "What am I most defensive about when others mention it?"
5. "If you could change only one thing and had to keep everything else the same, what would create the biggest positive impact?"

Pattern-Specific Amplifiers

Different ego faces have typical amplifiers:

Expert Pattern Amplifiers:

- Competitive work environments

- Academic settings
- Intellectual debates
- Professional recognition

Judge Pattern Amplifiers:

- Perfectionist backgrounds
- Critical relationships
- "Comparison culture"
- Leadership positions

Victim Pattern Amplifiers:

- Caretaker roles
- Financial dependence
- Chronic illness identity
- Past trauma

How Patterns Hijack Emotional Intelligence

Understanding how each pattern corrupts emotional intelligence helps identify when hijacking is occurring.

The Expert's Intellectual Bypass

The Expert converts emotions into concepts to avoid feeling them. Fear becomes "an interesting stress response." Love becomes "neurochemical bonding." This intellectualization corrupts:

- **Drive Strength** → Becomes drive for knowledge over accomplishment
- **Empathy** → Becomes analysis rather than connection
- **Communication** → Becomes lecturing rather than dialogue

The Judge's Emotional Weaponization

The Judge uses emotions as tools for criticism. Every feeling becomes evidence in the trial of self and others. This weaponization corrupts:

- **Commitment Ethic** → Becomes commitment to impossible standards
- **Social Awareness** → Becomes scanning for failures
- **Positive Influence** → Becomes demoralization through criticism

The Victim's Emotional Drowning

The Victim drowns in emotions without processing them. Feelings become proof of helplessness rather than information for action. This drowning corrupts:

- **Problem Solving** → Becomes problem attachment
- **Change Orientation** → Becomes proof change is impossible
- **Assertive Communication** → Becomes manipulation through suffering

The Pattern Stack Attack

When all three patterns activate together, emotional intelligence disappears entirely. My client demonstrated this perfectly intellectualizing his destruction (Expert), criticizing all help (Judge), while using responses as evidence of victimization (Victim). Complete hijacking with no authentic self-access.

For weeks, I focused on helping my client understand these hijacking mechanisms—how his Expert intellectualized, his Judge weaponized, his Victim drowned. We mapped every pattern, traced every trigger, analyzed every defensive move. Yet despite this deep understanding, his patterns remained firmly in control. He could explain his dysfunction brilliantly (Expert), judge it harshly (Judge), and feel hopeless about changing it (Victim). The patterns had incorporated our therapeutic insights into their defensive arsenal. That's when I realized we'd been fighting the wrong battle. Instead of trying to defeat his patterns directly, what if we simply removed what was giving them excessive power? When we shifted focus to his alcohol use—his pattern amplifier—something unexpected happened that changed my entire approach to treatment.

The Liberation Discovery

What I didn't expect was that removing his amplifier would reveal something else—five natural strengths that had been buried under the pattern activation that became the foundation of his healing.

As the alcohol-fueled pattern stack weakened, something remarkable emerged:

1. **Self-Integration** - His fragmented selves reconnected to his values and authentic self
2. **Relationship Health** - Love and empathy resurfaced as he salvaged crucial relationships with wife, children, employer, and self
3. **Personal Growth** - He could finally learn from mistakes and consider consequences before choosing
4. **Healthy Coping** - Growth-promoting strategies replaced destructive patterns, allowing him to step away from chaos
5. **Recovery Progress** - Each success provided evidence of capability, improving his sense of self without bias

These elements didn't require separate work—they emerged naturally as the patterns lost their amplified power. This discovery revealed a bidirectional healing system: reduce patterns and elements strengthen; strengthen elements and patterns weaken.

The Liberation Equation and Your Liberation Practice

Pattern Amplifier Removed (20%) → Patterns Lose Power →

Space Opens → Five Elements Emerge → Problems Resolve (80%)

Reclaiming emotional sovereignty begins with identifying and addressing your pattern amplifiers.

The Daily Sovereignty Check

Each morning, ask yourself:

1. What emotions am I carrying?
2. Are they informing or controlling me?
3. What might amplify my patterns today?
4. How can I strengthen the space between feeling and response?

The Pattern Interrupt Protocol

When you feel patterns activating:

1. **PAUSE** - Create space
2. **IDENTIFY** - Which pattern is activating?
3. **TRACE** - What's amplifying it?
4. **CHOOSE** - Let emotion inform, not control
5. **ACT** - Take one authentic action

When You Can't Remove the Amplifier

Sometimes your pattern amplifier can't be immediately removed. You can't abandon young children, quit a necessary job overnight, cure a chronic illness, or instantly resolve trauma. When removal isn't possible, the strategy shifts to **amplifier management**:

Dilution Strategy: If you can't remove the amplifier, dilute its power. A toxic workplace amplifier can be diluted with strong after-work recovery rituals, clear boundaries, and weekend restoration practices. The amplifier remains but loses concentration.

Buffer Building: Create protective factors between you and the amplifier. If caring for a difficult elderly parent is your amplifier, build in respite care, support groups, and daily self-care non-negotiables. These buffers prevent the amplifier from achieving full pattern activation.

Graduated Reduction: Some amplifiers can be slowly reduced rather than suddenly removed. Social media addiction might step down from 6 hours to 4 to 2 to 30 minutes daily. A toxic relationship might move from living together to separate spaces to limited contact to eventual termination.

Acceptance with Agency: For truly unchangeable amplifiers like chronic illness or past trauma, the work becomes accepting what can't be changed while maintaining agency over your response. "I have this condition AND I choose how to relate to it."

Remember: even reducing an amplifier's power by 30% can weaken patterns enough for the five elements to begin emerging. Perfect removal isn't required for liberation to begin.

Tracking Your 20%

Keep a simple log:

- When do patterns activate most strongly?
- What preceded the activation?
- What amplifiers were present?
- What helped create space for choice?

The Path Forward

Sobriety was not the destination; it was the doorway. By addressing the 20% that amplified everything else, my client could finally face the remaining 80% of his struggles without being overwhelmed by them. The patterns that had once controlled his life were still present, but no longer running at full volume.

Six months later, he sat in my office again—the same man but in control. "I feel everything now," he said, "but emotions don't control me anymore. They inform me. Is this what emotional intelligence really is?"

Yes. This is emotional sovereignty: feeling fully while choosing consciously.

Conclusion: Finding Your 20%

Every moment presents the same fundamental choice: Will your emotions control you through your patterns, or will you work with them as information for conscious choice?

The journey begins with identifying your pattern amplifiers—your 20%. What gives your ego patterns excessive power? What transforms manageable quirks into destructive forces?

Find your 20%. Address it. Watch as patterns lose their grip and something remarkable emerges—five key elements that naturally strengthen as patterns weaken. This is the promise of the Pareto Principle applied to emotional liberation: you don't have to fix everything at once. Address the vital few, and the useful many will follow.

Remember the man who couldn't stand himself? Today, he can look in the mirror with genuine self-respect. Not because he's perfect, but because he's sovereign.

>> Chapter 8 Key Takeaways

1. **The fundamental question** - Are emotions controlling you through patterns, or are you consciously working with emotions as information?
2. **The 80/20 Liberation Principle** - Most life problems (80%) are maintained by a few pattern amplifiers (20%).
3. **Pattern amplifiers** - Substances, stress, toxic relationships, extremes, trauma give patterns excessive power.
4. **Pattern-specific hijacking** - Expert intellectualizes, Judge weaponizes, Victim drowns in emotions.
5. **The space between** - Emotional sovereignty exists in the gap between feeling and response.
6. **Finding your 20%** - Identify what triggers your pattern stack most reliably.
7. **The liberation discovery** - Addressing amplifiers naturally strengthens five key recovery elements.
8. **Bidirectional healing** - Reduce patterns and elements strengthen; strengthen elements and patterns weaken.
9. **Daily practice** - Morning checks, pattern interrupts, and tracking create sustainable sovereignty.
10. **Hope in focus** - You don't need to fix everything, address your vital few and watch the many transform.

>> **Coming Next: Chapter 9 – The Five Elements of Recovery**

In the next chapter, we'll explore in greater detail the five elements that emerged —Self-Integration, Relationship Health, Personal Growth, Healthy Coping, and Recovery Progress. You'll discover how consciously building these elements creates a positive feedback loop that naturally weakens ego patterns and learn specific practices for strengthening each element regardless of where you are in your journey.

Chapter 9: The Five Elements of Recovery

Building What's Right Instead of Attacking What's Wrong

>> What You'll Learn in This Chapter

- The Reverse Engineering Formula
- The Five Elements in Detail
- Recovery Progress – The Evidence Trail
- The Restore Point Method: Understanding the Mechanism of Recovery
- Resourced Engagement: Carrying the Flashlight into the Dark

Reading Time: ~30 minutes

"Recovery is the act of reconnecting to real..."

The Reverse Engineering Formula

In the previous chapter, we saw how removing pattern amplifiers creates space for something new to emerge. This chapter explores what naturally fills that space when we consciously build it.

Traditional approaches attack patterns directly: identify, analyze, challenge, and change. This often fails because patterns incorporate therapeutic insights into their defenses and we have the tendency to adhere to the excuses. Therefore, the perceived change becomes too daunting a task. Rather than change we explore calibrating. Calibrating is the act of making incremental adjustments using the values that define us in the direction of growth, much like calibrating a thermometer back to its accurate settings. More specifically, it is to move the degree of acceptance in line with the authentic values that define who we are. Unlike change, which implies the abandonment of who we are, calibration honors the existing self as the starting point rather than the problem. This distinction is therapeutically significant because the client is not asked to become someone different, but rather to return to a more accurate expression of whom they have always been at their core.

The reverse engineering formula works differently—instead of attacking what's wrong, we build what's right. We acknowledge and work with the specific values that give rise to the influences of the very ego patterns that have controlled the frequency.

The Discovery

This approach emerged from observing clients who recovered despite never directly addressing their patterns. They had focused on building specific life elements, and their patterns had weakened as a side effect. Five elements consistently appeared in successful recoveries:

1. **Self-Integration** – Alignment between values, thoughts, feelings, and actions
2. **Relationship Health** – Authentic connections that reflect truth
3. **Personal Growth** – Continuous expansion beyond comfort zones
4. **Healthy Coping** – Adaptive strategies for managing life stressors
5. **Recovery Progress** – Measurable evidence of positive change

The remarkable discovery: these elements and pattern reduction work bidirectionally. Building elements weakens patterns;

weakening patterns strengthens elements. Start anywhere, and
the system supports itself.

The Five Elements in Detail

1. Self-Integration – Becoming Awareness

Self-integration is a transformative process that involves
aligning one's thoughts, feelings, and actions with their authentic
values and essence. It is a journey of self-discovery and personal
growth that requires intentionality, self-awareness, and a
willingness to embrace calibration.

At its core, self-integration is about reversing the fragmentation
and disconnection that ego patterns create within us. When we
are operating from a place of ego, we often find ourselves
reacting to perceived threats or challenges in ways that are not
aligned with our true values and desires. This can lead to internal
conflict, self-doubt, and a sense of being out of balance. This
clouds individual clarity and creates a self-induced negative bias
reaction within us.

The process of self-integration begins with exploring and
identifying our individual values. We then learn and understand
the lens by which we view and react to the world around us. And
then embrace a commitment to practicing self-awareness and
mindfulness through this calibrated lens. By tuning into our
inner world and observing our thoughts, feelings, and reactions
without judgment, we can begin to recognize the patterns and
habits that may be holding us back from living authentically.

As we develop this awareness, we can start to make intentional
choices about how we want to show up in the world. This
involves identifying the values and qualities that are most

important to us and making a conscious effort to embody them in our daily lives.

However, it's important to recognize that the very values that define our authentic self can also trigger ego patterns when we feel threatened or challenged. For example, someone who values kindness and compassion may find themselves slipping into people-pleasing behaviors or sacrificing their own needs in order to avoid conflict or disapproval.

This is where the concept of "dancing in the flow" comes in. Self-integration is not a one-time event, but an ongoing practice of navigating the space between our authentic self and our ego patterns with grace and flexibility. It involves learning to recognize when we are being triggered and choosing to respond from a place of love and alignment rather than fear and reactivity.

One powerful way to cultivate this skill is through a daily practice of intention-setting and reflection. By starting each morning with a clear intention to embody one or more of our core values, we can prime ourselves to show up in the world with greater authenticity and purpose.

Throughout the day, we can check in with ourselves to see if our actions are matching our intentions. Are we speaking and behaving in ways that are consistent with our values? Are we honoring our own needs and boundaries while also being present and compassionate with others?

At the end of the day, we can take a few moments to acknowledge and celebrate the ways in which we have aligned with our authentic self, without judgment or self-criticism. This practice of self-compassion and acceptance is essential for building resilience and maintaining a sense of balance on the journey of self-integration.

Ultimately, the goal of self-integration is to become the awareness that recognizes the opportunity of the space between experience and reaction. When we are fully integrated, we are able to respond to life's challenges with clarity, creativity, and compassion, rather than being swept away by our ego patterns and unconscious reactions.

This process of self-integration is not always easy or comfortable, but it is deeply rewarding. As we learn to align our thoughts, feelings, and actions with our authentic values and essence, we experience greater inner peace, clarity, and connection with ourselves and others. This is true freedom.

By embracing the journey of self-integration with curiosity, courage, and commitment, we can unlock our full potential and live a life that is truly authentic, meaningful, and fulfilling.

---

2. Relationship Health – The Mirror of Our Authenticity

Relationship health is a crucial aspect of our overall well-being and a powerful mirror of our progress in self-integration. When we can show up in our relationships with authenticity, vulnerability, and compassion, we create opportunities for deep connection, growth, and healing.

At its core, relationship health is about creating a safe and nurturing space where we can be seen, heard, and accepted for who we truly are. This requires a willingness to let go of the masks and defenses that we often wear in our interactions with others, and to express ourselves with honesty and openness.

One of the key ingredients of healthy relationships is vulnerability. When we are vulnerable to others, we are essentially saying, "I trust you enough to share my true thoughts, feelings, and experiences with you, even if it feels scary or uncomfortable."

This can be especially challenging for those of us who struggle with ego patterns such as the Expert, Judge, or Victim. These patterns often arise as a way of protecting ourselves from the pain of rejection, criticism, or abandonment, but they can also prevent us from forming deep and authentic connections with others, especially the ones that we love and care about deeply.

For the Expert, vulnerability might mean admitting that they don't always have all the answers, and that it's okay to ask for help or guidance from others. This can be a difficult step, as the Expert often prides themselves on their knowledge and expertise, and may fear losing respect or authority if they show any signs of uncertainty or fallibility.

For the Judge, vulnerability might involve letting go of the need for perfection, control and allowing others to see their flaws and struggles. This can be a terrifying prospect for the Judge, who often holds themselves and others to impossibly high standards, and may fear being judged or rejected if they reveal any weaknesses or imperfections.

For the Victim, vulnerability might mean taking responsibility for their own thoughts, feelings, and actions, rather than blaming others or circumstances for their difficulties. This can be a challenging shift, as the Victim often feels powerless and at the mercy of external forces, and may struggle to see their own agency and capacity for change.

Regardless of which ego pattern we struggle with, the path to greater relationship health involves gradually building our capacity for vulnerability and authenticity. One helpful tool for this process is the **Vulnerability Ladder**, which involves taking small steps towards greater openness and trust in our relationships.

The first step on the ladder is to share a small truth about ourselves without the influence of our ego patterns. This might be a simple statement of how we're feeling in the moment, or a brief anecdote about something that happened in our day. The key is to express ourselves honestly and without any agenda or expectation of how the other person will respond.

As we take this first step, it's important to pay attention to how the other person reacts. Do they listen with empathy and understanding, or do they dismiss or invalidate our experience? Do they reciprocate by sharing something vulnerable about themselves, or do they remain guarded and distant?

Based on the response we receive, we can choose to take another step up the ladder by sharing a slightly bigger truth about ourselves. This might involve revealing fear, insecurity, or challenge that we're facing, or expressing a deeper level of emotion or desire. The person's reaction to your initial step might be a good place to reveal a deeper truth.

As we continue to climb the ladder, we gradually build trust and intimacy with the other person, creating a foundation of safety and connection that allows us to be more fully ourselves in the relationship. For the deferent individual this only enhances their interpersonal skills.

Of course, this process is not always easy or linear. There may be times when we share something vulnerable and are met with rejection, judgment, or misunderstanding. In these moments, it's important to practice self-compassion and to remember that not everyone can meet us with the same level of openness and authenticity. Remember they are dealing with their own faces of Ego at various intensities. Always remind yourself that it's not you – it's them.

However, as we continue to practice vulnerability and authenticity in our relationships, we will naturally attract people who are able to reflect our true selves back to us with love and acceptance. This is one of the most powerful signs of progress in our journey towards greater relationship health and self-integration.

Now for individuals with high selfless, altruistic, harmonious and collaborative values this exercise should not be seen as permission to overextend yourself. On the contrary the exercise is to recognize your vulnerability and achieve balance within. Sharing with another that you struggle with saying "no" is a good start.

When we are surrounded by people who see and appreciate us for who we really are, we feel a sense of belonging, validation, and empowerment that allows us to show up more fully in all areas of our lives. We can let go of the masks and defenses that once held us back, and embrace the full range of our human experience with courage, compassion, and grace.

Ultimately, the path to greater relationship health is a journey of self-discovery and self-acceptance. As we learn to love and trust ourselves more deeply, we naturally become more open, authentic, and compassionate in our interactions with others. And as we create healthier and fulfilling relationships, we gain a powerful mirror of our own growth and evolution, reflecting to us the beauty, strength, and resilience of our true selves.

---

3. Personal Growth – The Pattern Antidote

Personal growth is a lifelong journey that challenges us to expand beyond our current limitations and become the best version of ourselves. It is a process of self-discovery, self-improvement, and self-actualization that requires courage, persistence, and a willingness to embrace calibration.

At the heart of personal growth is the development of a strong sense of self and overall self-esteem. These are not stand-alone concepts, but rather interconnected aspects of our overall well-being that require ongoing nurturing and validation.

One of the ways that we build self-esteem is through the achievement of goals, no matter how small or large they may be. When we set intentions for ourselves and follow through on them, we send a powerful message to our subconscious mind that we are capable, reliable, and worthy of success.

This process of goal attainment requires a strong individual drive and a commitment ethic that runs parallel to one another. We must be willing to put in the effort and energy required to pursue our dreams, while also staying true to our word and honoring the promises we make to ourselves and others.

As Don Miguel Ruiz emphasizes in his book "The Four Agreements," being impeccable with our word is essential for building self-esteem and maintaining integrity in our lives. When we say we are going to do something, it is crucial that we follow through and do it, even if it is challenging or uncomfortable, big or small. The most important aspect of this "contract" is getting it done.

Failing to keep our word, whether to ourselves or others, can result in subconscious messages that undermine our sense of self-worth and reliability. Over time, this can lead to hindered self-esteem, increased anxiety, and a greater susceptibility to the influence of ego patterns.

To combat these negative effects and promote personal growth, it is important to adopt a growth mindset and to engage in daily practices that challenge us to step outside of our comfort zone and expand our capabilities in a measured manner. Expanding our capability must be intentional but incremental in the early going because setting ourselves up for failure exacerbates the negative consequence of not being dependable.

One powerful approach is to set micro-challenges for ourselves each day, such as trying a new hobby, speaking up in a meeting, or reaching out to someone we admire. These small acts of courage and self-expression help to build our confidence and resilience, while also providing opportunities for learning and growth.

It is also important to celebrate our progress and achievements, no matter how small they may seem. Rather than striving for perfection or comparing ourselves to others, we can focus on the journey of personal growth and find joy in the process of becoming our best selves.

This means reframing mistakes and setbacks as valuable data points that help us to refine our approach and develop new skills and strategies. Instead of beating ourselves up for not getting it right the first time, we can view each challenge as an opportunity to learn, grow, and evolve.

As we embrace this growth mindset and engage in daily practices of self-improvement, we may find that our perspective on imperfection begins to shift. Instead of feeling ashamed or inadequate when we fall short of our own expectations, we can learn to laugh at our own humanity and find humor in the messiness of life.

This ability to choose growth over remaining small and tucked away in our comfort zone is a powerful sign of progress on the journey of personal development. It demonstrates a willingness to face our fears, take risks, and trust in our own resilience and potential.

Of course, personal growth is not always a linear or easy process. There will be times when we feel stuck, discouraged, or overwhelmed by the challenges we face. In these moments, it is important to practice self-compassion and to reach out for support from others who can provide guidance, encouragement, and accountability.

By surrounding ourselves with a supportive community of like-minded individuals who are also committed to personal growth, we can create a powerful network of inspiration, motivation, and mutual encouragement. Together, we can celebrate our successes, learn from our failures, and

Dimensional Rebalancing as Growth Practice

One particularly effective approach to personal growth involves identifying where your pattern's core values have become extreme, then intentionally practicing their dimensional opposites. This isn't about abandoning your authentic values but developing their complementary strengths.

For Experts with extreme Intellectual dominance, practicing Instinctive awareness—learning to trust intuition and embodied knowing—creates balance. For those whose Commanding value has become controlling, practicing Collaborative approaches develops partnership capacity.

Similarly, Judges with extreme Structured thinking benefit from practicing Receptiveness, while those with commanding tendencies can develop Collaborative skills. For Victims, practicing Resourcefulness counters extreme Selflessness, and practicing Intentionality balances Altruistic tendencies.

These rebalancing practices work because they develop genuine complementary strengths rather than fighting your authentic values. A simple weekly practice—researching what the opposite value looks like in healthy expression, then implementing one small element—gradually expands your capacity across the full spectrum.

Ultimately, the journey of personal growth is a deeply personal and unique experience that requires commitment to lifelong learning, self-reflection, and self-improvement. By cultivating a strong sense of self, healthy self-esteem, and a growth mindset, we can unlock our full potential and create a life that is rich in purpose, meaning, and fulfillment.

---

4. Healthy Coping – Replacing the Guards

Personal growth is a journey that challenges us to expand beyond our current limitations, but it also creates stress that requires effective coping strategies to maintain mental and emotional well-being. Just as a thermostat regulates the temperature and comfort of a room, healthy coping strategies help regulate our internal conditions, preventing burnout and promoting resilience.

Engaging in personal growth without addressing the stress it generates is like trying to run a marathon without proper training and support. It can lead to exhaustion, frustration, and even a sense of defeat. That's why it's crucial to replace pattern-based coping mechanisms—such as the Expert hiding behind wisdom, the Judge criticizing, or the Victim manipulating through helplessness—with proven coping strategies that promote authentic well-being.

Physical exercise is one such strategy that has been shown to improve mood, reduce stress and anxiety, and enhance cognitive function. When we engage in regular physical activity, our bodies release endorphins, which are natural mood-boosters that promote feelings of happiness and well-being. Exercise also helps to reduce cortisol levels, the hormone associated with stress, allowing us to better manage the challenges of personal growth.

Meditation is another powerful tool for managing stress and promoting emotional regulation. By practicing mindfulness and focusing on the present moment, we can cultivate a sense of calm and inner peace, even in the midst of the discomfort that often accompanies growth. Meditation has been shown to reduce symptoms of anxiety and depression, improve sleep quality, and enhance overall well-being, providing a strong foundation for personal development.

Breathing exercises are also highly effective for regulating the nervous system and promoting relaxation. By intentionally slowing down and deepening our breath, we activate the parasympathetic nervous system, which is responsible for the "rest and digest" response. This helps to counteract the effects of the sympathetic nervous system, which is activated during times of stress and triggers the "fight or flight" response. Breathing exercises can act as a storm door, shielding us from the turbulence of growth and allowing us to maintain a sense of inner calm.

Incorporating these strategies into our daily lives is like engaging in self-integration on a cellular level. By promoting physical, mental, and emotional well-being, we create a more harmonious and integrated internal environment that allows us to function at our best and show up more fully in all areas of our lives.

Some specific practices that can be incorporated into a personal growth journey include:

- Morning pages for mental clarity
- Box breathing for nervous system regulation
- Walking meditation for movement without judgment
- Creative expression without evaluation

Building a personalized toolkit of coping strategies is a crucial aspect of the personal growth process. By identifying what each ego pattern provides (such as a sense of control or avoidance), we can find healthier alternatives that meet those same needs in a more adaptive way. It's important to practice these strategies when we are feeling calm and centered, so that they become ingrained habits that we can easily access during times of stress or challenge.

The progress sign of choosing breath over pattern and tools over defense is a powerful indicator of growth and self-awareness. When we can pause in the midst of a stressful situation and consciously choose a healthy coping strategy instead of defaulting to an ego-driven response, we demonstrate a high level of emotional intelligence and self-regulation.

Ultimately, the journey of personal growth is not just about expanding our capabilities and achieving our goals, but also about developing a deep sense of inner peace, resilience, and well-being. By incorporating healthy coping strategies into our daily lives and building a robust toolkit of self-care practices, we can navigate the challenges of growth with greater ease and grace, becoming the best version of ourselves while maintaining our mental and emotional health.

Recovery Progress – The Evidence Trail

A. Clinical Decision Matrix: Self-Directed vs. Therapy-Supported Recovery

Recovery progress looks different depending on how deeply patterns have integrated into identity. Understanding which recovery strategies are genuinely accessible at each intensity level is essential to setting realistic expectations and recognizing where authentic change becomes possible.

The Fundamental Principle: As intensity increases, patterns become progressively more automatic and identity fused. At lower intensities, the restore point—the space between stimulus and response—remains accessible enough for conscious choice. At higher intensities, that space becomes increasingly obscured, making professional support essential.

Clinical Decision Matrix:

Intensity Level	Pattern Presentation	Restore Point Access	Recovery Approach
1: Pattern as Option	Conscious choice about patterns; temporary activation only when useful; authentic self-connection strong	Fully accessible; patterns activated consciously when genuinely useful	Maintenance through awareness
2: Pattern as Refuge	Go-to response for threats; beginning identity attachment; intermittent awareness "I am not my pattern"	Accessible in low-stress contexts; requires intentional recognition	Self-directed with optional professional support
3: Pattern as Necessity	Pattern required for self-worth; strong identity fusion; rare authentic glimpses in safe moments only	Accessible only in safe, non-triggering contexts; difficult to locate during stress	Therapy-supported self-directed work
4: Pattern as Identity	Pattern IS identity; no alternatives; complete disconnection from authentic self in most contexts	Marginally accessible in crisis or rare moments of unconditional acceptance; extremely fragile	Therapy-centered with supplementary self-directed homework

B. The Dual Nature of Values: Corrupted vs. Authentic Expression

Recovery progress is fundamentally about measuring the shift from pattern-driven behavior (where values are corrupted by ego protection) to authentically expressed values (where those same values serve growth and contribution).

Every pattern is fueled by values. The problem isn't the values themselves, it's whether they're being expressed authentically or defensively. The same values that create defensive patterns, when expressed cleanly, become the foundation of recovery.

Expert Pattern Values – Corrupted vs. Authentic

Pattern-Corrupted Expression (Ego Frequency):

- **Intellectual** becomes: Knowledge as identity armor; gaps in knowledge threaten existence
- **Resourceful** becomes: Efficiency as superiority; worth measured by optimization
- **Commanding** becomes: Control through expertise; must always be in charge of knowledge

Authentic Expression (Restore Point Frequency):

- **Intellectual** becomes: Genuine curiosity and love of learning; knowledge serves understanding
- **Resourceful** becomes: Helping others find their own solutions; efficiency serves contribution
- **Commanding** becomes: Confident guidance that enables others' capability

Judge Pattern Values – Corrupted vs. Authentic

Pattern-Corrupted Expression (Ego Frequency):

- **Structured** becomes: Rigid rules as control; flexibility = chaos
- **Commanding** becomes: Authority through enforcement; standards maintained via criticism
- **Objective** becomes: Emotions as weakness; rational superiority

Authentic Expression (Restore Point Frequency):

- **Structured** becomes: Healthy boundaries that enable flourishing
- **Commanding** becomes: Inspiring toward excellence; standards that elevate
- **Objective** becomes: Clear thinking integrated with emotional wisdom

Victim Pattern Values – Corrupted vs. Authentic

Pattern-Corrupted Expression (Ego Frequency):

- **Selfless** becomes: Self-abandonment as virtue; self-care = selfishness
- **Altruistic** becomes: Others' needs always first; your worth from sacrifice
- **Collaborative** becomes: Dependence as connection; need others to validate existence

Authentic Expression (Restore Point Frequency):

- **Selfless** becomes: Generous contribution from wholeness, not emptiness
- **Altruistic** becomes: Genuine care without self-erasure; both matter
- **Collaborative** becomes: Real partnership built on mutual capability

C. Intensity Levels 1-4: Understanding Pattern Depth and Restore Point Access

Understanding how patterns integrate at each intensity level is crucial to recognizing where recovery becomes possible and what it looks like.

Intensity 1: Pattern as Option

Pattern Presentation:

- Patterns are conscious tools used only when genuinely useful
- No identity fusion: clear awareness that patterns are something you do, not who you are
- Can observe patterns activating and choose different responses
- Authentic self remains easily accessible across most contexts
- Patterns are temporary and flexible; activated situationally, not reactively

Restore Point Accessibility: The restore point is fully accessible and essentially the default state. You can recognize when a pattern is activating and consciously choose whether to engage it. The space between stimulus and response is naturally open.

What recovery reveals at Intensity 1:

- Pattern activation is consciously noticed before or during its occurrence
- Genuine choice is always available; you're not compelled by the pattern

- Authentic self is the baseline; patterns are available as needed
- You can explain why you're using a pattern and can stop using it anytime
- Life flows from authentic values; patterns serve those values when useful

Recovery indicators:

- Patterns are employed strategically, not defensively
- People around you see you consistently as yourself
- You can laugh at your patterns and adjust them easily
- Stress doesn't automatically trigger pattern activation
- You feel fundamentally secure in your identity

Intensity 2: Pattern as Refuge

Pattern Presentation:

- Pattern becomes go-to response for perceived threats; provides temporary relief
- Beginning identity attachment; pattern creates thin veil over authentic expression
- Intermittent awareness of authentic self; can still recognize "I am not my pattern," though increasingly forgets this during stress
- Defensive neural pathways strengthening through repeated use

Restore Point Accessibility: The restore point is still accessible, especially in low-stress contexts. The key access point is the intermittent awareness—those moments when authentic self is visible, usually when not triggered. This is where recovery work begins.

What recovery reveals at Intensity 2:

- Pattern activation is noticeable; you can catch yourself in it, especially after the fact
- Moments of genuine choice appear, particularly in familiar, safe situations
- Self-awareness is possible but requires intentional attention
- The space between stimulus and response is still present, though narrowing under stress

Recovery indicators:

- Increasing ability to recognize when pattern is active
- More frequent moments of authentic self-awareness
- Growing capacity to choose differently when caught in pattern
- Evidence that pattern is optional, not inevitable

Intensity 3: Pattern as Necessity

Pattern Presentation:

- Pattern becomes required for self-worth and safety
- Strong identity fusion: "I am my pattern"
- Difficulty functioning without it; difficulty imagining functioning without it
- Rare authentic moments, usually only in safe, non-triggering contexts
- Pattern has become the primary filter through which life is experienced
- Defensive neural networks dominate response systems

Restore Point Accessibility: At Intensity 3, the restore point is accessible but only in very specific circumstances—certain safe people, particular activities, moments of genuine acceptance. It's as if the authentic self has retreated to protected spaces. The person can feel it there but accessing it during threat is extremely difficult.

What recovery reveals at Intensity 3:

- Authentic self is noticeably absent under any perceived threat
- Pattern activation feels like identity itself, not something "you do"
- Non-triggering contexts allow glimpses of authenticity
- Recognizing patterns require external reflection (others noticing it)
- The space between stimulus and response has largely collapsed

Recovery indicators:

- Noticing specific contexts where pattern doesn't dominate
- Receiving feedback from safe people about authentic moments they've witnessed
- Rare but real experiences of functioning differently with particular people
- Evidence that pattern is strong but not absolute (it's not active 100% of the time)

Intensity 4: Pattern as Identity

Pattern Presentation:

- Pattern IS the person's entire identity
- Cannot conceive alternatives; any threat to pattern feels like existential threat

- Complete disconnection from authentic self in most or all contexts
- Lives entirely in the "smoke" that obscures true self
- Cannot imagine existing without the pattern
- Demands that others enable the pattern; relationships structured around pattern need
- Pattern-driven neural networks have become so dominant they override most other systems

Restore Point Accessibility: The restore point is effectively closed during normal functioning. It may briefly appear in genuine crisis (when pattern fails to protect), during unconditional acceptance from another (rare), or during activities genuinely enjoyed (very specific contexts). These access points are fragile and easily lost.

What recovery looks like at Intensity 4:

- Authentic self is essentially inaccessible to the person without external support
- Pattern activation IS the person's experience of themselves
- No sense of choice; everything feels determined by necessity
- Others recognize the pattern more than the person does
- The space between stimulus and response is completely occupied by pattern

Recovery indicators:

- Brief moments when pattern grip loosens (crisis, unconditional acceptance, genuine engagement)
- Recognition from others that "something's different" in those moments
- Rare acknowledgment that something isn't working, even if fleeting

- These moments are fragile, rationalized away or forgotten

D. The Restore Point Method: Understanding the Mechanism of Recovery

The restore point is not a destination but a **space**—the gap between what happens and how you respond. It's the place where authentic choice becomes possible. It is where one's true essence should reside. Witnessing the innocence of a child to be free of judgement, victimization and the need to be right is an example of the beauty of this space. However, adults complicate it with their individual agendas that disconnect them from true essence and intent.

What is the Restore Point?

The restore point is the naturally occurring pause between stimulus and response where the authentic self has access to genuine choice. At Intensity 1, this space is relatively easy to find. As intensity increases, the space collapses under the weight of pattern activation until, at Intensity 4+, it's virtually inaccessible without external support.

Think of it like a doorway:

- **Intensity 1:** Door is open; you can see through it and step through with intention
- **Intensity 2:** Door is nearly closed; you can see the crack of light and occasionally slip through
- **Intensity 3:** Door is shut; only in rare moments does it crack open
- **Intensity 4:** Door appears locked with three impenetrable defenses (Expert, Judge, Victim)

How the Restore Point Works:

The restore point operates through what we might call
"frequency recognition "noticing which internal voice is
broadcasting: the ego frequency (pattern-driven, protective, fear-
based) or the authentic frequency (values-aligned, responsive,
truth-based).

When you access the restore point, you create a moment of
awareness where both frequencies are visible. You can see the
pattern activating, recognize what it's protecting, and choose a
different response. This choice is the beginning of recovery.

**The Restore Point is Always Theoretically Available—But
Practically Obscured:**

This is a critical distinction. The restore point doesn't disappear
at higher intensities; it becomes progressively hidden under
layers of pattern activation. Like a light switch in a dark room,
it's still there, but you can't find it without help.

**Resourced Engagement: Carrying the Flashlight into the
Dark**

Conventional wisdom tells us to face our fears head-on and to
confront what frightens us directly and push through. This
advice, while well-intentioned, misunderstands the fundamental
relationship between fear and ego patterns. Telling someone at
Intensity 3 or 4 to simply face their fear is like telling someone
to find that light switch in a pitch-black room with no tools—
they'll stumble, hit walls, and may conclude the switch doesn't
exist. Worse, each failed attempt reinforces the pattern's
narrative: *See? You can't do this. You need me to protect you.*

The ego intelligence framework offers a different approach:
resourced engagement. Rather than confronting fear unequipped

and alone, we face it carrying the resources that keep us connected to our authentic self. We don't eliminate the dark—we carry a flashlight.

Consider what this means practically. If someone fears public speaking, the conventional approach says: get on stage and push through. The ego pattern responds predictably—the Expert broadcasts inadequacy, the Judge catalogs every imperfection, the Victim confirms helplessness. Raw exposure without resources often strengthens the very patterns it was meant to weaken.

Resourced engagement asks a different question: What can you carry with you into that fear? The five elements aren't just abstract recovery concepts—they are the resources that make fear navigable rather than overwhelming. Self-Integration means entering the feared situation connected to your values rather than your patterns. Relationship Health means having genuine support—not rescue, but witness. Personal Growth means reframing the experience as expansion rather than threat. Healthy Coping means having tools ready before the pattern activates. Recovery Progress means carrying evidence that contradicts the pattern's predictions.

This distinction explains why the five elements work bidirectionally. Each element you build becomes a resource you carry into the next feared situation. Each feared situation you navigate "resourced" becomes evidence that strengthens the elements further.

This isn't merely metaphor—it reflects the structural mechanism by which resilience develops. Research on self-complexity demonstrates that individuals who maintain multiple distinct, well-developed self-aspects are more resistant to psychological collapse when any single domain is threatened. Each element you build creates an additional dimension of self that exists independently of your patterns. When fear threatens one area, the others hold. The person operating from a single pattern-driven identity has no structural redundancy—one threat cascades through everything. But the person who has built across the five elements has created the internal architecture that distributes impact rather than concentrating it. This is resilience—not the absence of fear, but the complexity to carry it without collapse.

The person who fears the dark doesn't need to love the dark—they need a flashlight that lets them walk through it while remaining themselves.

The principle also illuminates why recovery stalls when people attempt to face fears at intensity levels beyond their current resource capacity. At Intensity 2, the person may have enough internal resources to face moderate fears with minimal external support—their flashlight is dim but functional. At Intensity 3, the darkness is deeper, and the flashlight needs to be stronger and therefore therapy provides additional light. At Intensity 4, the darkness is so complete that professional support essentially becomes the flashlight until the person can trust their ability to use the light.

This is where the Quality of Motivation becomes visible. Motivation doesn't improve through willpower applied against fear. It improves incrementally as each resourced encounter with fear displaces pattern-driven motivators—the self-defeat, sabotage, the punishment, the martyrdom—with something real. Every time someone faces a fear carrying their values rather than their patterns, they prove to themselves that the pattern was never necessary for survival in that moment. The pattern's grip loosens not because it was defeated, but because it was rendered unnecessary by something more authentic.

The flashlight doesn't fight the dark. It simply makes the dark irrelevant.

Recovery is the process of progressively clearing the interference until the restore point becomes accessible again.

E. Recovery Progress: The Five Elements as Measurable Evidence

Recovery progress is measured by building evidence that contradicts pattern narratives and gradually expanding access to the restore point.

The Five Recovery Elements Work Together:

These aren't separate tracks but an integrated system where building in one area creates openings in others:

- **Self-Integration** establishes who you are beyond patterns
- **Relationship Health** provides external mirrors of authentic self
- **Personal Growth** proves capability exists independent of patterns
- **Healthy Coping** regulates nervous system so restore point becomes more accessible
- **Recovery Progress** documents objective evidence that patterns are optional

Tracking Recovery: The Evidence Trail

Recovery progress is best measured through specific, documented evidence that contradicts your pattern narrative:

Expert Pattern Narrative: "I must be the most knowledgeable or I have no value"

Recovery Evidence (Weekly):

- Times I asked genuine questions: ___
- Times people valued my presence without my expertise: ___
- Times I admitted "I don't know" and stayed present: ___
- Times I learned something new from someone else: ___

Judge Pattern Narrative: "If standards aren't perfect, everything falls apart"

Recovery Evidence (Weekly):

- Things that worked despite imperfection: ___
- People I accept without criticizing: ___
- Times flexibility led to better outcomes: ___
- Times I enjoyed something imperfect: ___

Victim Pattern Narrative: "I'm helpless; I can't do things without others"

Recovery Evidence (Weekly):

- Things I completed independently: ___
- Problems I solved myself: ___
- Skills I'm developing: ___
- Times I acted before waiting for help: ___

What Makes Evidence Count:

Specificity matters. "I was less critical" isn't evidence. "I watched my friend make a mistake and said nothing, let them learn from it" is evidence. Objective facts defeating subjective pattern narratives is what transforms recovery from intellectual understanding into neurological change.

As patterns weaken and restore point access expands, you'll notice your core values naturally realigning from corrupted expression to authentic expression. This shift in values is evidence that recovery is occurring.

Summary: Recovery as Concept

Recovery is the progressive expansion of access to the restore point—the space between stimulus and response where genuine choice lives. It happens through systematically building the five elements (Self-Integration, Relationship Health, Personal Growth, Healthy Coping, Recovery Progress) which collectively weaken patterns and strengthen access to authentic voice.

The process looks different at each intensity level. At Intensity 1, recovery is primarily self-directed with optional professional support. At Intensity 2, therapy becomes valuable for creating safe contexts where the restore point becomes accessible. At Intensity 3, therapy becomes primary, with self-directed work supportive. At Intensity 4, professional intervention is non-negotiable.

Throughout, the fundamental mechanism remains the same: patterns weaken when evidence contradicts their narratives, when values express authentically, and when the restore point becomes progressively more accessible. Recovery isn't about becoming different, it's about clearing the interference that obscures what was always there: your authentic self, your genuine values, your real capacity for choice.

1. **Calibration, not change** — Recovery works by making incremental adjustments toward authentic values, not by dismantling who you are. The goal is returning to a more accurate expression of who you have always been at your core.

2. **The reverse engineering formula** — Instead of attacking what's wrong, build what's right. Patterns weaken as a side effect of deliberately strengthening the five recovery elements.

3. **The five elements work bidirectionally** — Self-Integration, Relationship Health, Personal Growth, Healthy Coping, and Recovery Progress each reinforce the others. Start anywhere, and the system supports itself.

4. **Self-Integration is becoming the awareness** — The goal is not to eliminate patterns but to develop the capacity to observe them activating and respond from values rather than fear.

5. **Relationship Health as mirror** — Authentic connection is both an indicator and an accelerator of recovery. The quality of your relationships reflects — and shapes — your access to your authentic self.

6. **Values have two expressions** — Every pattern is fueled by genuine values. Recovery is the shift from pattern-corrupted expression (defensive, fear-driven) to authentic expression (contribution-driven, genuinely chosen).

7. **The restore point is always theoretically available** — At every intensity level, the space between stimulus and response exists. What changes across intensities is how

accessible it is — and whether self-directed work or professional support is needed to reach it.

8. **Resourced engagement, not raw exposure** — Facing fear unequipped often strengthens patterns. Recovery happens by carrying resources into difficult situations — values, relationships, evidence, coping tools — not by confronting the dark alone.

9. **Recovery evidence must be specific** - "I was less critical" isn't evidence. "I watched my friend make a mistake and said nothing, let them learn from it" is evidence. Concrete facts that contradict pattern narratives are what create neurological change.

10. **Intensity determines the recovery path** — At Intensity 1–2, self-directed work is primary. At Intensity 3, therapy becomes essential. At Intensity 4, professional intervention is non-negotiable before meaningful self-directed work can gain traction.

>> Coming Next: Chapter 10 – The Therapeutic Connection

In the next chapter, we'll explore how various therapeutic approaches (CBT, ACT, DBT, humanistic, and others) all fundamentally work the same way: they create safety sufficient for patterns to become optional and rebuild access to the restore point. You'll discover that recovery happens not through one "correct" therapy but through any approach that helps reconnect you with the space between stimulus and response—the restore point where authentic choice lives.

Chapter 10: The Therapeutic Connection

Every Therapy Hands You a Flashlight

>> **What You'll Learn in This Chapter**

- **The Resourced Engagement Principle:** How all effective therapies work by equipping clients with specific resources to use into feared situations—not by sending them into the dark alone

- **EJV Patterns as Perceptual Filters:** Understanding how Expert, Judge, and Victim patterns distort perception and why shifting perception is the universal mechanism of change

- **Different Flashlights for Different Darkness:** How humanistic and cognitive-behavioral therapies each build distinct resources matched to specific pattern configurations

- **The Clinician's Decision Framework:** How to select therapeutic approaches based on which resource the client most needs, rather than theoretical allegiance

- **Practical Integration:** Daily practices that build and maintain the resources you carry into your own pattern work

Reading Time: ~25 minutes

Clinical Foundation: Connecting EJV framework to established therapeutic traditions through the resourced engagement principle

In Chapter 9, we introduced the concept of resourced engagement, the principle that recovery happens not by confronting fear unequipped and alone, but by carrying resources that keep us connected to our authentic self. We used the flashlight metaphor: you don't eliminate the dark, you carry a light into it. Each of the five elements—Self-Integration, Relationship Health, Personal Growth, Healthy Coping, and Recovery Progress—serves as a resource you carry into the next feared situation, and each feared situation you navigate resourced becomes evidence that strengthens the elements further.

This chapter reveals something remarkable: every major therapeutic approach, despite different languages and techniques, works because it builds a specific type of flashlight. None of them tell the client to walk into the dark alone. They just build different flashlights calibrated to different kinds of darkness.

Counseling theory has evolved significantly since Freud's introduction of psychoanalysis in the late 19th century. Neo-Freudian theorists like Erikson and Adler continued this evolution, leading to advancements not only in approaches and perspectives on human behavior but also in the accountability of the subject. During the Freudian era, accountability and expertise fell on the therapist. However, the rise of Behaviorism and Humanism shifted focus to the client being the expert of their own lives. Behaviorism reshaped the emphasis on behavior, while Humanism focused on individual potential and client experience.

The emergence of perception-based approaches, particularly Cognitive-Behavioral Therapy and its variations, marked a significant milestone. These approaches have become the standard in evidence-based practice, focusing on how individuals perceive and interpret their experiences. The Ego Intelligence framework draws upon the entire evolution of the field, from Freudian defense mechanisms to modern interpretations of cognitive distortions, and much in between.

What unites this entire evolution is a single principle: every effective therapy equips the client with perceptual tools, relational experiences, cognitive skills, embodied awareness—that they carry into the situations where their patterns previously operated unchallenged. The therapist's task is not to fix the client but to help them build the right flashlight for their specific darkness.

Dr. Low and Hammett define a process that may be crucial to Ego Intelligence in their book Transformative Emotional Intelligence. The process is known as the Emotional Learning System and it encompasses five core stages—Explore, Identify, Understand, Learn, and Model/Apply. While we will not be formally exploring the ELS model in this chapter, it is assumed that we are engaging in the process of exploring, identifying what may work for us, understanding the processes, and learning. The students I have worked with have successfully modeled and applied these concepts with great results, demonstrating the transformative potential of this approach. This approach seems to organize and align well with the counseling approaches that we will explore in this chapter. Think of the ELS as the filing cabinet that organizes what each therapeutic approach brings out — without a system to sort and integrate those discoveries, the insights remain scattered rather than transformative.

Let's begin by understanding the perceptual prisons that make these therapeutic flashlights necessary.

The Perceptual Prison

Every ego pattern is fundamentally a perceptual distortion that becomes a self-fulfilling prophecy. The perception is influenced by several factors, but at the heart of the perception are the hidden motivators or values that we defined in earlier chapters. These hidden motivators or values are the essence of our authentic self, so we lean on these to arrive at our perceptions. When we are under pressure, fatigued, or feeling the effects of anxiety, these values activate the defenses of patterns, and the perception evolves through the intent of the ego patterns. The intent is to protect and defend against a perceived threat. Absolutely no one is exempt from the patterns of the ego as they will continue to be a part of the human element.

The Expert's Perceptual Filter

When focusing on distinct perceptions it is necessary to understand how these perceptions typically manifest distorted thinking. The Expert's Perceptual Filter creates a complex web of interpersonal and intrapersonal dynamics that shape their interactions and inner emotional landscape.

Interpersonally, the Expert's constant drive to demonstrate superior knowledge sets up a competitive dynamic in their relationships. They may inadvertently alienate others by coming across as condescending or dismissive when they feel compelled to correct or lecture. Genuine connection becomes difficult as the Expert evaluates each interaction through the lens of who knows more. Others may feel shut down or intellectually intimidated, leading to resentment or avoidance.

If avoidance is not an issue, questions posed to the Expert carry a perceived undertone of threat, as they are filtered through the lens of defending expertise, having the answers and leading with knowledge. So, when the Expert doesn't have the answer, they resort to responding with an overwhelming barrage of information to recover their perceived superior knowledge, rather than engaging in open dialogue. This defensiveness prevents authentic communication and collaboration. The Expert also struggles to be truly present with others, as they are constantly analyzing the interaction for potential challenges to their intellectual standing.

On an intrapersonal level, the Expert's perceptual filter generates a constant undercurrent of anxiety which circuitously fuels the pattern. The need to always have the right answer or the most knowledge places immense pressure on the Expert. They may fear being exposed as a fraud, not measuring up to their own impossible standards. This fear of vulnerability can lead to procrastination, perfectionism, or avoidance of situations where their expertise could be questioned.

The Expert's self-worth becomes contingent on maintaining the facade of superior knowledge. They may neglect self-care or relationships in the relentless pursuit of more information and accolades. Internally, the Expert is plagued by doubt and insecurity, as the filter of knowledge hierarchy leaves no room for the inherent vulnerability of being human.

This inner turmoil can manifest stress, burnout, and difficulty regulating emotions which fueled the initial pattern manifestation. The Expert may lash out when challenged or withdraw entirely. Imposter syndrome is common, as the Expert's filter discounts their actual competence and fixates on potential gaps in knowledge.

Transformative growth for the Expert involves recognizing the limitations and costs of their perceptual filter. By learning to embrace vulnerability as a strength and to approach interactions with curiosity rather than defensiveness, the Expert can develop more authentic connections and internal peace. This shift allows the Expert to access their vast knowledge with flexibility and compassion, becoming a true leader and collaborator.

The Judge's Perceptual Filter

The Judge's perceptual lens of constant evaluation and rigid standards creates a complex interplay of interpersonal and intrapersonal dynamics.

Interpersonally, the Judge's critical stance can lead to strained relationships. As the Judge perceives others through the lens of their own rigid standards, they may frequently express disapproval, criticism, or judgment. This can lead others to feel constantly scrutinized and found wanting. The Judge's binary thinking leaves little room for empathy or understanding, as they categorize others' actions as either right or wrong.

In interactions, the Judge may take on a tone of moral superiority, positioning themselves as the arbiter of what is acceptable. This can lead to conflicts and power struggles, as others feel judged and controlled. The Judge's need for perfection can also make them highly critical of themselves, leading to a projection of their own insecurities onto others.

Intrapersonally, the Judge's constant evaluation creates a backdrop of internal tension and self-judgment. The Judge may hold themselves to impossibly high standards, leading to feelings of inadequacy and self-doubt when they inevitably fall short. This can manifest as self-criticism, guilt, and shame.

The Judge's binary thinking can lead to mental rigidity and difficulty adapting to change. They may struggle with decision-making, getting stuck in analysis paralysis as they evaluate every option against their strict criteria. This rigidity can also contribute to feelings of anxiety and a need for control.

The Judge's perception of emotions as weakness can lead to emotional suppression and difficulty with vulnerability. They may see their own emotions as a sign of failure and strive to maintain the illusion of perfect control. This emotional disconnection can contribute to feelings of isolation and difficulty forming close relationships.

Internally, the Judge may experience a constant sense of pressure to meet their own high standards. They may drive themselves to perfection, neglecting self-care and work-life balance in the process. This can lead to burnout, stress-related health issues, and a pervasive sense of never being good enough.

Growth for the Judge involves learning to recognize the limitations of binary thinking and cultivating self-compassion. By practicing empathy and perspective-taking, the Judge can learn to see shades of grey and approach others with more understanding. Embracing vulnerability and emotions as natural parts of the human experience can help the Judge form more authentic connections and develop a more balanced sense of self.

By recognizing the impact of their perceptual lens on their internal world and relationships, the Judge can learn to reframe their experiences and choose more flexible, compassionate responses. This growth allows the Judge to channel their discernment and high standards in a more productive and balanced way.

The Victim's Perceptual Filter

The Victim's perceptual lens of powerlessness and persecution creates dysfunctional interpersonal dynamics, such as dependency, blame, and conflict. They may seek constant validation, struggle with assertiveness, or lash out at others seen as persecutors.

Intrapersonally, the Victim's negative self-perception leads to harsh self-criticism, learned helplessness, and self-sabotaging behaviors. They may feel stuck, avoiding decisions or setting themselves up for failure to confirm their sense of being broken.

Emotionally, the Victim experiences despair, shame, and resentment, with their pain reinforcing the cycle of powerlessness.

Growth involves challenging beliefs about powerlessness, developing assertiveness and self-compassion, and reframing obstacles as opportunities. By taking responsibility for their emotions and needs, the Victim can break patterns of dependency and blame.

Transforming the Victim's perceptual lens from powerlessness to empowerment is challenging but leads to more authentic relationships and a sense of agency in crafting a life aligned with their values. This growth process is essential for moving from suffering to resilience and self-actualization.

These perceptual filters don't just interpret reality—they create it. The Expert's superiority drives others away, confirming their isolation. The Judge's criticism creates resistance, proving others are difficult. The Victim's helplessness exhausts support, validating abandonment.

Understanding these perceptual prisons reveals why therapeutic intervention matters—and why different prisons require different keys. Each therapeutic approach we'll examine builds a specific resource that addresses a specific dimension of perceptual distortion. The clinician's task is to match the flashlight to the darkness.

Part I: Humanistic Approaches — Building the Flashlight of Experience

Humanistic therapies work by gently dissolving the perceptual filters that maintain ego patterns. They don't attack patterns directly but create conditions where authentic perception naturally emerges. Through the reverse engineering approach, one can identify whether the authentic self is coming through or if the ego has emerged. If the ego pattern persists then perceptions need to change.

In the language of resourced engagement, humanistic approaches build their flashlight through experience rather than instruction. They don't hand the client a cognitive tool and say "use this"—they create a relational environment where the client experiences something that contradicts the pattern's narrative, and that experience itself becomes the resource they carry forward.

Person-Centered Therapy: The Flashlight of Unconditional Acceptance

Carl Rogers understood that problems arise from incongruence between self-perception and actual experience. The Expert maintains incongruence by perceiving only importance in their knowledge and disregarding their humanity. The Judge's incongruence arises by perceiving only flaws, not wholeness or the potential in failing. The Victim's incongruence manifests by perceiving only helplessness will yield acceptance and omits individual agency.

Person-centered therapy provides what patterns can't: unconditional positive regard, accurate empathetic understanding, growth promoting environments and connection to genuineness (authentic self). The resource being built here is the internalized experience of being valued without performing a pattern. Once a client has genuinely felt accepted without being the Expert, the Judge, or the Victim, they carry that experience—that flashlight—into every future situation where their pattern insists acceptance requires performance.

Pattern dissolution through acceptance and the establishment of a growth promoting environment:

The Expert discovers they're valued for being and not solely for knowing. Individual growth is a product of remaining true to authentic living and aligning with values and skills that allowed the elements of inspired intelligence.

The Judge experiences acceptance within their imperfection. And growth embraces failures as opportunities through self-forgiveness.

The Victim can recognize and align with personal agency despite struggles. Individual growth is seen in self-compassion but a commitment to accountability by omitting the blame strategy.

Gestalt Therapy: The Flashlight of Present Awareness

Fritz Perls recognized that problems maintain themselves through avoiding full awareness of present experience. The embrace of present focus and collaborative relationship is seen in filling the space between experience and reactivity with holistic integration. Ego patterns are masters of perceptual avoidance because they aim to push their agenda at whatever cost to the authentic self.

The resource Gestalt builds is embodied present-moment awareness—the ability to notice what is happening in your body, your emotions, and your relational field right now, rather than what the pattern insists is happening. This is a flashlight that illuminates the present instead of the pattern's projected past or feared future.

The Expert avoids perceiving their defensive needs by remaining true to present focus and not what could happen if answers are not found.

The Judge avoids perceiving their own imperfections as all or nothing concepts and fills the space with potentiality and empowerment.

The Victim avoids trading sympathy for solace and making connections through helplessness with genuine accountability.

Gestalt's here-and-now awareness cuts through these avoidances. When James was asked to notice his body sensations while lecturing (Expert), he felt the tension of maintaining superiority. When criticizing (Judge), he felt the loneliness of separation. When collapsing (Victim), he felt the effort required to maintain helplessness.

The Empty Chair Revolution

James sat facing an empty chair representing his patterns. As he spoke to each one, his perception shifted. The Expert wasn't protecting him—it was isolating him. The Judge wasn't maintaining standards—it was destroying connection. The Victim wasn't keeping him safe—it was keeping him stuck.

Adlerian Therapy: The Flashlight of Social Connection

Alfred Adler understood that we operate from "private logic"—subjective perceptions that may be completely disconnected from reality. Each ego pattern has its own faulty private logic:

- Expert: "If I don't know everything, I'm worthless"
- Judge: "If I'm not perfect, I'm unacceptable"
- Victim: "If I take responsibility, I'll fail"

Adlerian therapy gently exposes these perceptual errors. James discovered his Expert's private logic came from childhood experiences where intelligence was his only source of approval. His Judge from a family where love was conditional on performance. His Victim from early failures that felt catastrophic. Learning that although there may be a reason for the private logic, applying it in all experiences moving forward is faulty and places us in a state of dormancy.

Understanding these origins didn't eliminate the patterns, but it revealed them as outdated perceptual habits rather than truth. What he perceived as proof turned out not to be the truth.

But Adler's contribution extends beyond exposing private logic. His concept of social interest reveals something essential about resourced engagement: genuine social connection is not merely one resource among many. It is a fundamental category of resources that makes all other therapeutic work possible. When someone carries authentic relational connection into a feared situation, they carry something the pattern cannot replicate—the experience of being witnessed, understood, and valued by another human being without the pattern's performance requirements.

This is why isolation is so devastating at higher intensity levels. It isn't just loneliness—it's the removal of an entire category of resource. The person at Intensity 3 or 4 who has withdrawn from authentic connection has essentially dropped their flashlight in the dark. Another person can hold the light when you cannot hold it yourself. Adler understood this intuitively: psychological health is inseparable from social embeddedness. We develop, heal, and find meaning through our connections with others.

Existential Therapy: The Flashlight of Freedom

Existential therapy addresses the fundamental perceptions we avoid: freedom to choose and the consequences of that choice, anxiety caused by death, isolation. The death concept moves further as it considers not solely our own mortality but the death of individual roles as we age. Ego patterns are elaborate defenses against these existential realities:

Experts avoid freedom by hiding in knowledge and not facing not knowing. The expert embraces the role of the intellectual or academic and fears that power in that role will expire.

The Judge avoids the freedom of not having to lower the expectations or standards. They embrace perfection and disregard the consequences to their sense of self riddled in bias.

Victim avoids responsibility by denying choice which fosters dependence rather than independence.

When James confronted these existential givens directly, his patterns lost their purpose. If death of my role is inevitable, why waste life performing expertise? If we're ultimately alone, why push others away through judgment? If we're truly free, why pretend to be helpless and why not embrace independence?

The resource existential therapy builds is the direct experience of freedom itself, the recognition that choice exists even when patterns insist it doesn't. This flashlight illuminates the exits that patterns have spent a lifetime concealing.

Part II: Cognitive-Behavioral Approaches — Building the Flashlight of Cognitive Clarity

While humanistic approaches build flashlights through relational experience, cognitive-behavioral therapies build them through cognitive skill. They equip the client with specific tools— evidence testing, demand detection, narrative reauthoring—that become resources carried into every situation where distorted perception would otherwise operate unchallenged.

The CBT framework was instrumental in developing the Ego Intelligence model as it defined the typical cognitive distortions of the patterns.

CBT: The Flashlight of Evidence Testing

Cognitive Behavioral Therapy recognizes that emotional distress comes from distorted perceptions, not events themselves. If we can acknowledge a different viewpoint each ego pattern specializes in specific cognitive distortions:

Expert Distortions:

Mental filter (seeing only intellectual aspects): "I don't have time to deal with emotions right now. Let's focus on the facts and figure out a logical solution." This example shows how the Expert's mental filter leads them to prioritize intellectual aspects while dismissing or avoiding emotional considerations. The Expert attempts to bypass emotions entirely, seeing them as irrelevant or distracting from the task at hand.

Discounting the positive (dismissing others' contributions): "While everyone's input is appreciated, I think it's best if I handle this project myself to ensure it meets the highest standards." This example illustrates how the Expert discounts the value of others' contributions, implicitly assuming that their own expertise is superior. The dismissal is couched in polite language, but the underlying message is that others' input is not truly necessary or valuable.

Labeling (categorizing people as "intelligent" or "ignorant"): "I don't think John has the intellectual capacity to grasp the complexities of this issue. It's best if we consult with someone who has a deeper understanding. This example demonstrates the Expert's tendency to categorize people based on their perceived level of knowledge or intelligence. The Expert assigns labels to others, using these categories to determine whose opinions and contributions are worthy of consideration.

Judge Distortions:

All-or-nothing thinking (perfect or worthless): "If the project isn't executed flawlessly, it's a complete failure, and I'm a total incompetent." This example highlights the Judge's binary thinking, where outcomes are seen as either perfect or utterly worthless, with no middle ground. The self-evaluation is also extreme, equating a less-than-perfect result with personal inadequacy.

Should statements (rigid rules for everything): "I should have anticipated every potential problem. I should have worked harder to make sure everything was perfect." This example illustrates the Judge's use of rigid, unrealistic expectations as a basis for self-criticism. The "should" statements imply a set of inflexible rules that the individual holds themselves to, setting the stage for inevitable self-judgment when these standards are not met.

Personalization (taking excessive responsibility for negative outcomes): "If I had been more diligent, the project would have been a resounding success. The fact that it wasn't is a clear sign of my inadequacy as a leader." This example demonstrates how the Judge distortion of personalization leads to taking disproportionate responsibility for negative outcomes, even when other factors are involved. The individual exclusively blames themselves, interpreting the result as a direct reflection of their own shortcomings.

Victim Distortions:

Catastrophizing (worst-case scenario thinking): "I made a mistake at work today. I'm going to get fired, lose my house, and end up on the streets. My life is falling apart. This example shows how the Victim's catastrophic thinking leads them to extrapolate a single negative event into a cascade of disastrous consequences. The Victim jumps to the worst possible outcome, magnifying the severity and implications of the situation.

Mind reading (assuming others' negative thoughts): "My friend didn't respond to my text message. They must be angry with me and no longer want to be my friend." This example illustrates how the Victim engages in mind reading, assuming they know what others are thinking without evidence. The Victim interprets the absence of a response as a definite sign of rejection or disapproval, rather than considering alternative explanations.

Fortune telling (predicting failure): "I was thinking about applying for that promotion, but I know I won't get it. I never have any luck, and I'm just not good enough." This example demonstrates the Victim's tendency to predict negative outcomes and failure based on their own self-defeating beliefs. The Victim assumes a future rejection without even trying, based on a generalized sense of personal inadequacy and helplessness.

Cognitive Behavioral Therapy helps clients identify these distorted perceptions in real-time and the therapist challenges these distortions helping the client reframe the thoughts and messages of the internal dialogue with messages that consider both content and context of the situation. CBT teaches a client how to catch, dispute and reframe their distorted ego frequency messages which are riddled with cognitive distortions. The resource being built is the skill of evidence testing—the ability to pause before a distorted perception and ask, "What are the actual receipts here?" This becomes a flashlight the client carries into every situation where the pattern would otherwise operate unchallenged.

Pattern-Specific Reframes:

Expert Dialogue – Internal Dialogue states: "They're asking questions because they're ignorant"

Reframe: Often, people ask questions because they are interested, not ignorant.

Judge Dialogue – Internal Dialogue states: "If I don't achieve perfection, I'm a complete failure."

Reframe: "Perfection is an unrealistic standard. I can strive for excellence while still allowing room for growth and learning."

Victim Dialogue – Internal Dialogue states: "There's no point in trying; I always fail."

Reframe: "Every attempt is an opportunity to learn and improve. Failure is not a reflection of my inherent worth."

Advanced Intervention: Turning the Distortion Against Itself

A powerful technique to challenge the distorted thinking of the Expert, Judge, and Victim patterns is to turn the power of the distortion against itself. After reframing the initial distortion, the therapist can take it a step further by questioning how the ego pattern, with its supposed logic, could fail to recognize the alternative explanation. However, it is crucial to consider the timing and appropriateness of using this intervention. The therapist must assess the level of client engagement, readiness, and openness to allow the technique to be successful. Attempting to turn the distortion on itself prematurely or without sufficient rapport could have negative consequences, particularly when dealing with deeply entrenched patterns, as it may inadvertently fuel the pattern by making the client feel attacked or defensive.

Expert Pattern:

Initial distortion: "They're asking questions because they're ignorant."

Reframe: "Often times, people ask questions because they are interested, not ignorant."

Turning the distortion against itself: "If you're truly the expert, how could you not see that curiosity, rather than ignorance, drives many questions?"

Judge Pattern:

Initial distortion: "If I don't achieve perfection, I'm a complete failure."

Reframe: "Perfection is an unrealistic standard. I can strive for excellence while still allowing room for growth and learning."

Turning the distortion against itself: "I wonder why the Judge didn't catch that perfection isn't achievable. How could an astute judge overlook such an obvious reality?"

Initial distortion: "I'm worthless because I made a mistake."

Reframe: "Everyone makes mistakes. It doesn't define my overall worth."

Turning the distortion against itself: "I wonder why you have kept your job for so long if you are truly worthless. Wouldn't a worthless person have been fired by now?"

Victim Pattern:

Initial distortion: "There's no point in trying; I always fail."

Reframe: "Every attempt is an opportunity to learn and improve. Failure is not a reflection of my inherent worth."

Turning the distortion against itself: "If things always turn out badly for you, how do you explain the times when you've overcome challenges or achieved success? Doesn't that contradict the notion of inevitable failure?"

This technique challenges the ego patterns' assumptions and distorted logic, encourages the client to question the validity of their automatic thoughts, introduces nuance and flexibility into rigid thinking patterns, and invites meta-cognitive reflection.

By using the ego patterns' own logic against themselves, the therapist creates a dissonance that can help the client break free from the grip of these cognitive distortions. It's a way of highlighting the inconsistencies and limitations in the client's habitual thinking patterns.

This paradoxical intervention can be a powerful catalyst for change, using the client's own cognitive patterns as a lever for growth and transformation. However, it should be used judiciously and collaboratively, attuned to the client's readiness and ability to engage in this level of meta-cognitive reflection.

As an advanced intervention, turning the distortion against itself can be a valuable tool in the CBT toolkit, helping clients break free from the limiting patterns of the Expert, Judge, and Victim, and move towards more flexible, adaptive thinking. It's crucial to establish a foundation of reframing and alternative thinking before moving to this more advanced challenge.

REBT: The Flashlight of Demand Detection

Albert Ellis's Rational Emotive Behavior Therapy targets the absolutistic demands that fuel patterns and uses an easy-to-follow ABC plan where the Activating event (A) is defined. The Belief/perception (B) is defined, and the Consequence (C) of that belief is interpreted. The therapist will extend the model by including D and E. Disputing (D) the client's belief/perception successfully will Effect (E) change by replacing the belief. As a therapist uses the techniques it is recommended that one starts by defining information that is already obvious such as the Activating Event (A) What was the experience/Situation that occurred? And the Consequence (C) What happened and how did you feel? Once this is established then the Belief (B) can be introduced into the equation to shed light on the distorted WHY?

Let's consider a common workplace scenario where a project fails to meet its objectives. Here's how the Expert, Judge, and Victim patterns might respond:

A (Activating event): The team project fails to meet its objectives.

B (Belief/Perception) and C (Consequence):

Expert: "I am the smartest person on this team. I should have been able to prevent this failure." (B). This leads to feelings of inadequacy and a compulsion to prove their expertise by dominating future projects (C).

Judge: "This failure is unacceptable. Everyone on this team is incompetent." (B). This results in harsh criticism of team members and a refusal to acknowledge any external factors that contributed to the failure (C).

Victim: "I knew this project was doomed from the start. I'm just unlucky and always end up on failing teams." (B). This leads to feelings of helplessness, disengagement, and a reluctance to take on future projects (C).

D (Dispute Distortion): In each case, the therapist would challenge the irrational beliefs driving these responses. For example:

Expert: "Is it realistic to expect yourself to single-handedly prevent all failures? Can you learn from this experience and collaborate more effectively in the future?"

Judge: "Are there any external factors that contributed to this outcome? Is it fair to label everyone as incompetent based on one project?"

Victim: "Have you ever been on a successful team project? What actions could you take to contribute to a more positive outcome in the future?"

E (Effect Change): By disputing these distorted beliefs, the therapist helps the client develop a more balanced and adaptive perspective, leading to healthier emotional responses and more constructive behaviors in future team projects.

The resource REBT builds is demand detection—the ability to recognize when absolutistic thinking ("I must," "they should," "life must not") is driving the pattern rather than genuine values. This flashlight reveals the difference between authentic standards and pattern-manufactured demands.

Narrative Therapy: The Flashlight of Alternative Stories

Narrative therapy recognizes that we live within the stories we tell about ourselves. Ego patterns are rigid narratives that filter all perception:

- Expert story: "I am my knowledge"
- Judge story: "I maintain standards"
- Victim story: "I am helpless"

The client is taught to separate themselves from these problem-saturated narratives. The client learns that the Expert, the Judge, the Victim wasn't about them, it was an embellished story about them. By finding "unique outcomes" (times the story didn't fit), they can begin reauthoring their narrative. Clients are then asked to reflect on times lessons are learned from others, when there were moments of acceptance and instances of capability internally and with others.

Externalization is a Narrative Therapy technique that is very effective. I have used externalization by encouraging the client to name the voice of their internal dialogue.

Integrating the externalization technique from narrative therapy into work with ego patterns is a powerful way to help clients separate their authentic self from the internalized critic. By having clients name the ego dialogue, especially when it echoes the voice of a significant figure from their past, they create a clear target for disputation and gain distance from the negative self-talk.

Naming the ego voice helps clients recognize the critical messages as learned scripts rather than inherent truths, focus their efforts to dispute and counter the negative self-talk, gain insight into the origins of their self-limiting beliefs, reduce the power of the critic over their sense of self, and develop a stronger sense of agency and autonomy.

The resource Narrative therapy builds is the alternative story itself—a reauthored identity that the client carries as evidence against the pattern's dominant narrative. Each "unique outcome" discovered becomes another beam of light in the flashlight, making the pattern's story progressively less convincing.

Brief Solution-Focused Therapy: The Flashlight of Exceptions

Brief Solution-Focused Therapy (BSFT) offers several techniques that can be effectively applied to reshape and manage the internal dialogue tuned to Ego Frequency. BSFT emphasizes goal clarification, helping clients define their desired outcomes and the strategies, objectives, and commitment needed to achieve them. This process is supported by cultivating an "Unbending Intent" mindset, which prioritizes goal pursuit over the distractions and obstacles posed by ego patterns.

BSFT also utilizes the technique of exception finding, which encourages clients to identify and explore times when the ego patterns were not active or influential. By recognizing these exceptions, clients can challenge the perceived dominance of the patterns and recognize their own capacity for control and change. Examples of exceptions might include:

- The Expert being controlled when a father speaks to his depressed daughter
- The Judge being silent when an artist engages in their craft
- The Victim transforming into capable action during crisis and true pressure

The resource BSFT builds is the exception itself—concrete proof that the pattern doesn't always win. These exceptions become flashlights of possibility that the client carries into moments of hopelessness. If the pattern wasn't active then, it doesn't have to be active now.

DBT: The Flashlight of Dialectical Balance

Dialectical Behavior Therapy offers valuable techniques for addressing ego patterns and challenging rigid thinking, particularly using the "both/and" perspective. This approach encourages individuals to recognize that seemingly contradictory truths can coexist, helping them move beyond the black-and-white, all-or-nothing thinking that often underlies ego patterns.

The relationship between the authentic self and ego patterns can be understood through the sibling rivalry metaphor. Like siblings, the authentic self and ego patterns can compete, shape each other's development, and create internal struggle. Yet they share a fundamental connection as part of the same individual. Personal growth allows for the transformation of this rivalry into a more collaborative relationship. By understanding ego patterns as learned adaptations, individuals can heal wounds, challenge beliefs, and integrate these aspects of self, leading to the and emerging authentic self that fosters self-acceptance, purposeful action, and emotional resilience.

The "both/and" perspective can be applied to each ego pattern:

- One could be knowledgeable AND still be capable of learning (challenging the Expert)
- One could have standards AND accept imperfection (challenging the Judge)
- One could feel vulnerable AND be capable (challenging the Victim)

By embracing dialectical thinking, individuals can break free from the rigid, self-limiting beliefs associated with ego patterns and develop a more balanced understanding of themselves and their experiences. The goal is not to remove the ego entirely but to lessen and manage it, recognizing that ego patterns are learned adaptations that can be integrated into a more cohesive sense of self.

Focused self-disclosure can be used to strengthen the "both/and" perspective, with therapists sharing personal examples of how they have navigated similar challenges. This technique normalizes the struggles associated with ego patterns and inspires hope for change.

The resource DBT builds is dialectical balance—the ability to hold two truths simultaneously. This flashlight illuminates the middle ground that binary pattern thinking has erased, revealing that strength and vulnerability, standards and acceptance, knowledge and humility can coexist.

ACT: The Flashlight of Observer Consciousness

Acceptance and Commitment Therapy offers valuable techniques for helping clients shift their relationship with ego patterns, focusing on the process of thinking rather than the content of thoughts. ACT encourages clients to perceive patterns as mental events, not as part of their identity. For example:

- "I'm having the thought that I need to be superior" (observing the Expert pattern)
- "I notice my Judge is active right now" (observing the Judge pattern)
- "The Victim story is playing" (observing the Victim pattern)

This shift in perspective, from being the pattern to observing it, creates space for choice and agency. By learning to observe their patterns rather than being controlled by them, clients can develop a more flexible and adaptive relationship with their thoughts and emotions.

Values clarification is another key technique in ACT. Therapists help clients identify their core values and use them as a guide for action, supporting them in aligning their behaviors with their authentic selves rather than being driven by ego patterns. An extension of this technique involves asking clients to recall the values and hidden motivators identified through their assessments, integrating these insights into the therapeutic process. By doing so, clients can develop a stronger sense of their authentic self and use this awareness to guide their actions in a more proactive, values-driven way.

The concept of "value-driven proactivity" captures the goal of this approach: helping clients cultivate a more intentional, self-directed way of engaging with their thoughts, emotions, and behaviors. By prioritizing their core values and using them as a compass, clients can learn to respond to their ego patterns with greater flexibility and choice.

The resource ACT builds is observer consciousness—the ability to watch the pattern activate without being consumed by it. This may be the most fundamental flashlight of all, because it creates the very space—the restore point—where all other resources can be accessed.

The Universal Mechanism: One Principle, Many Flashlights

Different therapeutic approaches, despite their unique languages and techniques, share a common mechanism: they all equip the client with specific resources to carry into situations where their patterns previously operated unchallenged. The clinician's task is not to choose the "right" therapy but to identify which resource the client most needs and select the approach that builds that flashlight most effectively for that person's pattern configuration and intensity level.

Patterns as Constructions, Not Truth

Humanistic and cognitive therapies help individuals recognize that their ego patterns are not fixed realities but rather constructed ways of interpreting and interacting with the world. Humanistic therapy, through its emphasis on unconditional positive regard and the exploration of alternative ways of being, encourages individuals to experience themselves beyond the limits of their patterns. Cognitive therapy takes a more direct approach by helping individuals identify the distortions and irrational beliefs that underline their patterns and test these constructions against reality. Through techniques such as cognitive restructuring and behavioral experiments, individuals learn to recognize the ways in which their patterns are based on faulty or exaggerated interpretations of their experiences.

Choice Where We Perceived None

Existential therapy and Reality Therapy both work to help individuals recognize the choices available to them, even in the face of seemingly overwhelming patterns. Existential therapy does this by directly confronting individuals with their inherent freedom and responsibility. Reality Therapy similarly helps individuals recognize the options available to them in the present moment, encouraging them to assess their current needs, wants, and choices.

Possibility Beyond Pattern Limits

Solution-Focused therapy and Narrative therapy both work to expand individuals' sense of possibility. Solution-Focused therapy shifts attention toward exceptions, resources, and future goals. Narrative therapy helps individuals explore alternative stories and interpretations of their experiences. Both reveal that patterns are not all-encompassing; they are contextual, and the client already has evidence of life beyond the pattern's narrative.

Self as Larger Than Patterns

Gestalt therapy and Acceptance and Commitment Therapy both emphasize that the self is larger than any pattern. Gestalt fosters holistic awareness through present-moment attention to the full range of experience. ACT cultivates observer consciousness—the ability to notice thoughts and patterns from a distance without being consumed by them. Both help individuals connect with a sense of self that transcends their momentary patterns.

In every case, the therapy is building a resource the client didn't have before—or couldn't access. The humanistic approaches provide experiential resources (what it feels like to be accepted, present, connected, free). The cognitive approaches provide cognitive resources (skills for testing evidence, detecting demands, reauthoring stories, finding exceptions, holding paradox, observing thoughts). Together, they equip the client with a full toolkit of flashlights for navigating whatever darkness their pattern configuration creates.

Practical Troubleshooting

Understanding how therapeutic approaches build resources empowers us to use their insights even without formal therapy. Each practice below is a way of building and maintaining a specific flashlight:

Daily Perceptual Practices

Morning Reality Check:

- What story am I telling myself today? (Narrative)
- What am I demanding must happen? (REBT)

- What exceptions might I notice? (Solution-Focused)

Midday Perception Shift:

- How would unconditional positive regard see this? (Person-Centered)
- What would wise mind say? (DBT)
- What choice do I have here? (Reality/Existential)

Evening Integration:

- What distortions were active today? (CBT)
- When were patterns absent? (Solution-Focused)
- What did I observe about my patterns? (ACT)

Meta-Perception

The ultimate perceptual shift is seeing that all ego patterns are perceptual habits that can be changed. They're not character flaws, mental illness, or permanent conditions. They're outdated ways of seeing that once protected us but now imprison us. Every therapeutic approach, in its own language, hands you a flashlight and says the same thing: you don't have to walk into the dark alone.

After understanding the connection between their ego patterns and therapeutic approaches, students often emerge with a transformed perspective and a powerful set of tools for personal growth. They no longer see themselves as mere learners of theories, but rather as individuals who have gained a deep understanding of how to apply these concepts to their own lives and the lives of others.

"I realized every therapy was trying to help me see the same thing," they might say. "That my patterns were just old glasses

I'd forgotten I was wearing. Once I saw that, I could take them off."

But more than that, they recognize what each therapy was doing: handing them a resource to carry into the dark. When the Expert pattern activates, they can draw upon CBT's evidence testing. When the Judge emerges, they can carry Person-Centered self-compassion. When the Victim appears, they can hold existential freedom. The therapies hadn't failed—the patterns had been refusing the flashlight. Once these students grasped that all approaches equip them with resources for navigating their specific darkness, they could select and carry whichever flashlight the moment required.

Moreover, these students have developed a nuanced understanding of how values, quality of motivation, and behavioral styles interact with ego patterns. They can recognize how their patterns may have been influencing their values, motivations, and behaviors, and they can consciously choose to align these elements with their authentic selves.

At their core, ego patterns are deeply ingrained perceptual habits. They color the way individuals see themselves, others, and the world around them. Every therapeutic approach, in its own unique language and style, offers the same fundamental invitation: to see differently, and to allow that new vision to transform one's life. But seeing differently requires more than insight. It requires carrying our resources such as a skill, an experience, a connection into the very situations where the pattern has always operated unopposed.

By recognizing the constructed nature of their patterns, the choices available to them, the possibilities beyond their current limitations, and the expansive nature of their true selves, students can break free from the constraints of their ego patterns.

They can move towards greater authenticity, flexibility, and empowerment, armed with a comprehensive understanding of therapeutic strategies and how they relate to personal growth.

In essence, the educational journey is one of learning to carry light—to carry the flashlights of acceptance, presence, connection, freedom, evidence, clarity, alternative stories, exceptions, balance, and observation into the darkness that patterns create. As students develop this capacity and integrate their understanding of values, motivations, and behavioral styles, they become increasingly able to navigate life's challenges with grace, resilience, and a deep sense of personal agency.

Graduating with this transformative knowledge, these students are prepared not only to apply these insights to their own lives but also to support others in their growth and development. They become powerful agents of change, equipped with wisdom and tools to help themselves and others break free from limiting patterns and embrace the fullness of their authentic selves.

The flashlight doesn't fight the dark. It simply makes the dark irrelevant.

>> Chapter 10 Key Takeaways

1. Every therapy builds a flashlight—Different approaches equip clients with specific resources to carry into feared situations

2. Patterns are perceptual filters—Expert sees hierarchy, Judge sees flaws, Victim sees helplessness

3. Humanistic approaches build experiential resources— Acceptance, present awareness, social connection, freedom

4. Cognitive approaches build cognitive resources—
    Evidence testing, demand detection, alternative stories,
    exceptions, dialectical balance, observer consciousness

5. The clinician's task is resource matching—Identify
    which flashlight the client needs for their specific pattern
    darkness

6. Social connection is foundational—Adler's insight that
    relational resources make all other therapeutic work
    possible

7. Patterns hijack therapies—Without awareness, patterns
    use therapeutic insights as ammunition rather than
    resources

8. Meta-perception liberates—Seeing that you're seeing
    through filters is the beginning of freedom

9. Advanced assessment reveals access points—EJV data
    can identify where restore point access naturally exists

10. Daily practice builds and maintains resources—Simple
    perception checks keep your flashlights charged

>> Coming Next: Chapter 11 – What Patterns Taught Us

In the next chapter, we'll explore the EJV assessment, a tool that measures not just your pattern intensity but also your recovery potential.

Chapter 11: What Patterns Taught Us

>> What You'll Learn in This Chapter
- How clinical observation of real patterns across three cohorts informed the theoretical framework
- What the Wounded Healer signature reveals about who is drawn to helping work — and why
- Three key clinical signals that emerged from observing how patterns organize across individuals and groups
- Why the recovery paradox is one of the framework's most important theoretical insights
- How the Ego Intelligence theory positions itself as a first contribution to an ongoing conversation
- Where this work grows next and what questions it opens for the field

Reading Time: ~20 minutes

Clinical Foundation: How clinical observation grounded the theory — and what real patterns revealed about how ego intelligence works

"Theory without observation is speculation. Observation without theory is noise. The Ego Intelligence framework emerged from the space between them — from watching real people navigate real defensive patterns and asking what that behavior reveals about how the mind protects itself."

The patterns in this book were not discovered in a research laboratory. They were observed across years of clinical practice — in hundreds of assessment debriefing sessions, in classrooms full of counseling students, in private practice with clients whose intelligence and self-awareness could not protect them from the defensive patterns that hijacked both. The Expert, the Judge, and the Victim emerged from watching real people in real distress and asking what their behavior had in common.

That observational history matters for understanding what this chapter is and what it is not. The Ego Intelligence framework did not begin with a hypothesis to be tested. It began with patterns so consistent across so many people and settings that they became impossible to ignore — and only then did the work of naming them, theorizing about them, and examining them more systematically begin. The assessment instrument developed in the later stages of this journey was a tool for looking more carefully at what years of trained observation had already revealed. It was built to examine the patterns, not to discover them.

Beginning in 2008, working alongside Brian Humphries in assessment debriefing sessions for the Texas Rehabilitation Commission, the pattern recognition work that would eventually become this framework began in earnest. Over six years of reviewing hundreds of Trimetrix, DISC, and Quality of Motivation assessments together, the same signatures appeared repeatedly: brilliant people who could not access their intelligence under threat, high-EQ individuals whose emotional skills disappeared in specific situations, talented professionals who sabotaged themselves repeatedly despite genuine insight into what they were doing. The assessments were not generating these observations — they were making visible what trained clinical eyes were learning to recognize.

The three faces of ego — Expert, Judge, Victim — were named in 2015, after Don Miguel Ruiz's framework provided the conceptual language to describe what six years of observation had already documented. By the time the EJV Pattern Assessment was developed, the patterns it was designed to measure had been observed across hundreds of individuals over more than a decade. What the assessment provided was a systematic way of examining those patterns across groups — of asking whether what appeared consistently in clinical observation also appeared consistently when examined more formally.

The question was whether these patterns — so consistent in clinical observation — would appear with similar consistency when examined systematically across independent groups. The answer, across three cohorts of graduate counseling students at Sul Ross State University, was yes. This chapter describes what that examination found, why it matters for the framework, and what the consistency of those findings across groups suggests about the theory's core propositions.

Who We Observed — and Why It Matters

Think about who chooses to become a counselor.

They have often been through difficulty themselves. They understand suffering from the inside. They are drawn to help others carry weight they know from personal experience. The qualities that make them effective in the therapeutic room — deep empathy, the capacity to absorb pain, the willingness to set aside their own comfort for someone else's healing — are often the same qualities that organize their most entrenched defensive patterns.

This connection between the values that draw people to helping work and the patterns those values generate under threat was one of the earliest and most consistent observations in the clinical pattern recognition work that preceded this book. Long before the EJV assessment existed, debriefing sessions with helping professionals consistently revealed the same signature: Selfless and Altruistic values at the top of the Trimetrix profile, combined with a defensive organization that had built itself around protecting those values from the threat of being perceived as inadequate, selfish, or incompetent. The Wounded Healer was not a theoretical prediction — it was a clinical observation made repeatedly before it had a name.

Examining graduate counseling students across three cohorts provided a way to look at this pattern more systematically. What appeared in those examinations was consistent with what clinical observation had already shown: 97% of participants showed the Victim pattern as their primary or most strongly co-activated pattern. Every single participant developed all three patterns simultaneously — Stage 3 tri-pattern activation. More than 40% showed the Victim-Expert fusion as their dominant configuration — the Wounded Healer pattern appearing not as an exception but as the norm in a population of people who had chosen counseling as their life's work.

When participants received their individual results and debriefing, 91.9% confirmed that the framework accurately captured their experience. That recognition rate is not a psychometric finding — it is people saying, in their own words, that the patterns described in this book reflect what they already knew about themselves but had never had language precise enough to work with. Seeing that recognition systematically across three independent groups was a meaningful corroboration of everything the clinical work had suggested.

*** What Systematic Observation Revealed Across N=32**

91.9% of external validation rate participants confirmed the framework accurately described their experience through structured debriefing

97% showed Stage 3 tri-pattern activation — all three patterns simultaneously active across all three cohorts

82% showed compressed configurations — patterns operating as a unified defensive system rather than independently

43% showed Victim-Expert (Wounded Healer) as dominant fusion — consistent across all three independent groups

Fusion consistency coefficient $R^2=0.70$ — indicating 70% configuration stability across groups

in all three cohorts assessed at different times

86.0% combined assessment quality score across N=32

These figures corroborate years of clinical observation and iterative assessment development. They are presented as meaningful confirmatory evidence, not as the source of the theoretical framework.

Assessment as a Development Partner

The EJV Pattern Assessment did not arrive at the end of this work as a documentation tool. It arrived in the middle of it — as a working partner in the framework's development, asking questions that clinical observation alone could not answer and returning findings that shaped the model into its current form.

The earliest versions of the assessment were built to examine patterns that years of clinical observation had already made visible. But what happened when those patterns were examined systematically was not simply confirmation. The assessment revealed structure that observation had suggested but not fully resolved. The specific relationship between pattern pairs — how tightly Expert and Judge tended to link, how differently Victim-Expert fusion functioned from Judge-Victim fusion, how compression ratio predicted intervention response more reliably than any single pattern score — these were not things that debriefing sessions alone had made precise. The assessment made them precise.

Each cohort of findings fed back into the framework. Early data revealed that the three patterns did not simply coexist — they organized into configurations that behaved differently from one another in clinically meaningful ways. That finding produced profile descriptions. Later data revealed that restore point accessibility and recovery capacity were partially independent of pattern intensity — that someone could show very high pattern engagement and very high growth motivation simultaneously. That finding produced the recovery paradox as a named clinical concept rather than an occasional observation. The model in this book is more differentiated, more precisely articulated, and more clinically useful than it would have been if the assessment had never been developed.

This is how frameworks mature. Not through a single moment of theoretical insight, or through a single study that proves the concept, but through the iterative back-and-forth between careful observation and systematic examination — each informing the other, each making the other more precise. The Ego Intelligence framework is at an early stage of that iterative process. What the assessment has contributed so far is already significant. What it will contribute to as it is used more broadly, across more populations and contexts, is part of what makes this work worth continuing.

What Observation and Examination Revealed

The following observations are not conclusions drawn from a single study. They are patterns that appeared repeatedly across years of clinical practice, were made more precise through iterative assessment development, and were then examined systematically across three independent groups. The systematic examination did not generate these insights — it corroborated and sharpened them. That distinction matters, and it is the reason the findings can be stated with more confidence than a single preliminary study would ordinarily warrant.

* Patterns Organize as a System, not as Independent Forces

One of the earliest and most consistent clinical observations was that the Expert, Judge, and Victim rarely appeared in isolation. When someone's Expert pattern activated, the Judge was typically close behind — enforcing the standards the Expert needed to meet, criticizing the failures the Expert needed to explain away. The Victim absorbed what neither the Expert nor the Judge could resolve. Each face of ego served the others in a mutually reinforcing architecture that functioned as a single integrated system rather than three separate defenses.

Systematic examination across three cohorts was consistent with this observation. Eighty-two percent of participants showed compressed configurations — all three patterns operating within a narrow range of each other. Every single participant showed all three patterns simultaneously active. The fusion consistency coefficient remained stable at $R^2=0.70$ indicating 70% configuration stability across groups assessed at different times, suggesting this unified architecture is a genuine structural feature of how ego defense organizes rather than an artifact of any group or moment.

The theoretical implication is significant: you cannot work effectively with the Expert pattern without understanding its relationship to the Judge and the Victim. The three faces of ego are not alternative descriptions of the same person at different times — they are simultaneous dimensions of a single defensive architecture operating together in every triggered moment.

* The Wounded Healer Is a Pattern, not a Coincidence

Across hundreds of Trimetrix debriefings with helping professionals over more than a decade, the same configuration appeared with striking regularity: Selfless and Altruistic values at the top of the profile, Victim pattern elevated, Expert pattern linked tightly to the Victim in a fusion that organized personal suffering and hard-won competence into a single defensive complex. Long before it had a name, the Wounded Healer was a pattern observed and documented.

Systematic examination confirmed this with notable consistency. The Victim-Expert fusion appeared as the dominant configuration in 43% of participants across all three cohorts, with a mean fusion score of 67.6%, the highest of any pattern pair across the entire sample. The Wounded Healer was not an exception in this population. It was the most common single configuration observed.

What makes this finding clinically important is not its prevalence but its implications. A practitioner whose personal suffering and professional competence are fused at the defensive level will bring both into the therapeutic relationship — the empathy and the cost of it, the skill and the depletion it generates. Understanding this pattern in oneself is not optional for a helping professional. It is foundational. The Ego Intelligence framework exists, in part, because years of observation made clear that helping professionals are among those who most need access to it.

* Insight and the Capacity to Change Are Not the Same Thing

Perhaps no clinical observation was more consistent across years of debriefing work than this one: the people with the most insight into their patterns were not reliably the people making the most progress in changing them. Clients who could articulate their defensive architecture with precision — who understood exactly what triggered the Expert pattern, exactly what the Judge was protecting against, exactly how the Victim organized their helplessness — often found themselves just as trapped by those patterns as people with far less self-awareness.

The systematic examination produced a striking corroboration of this observation. The participant with the highest overall pattern engagement across the entire study simultaneously showed among the strongest recovery indicators. They understood their patterns with exceptional clarity. They were deeply motivated to change. And the gap between that understanding and their capacity to interrupt the patterns in real time was the defining feature of their clinical presentation.

This is the recovery paradox, and it is one of the framework's most important theoretical contributions. The space between stimulus and response — the restore point — can be compressed to the point where even genuine self-awareness cannot reach it. Insight is necessary. It is not sufficient. This observation fundamentally shaped the framework's emphasis on restore point accessibility as a distinct clinical target, and on the difference between developing understanding and rebuilding neurobiological flexibility.

* Recovery Exists Alongside Defensiveness — Not After It

A second observation that clinical work made consistently clear: waiting for defensive patterns to diminish before beginning recovery work is waiting for the wrong thing. Growth capacity and defensive activation coexist in the same person at the same time. The most defended individuals in a debriefing session were often simultaneously the most motivated, the most self-aware in their better moments, and the most capable of genuine change when the conditions were right.

Systematic examination reflected this consistently. Self-Integration appeared as the strongest recovery domain across all three groups, even in the most defensively organized profiles. People who showed highly compressed pattern configurations — suggesting globally activated defensive systems — often retained meaningful capacity for self-awareness and personal coherence alongside that activation.

The practical implication is hopeful and important: the resource base for recovery is usually present even when it is not immediately visible. The work of Ego Intelligence is not to create recovery capacity from nothing. It is to identify where genuine flexibility already exists and build deliberately from there — carrying the resources into the difficulty rather than waiting for the difficulty to clear before the resources can be used.

Six Profiles That Emerged from Clinical Observation

As patterns were observed across individuals and groups, six recurring configurations emerged that appeared to describe meaningfully different ways defensive patterns can organize. These profiles are offered as clinical orientation tools — ways of thinking about where a person may be in their defensive organization and what that might suggest about the most productive direction for the work. They are not diagnostic categories. They are working descriptions that emerged from watching real people and asking what their patterns had in common.

Profile 1: *The Compressed Tri-Stack*

All three patterns operating together at similar intensity — the most common configuration in helping professions

The entire defensive system has become unified and automated. Insight is often very high — these individuals frequently understand their patterns clearly. But integrated architecture means self-directed work alone tends to have limited traction. External relational scaffolding is usually more useful than additional psychoeducation. The clinical challenge is not lack of understanding but the decoupling of insight from the capacity to interrupt.

Profile 2: *The Expanded Single Dominant*

One pattern prominent, others less activated — defended in one area, flexible in others

This person is not defending everything — they are defending something specific. Flexibility in less-dominant areas is the key clinical resource. The work is about helping them recognize that flexibility and bring it deliberately into the defended area. Not teaching something new but extending what they are already capable of.

Profile 3: *The Dual Fusion*

Two strongly linked patterns, a third offering possible leverage

Two patterns have been organized together in a mutually reinforcing way that makes them difficult to address directly. The third pattern — the one with less fusion — tends to be where the most restore point access lives. Working through the path of least resistance often creates surprisingly significant movement in the locked pair.

Profile 4: *The High Restore Point Profile*

Patterns present but significant flexibility retained — already moving toward health

This person has developed defensive patterns but retained meaningful access to the restore point. They are likely already interrupting their patterns with some regularity without necessarily having language for it. What tends to be most useful here is direction and clarity — helping them understand what they are already doing when they function well and building their capacity to do it more intentionally.

Profile 5: *The Critical Mass / Low Restore Point Configuration*

"I understand it completely — and I still cannot stop it"

High pattern engagement coexisting with high insight and strong recovery motivation — but very low restore point access. This is the recovery paradox in its clearest form. More work on individual awareness is not what this person needs. What they need is external scaffolding to rebuild neurobiological flexibility before self-directed work can gain meaningful traction.

Profile 6: *The Context-Specific Configuration*

Defended in some situations, more flexible in others

The defensive system is context-sensitive rather than globally activated — which is itself a positive indicator. This person is already demonstrating the capacity to function without the dominant pattern in some areas of their life. The clinical work is about expanding that existing capacity into the contexts where the pattern currently dominates.

* Key Insight
How to Use the Profiles

These profiles are starting points for clinical thinking, not finishing points. Every assessment result should be held lightly and revised as the therapeutic conversation develops. A profile is a hypothesis about where someone may be — not a verdict about who they are.

Three Signals Worth Attending To

Three observations emerged consistently across the full range of pattern configurations encountered in clinical work. They are offered not as diagnostic rules but as clinical orientations that have proven useful in practice.

Compression tells you more than any single pattern score

How tightly the three patterns cluster together — the spread between highest and lowest scores — tends to be a more informative signal than any individual pattern score. Tight clustering suggests the defensive system is globally activated and highly integrated. Wider differentiation suggests more selective defensiveness and greater flexibility. In general, tighter compression indicates the value of external professional support, while wider differentiation suggests self-directed work has more traction.

The weakest fusion is usually the strongest entry point

Where two patterns are strongly fused, working on that fusion directly tends to be slow. Where a pattern has lower fusion with the others — where it feels more separate, more accessible — that is usually where intervention gains the most leverage. Small genuine changes in the less-defended area often create movement in the patterns that feel most locked. The path of least resistance is frequently the most productive clinical path.

Restore points and insight are independent — both matter

A person can understand their patterns with exceptional clarity and still have very limited access to the restore point in the moment of activation. Conversely, someone with lower insight may have meaningful neurobiological flexibility and respond rapidly to relatively simple interventions. Both dimensions matter and both can be developed. The mistake is treating insight as the primary lever when restore point access may be the more fundamental one.

Where This Work Grows Next

The clinical observation work that generated this framework continues. Every cohort of students assessed, every practitioner who completes the EJV and brings the results into supervision, every debriefing conversation that produces a moment of recognition — each adds to the accumulated picture of how ego patterns organize across individuals and populations. That accumulation is how the framework's precision will deepen over time, the same way it deepened through the years of pattern recognition that preceded this book.

The natural next questions are ones this book opens rather than answers. Do the same pattern signatures appear in other helping professions — physicians, social workers, teachers, first responders? Does identifying a client's dominant configuration at the beginning of treatment change how that treatment unfolds and how quickly meaningful progress occurs? Does the framework's emphasis on restore point accessibility as distinct from insight lead to more effective intervention planning for clients in whom insight alone has not been sufficient?

What this book offers is a foundation grounded in extensive clinical observation, refined through years of collaborative assessment work, and examined systematically enough to be presented with genuine confidence. It is the beginning of a conversation the field is ready to have — about how defensive patterns organize, why they resist change even in the most insightful people, and what it actually takes to develop the capacity to see them clearly enough to choose differently.

A Beginning Built on Fifteen Years

The graduate counseling student who came to the program because she had lived through depression and wanted to use that experience to help others — she is not an unusual case. She is, based on years of clinical observation and three cohorts of systematic examination, a fairly typical one. Her Victim-Expert fusion, her Stage 3 tri-pattern activation, her high insight combined with limited restore point access — these were being observed and documented in debriefing sessions years before the assessment instrument existed to examine them more formally. What systematic examination added was not the discovery of her pattern but the confirmation that it was not hers alone.

The Ego Intelligence framework offers her something specific: language for what she already knows about herself, a map of how her defensive patterns appear to be organized, and a theory of where change is most accessible. Not a verdict. Not a label. The same thing skilled clinical debriefing always tried to offer — a way of seeing clearly enough to work with what is there.

That is what this book has tried to offer across every chapter. A framework grounded in extensive clinical observation and refined through years of collaborative pattern recognition. A vocabulary precise enough to be clinically useful. A set of propositions about how defensive patterns form, how they intensify, how they interact with values and motivation, and how change actually happens — not through dismantling defenses but through building the resources, the flexibility, and the conscious relationship with patterns that allows the restore point to become genuinely accessible again.

The journey from unconscious reaction to conscious response — from being driven by patterns to having genuine choice about how to engage with them — is what Ego Intelligence is ultimately about. It is the work of authentic living. It is never fully finished. And understanding it better, in clinical rooms and classrooms and research conversations, is work that belongs to everyone willing to look honestly at what drives them.

This is the beginning of that conversation. The rest is an open invitation.

1. **Clinical observation preceded the measurement** — the Expert, Judge, and Victim patterns were identified through hundreds of assessment debriefings and clinical encounters; the EJV instrument was built to examine those observations more systematically, not to generate them

2. **The systematic examination corroborated what clinical observation had long suggested** — across three independent cohorts, the findings were consistent with the framework's core propositions, including the unified defensive architecture, the Wounded Healer signature, and the recovery paradox

3. **A 91.9% external validation rate through structured debriefing** is meaningful clinical corroboration — participants across all three groups confirmed in their own words that the framework accurately described their experience

4. **The Wounded Healer is a pattern, not a coincidence** — Victim-Expert fusion as the dominant configuration in 43% of helping professionals, consistent across three independent groups, reflects the direct relationship between the values that draw people to this work and the patterns those values generate under threat

5. **The recovery paradox is one of the framework's most important insights:** insight and restore point access are independent dimensions, and high insight with low restore point access requires a fundamentally different intervention approach than building more understanding alone

6. **Growth and defensiveness genuinely coexist** — recovery does not wait for patterns to diminish; the resource base for change is almost always present alongside active defensive organization, and finding it is where the clinical work begins

7. **The six clinically derived profiles** emerged from observation across individuals and groups — they are orientation tools for clinical thinking, not diagnostic categories, and should be held lightly and revised as the therapeutic conversation develops

8. **This framework is offered with confidence —** grounded in extensive clinical observation, refined through systematic examination, and presented as a first contribution to a conversation the field is ready to have

A Final Note: The work of Ego Intelligence does not end with a book. It continues in every clinical encounter where a practitioner recognizes a pattern activating in real time, in every supervision session where a student names what is happening before it has fully played out, and in every research conversation where someone asks whether the framework's propositions hold up under independent scrutiny. That work belongs to a community — and this book is an invitation to join it.

APPENDIX - A

EJV Pattern Profile Taxonomy

A Reference Guide to EJV-Motivated Descriptive Terms

NOTE: **Important Notice-**: The terms in this reference guide are EJV-motivated descriptive terms — not clinical diagnoses, personality classifications, or replacements for established diagnostic or psychometric terminology. They describe defensive pattern configurations as observed and measured by the EJV Pattern Assessment within the Ego Intelligence theoretical framework.

I. Taxonomy Overview

The EJV Pattern Profile Taxonomy provides a shared vocabulary for understanding how ego defensive patterns manifest in observable behavior. It organizes descriptive terms into six categories, moving from foundational pattern combinations to complex dynamic sequences. All terms describe defensive pattern configurations — not clinical diagnoses, personality classifications, or fixed labels.

These terms emerged from three converging sources: seventeen years of clinical observation, pattern configurations consistently measured by the EJV Pattern Assessment across multiple independent cohorts, and participant self-recognition during structured debriefing sessions. They are a new vocabulary for a new construct, and will continue to be refined as research expands.

Category	What It Describes	Terms	Status
Primary Fusion Profiles	Core two-pattern combinations	3	* Confirmed
Behavioral Expressions	How fusions manifest in observable behavior	8	* Confirmed
Configuration Types	System-level defensive architectures	4	* Confirmed

II. Primary Fusion Profiles

Fusion profiles describe how two EJV patterns collaborate to form a dominant defensive strategy. Approximately 82% of participants show compressed configurations where all three patterns operate within a narrow range. These profiles describe emphasis within a unified architecture, not separate conditions.

1. The Wounded Healer | Victim + Expert *

Personal suffering becomes the foundation for professional expertise. The Victim pattern's experience of pain merges with the Expert pattern's drive for knowledge, creating a self-reinforcing loop: I suffer, therefore I understand; I understand, therefore I can help; my helping proves my suffering had meaning.

Internal Voice: "My wounds make me a better healer."

Example: A counselor who feels most confident in sessions when drawing from personal trauma, and subtly resists resolution of their own pain because healing it feels like losing their authority.

2. The Self-Critical Martyr | Judge + Victim *

Harsh internal standards automatically trigger self-sacrificing behavior. The Judge pattern's relentless evaluation merges with the Victim pattern's helplessness: I can never meet my own standards; my failure proves my inadequacy; my suffering is evidence of how hard I'm trying.

Internal Voice: "Nothing I do is ever good enough — but at least I'm trying harder than anyone else."

Example: A graduate student who holds themselves to impossible standards, then works to exhaustion as both punishment and proof of effort, while feeling chronically unappreciated.

3. The Analytical Perfectionist | Expert + Judge *

Intellectual rigor becomes the instrument of self-evaluation and other evaluation. The Expert pattern's need to demonstrate knowledge merges with the Judge pattern's compulsion to evaluate - I must know everything; imperfect knowledge means I have failed.

Internal Voice: "If my knowledge isn't comprehensive and flawless, it's worthless."

Example: A clinician who corrects colleagues' conceptual framing in team meetings and delays writing reports until they've reviewed every relevant source, never feeling adequately prepared.

III. Behavioral Expression Terms

Behavioral expressions describe how fusion profiles manifest in what others observe — and what the individual actually does. Multiple expressions can operate within a single fusion profile, and a single individual may exhibit different expressions across contexts. These are descriptive, not fixed traits.

Expression	Ego Faces	Definition	Example
Sacrificial Expertise	Victim + Expert	Deploying professional knowledge at personal cost; helping others while depleting self	Takes on every student crisis, exhausted but unable to say no because "they need me"
Intellectual Victimhood	Victim + Expert	Using analytical frameworks to validate helplessness; intellectualizing perceived unfairness	Constructs sophisticated explanations for why change isn't possible in their situation
Scholarly Suffering	Victim + Expert	Becoming an expert in one's own trauma; using mastery of personal pain to avoid healing	Can detail their attachment style and neurobiology fluently, but uses it to explain why they can't change
Self-Critical Caretaking	Judge + Victim	Harsh self-judgment driving compulsive caretaking; punishing self through service to others	Internally criticizes own adequacy while over-functioning for everyone around them

Expression	Ego Faces	Definition	Example
Self-Critical Martyrdom	Judge + Victim	Self-punishment expressed through visible sacrifice; suffering displayed as moral evidence	"I stayed up all night finishing it because no one else would." Rejects all offers of help
Values-Driven Martyrdom	Judge + Victim	Core values hijacked to justify chronic self-sacrifice framed as moral imperative	"If I don't do it, who will? These people need someone who actually cares."
Evaluative Knowledge	Expert + Judge	Knowledge deployed primarily to assess and grade rather than to understand	Corrects others' information in group discussions; maintains running evaluative commentary
Knowledge-Based Perfectionism	Expert + Judge	Knowledge gaps treated as personal failures; intellectual standards applied as perfectionist criteria	Researches exhaustively before acting; cannot tolerate being the non-expert in any room

Quick Reference Summary

The table below consolidates the three primary fusion profiles with their associated ego faces, core dynamic, internal voice, and key behavioral indicator for rapid clinical reference.

Profile	Ego Faces	Core Dynamic	Internal Voice	Key Indicator
The Wounded Healer	Victim + Expert	Suffering validates expertise	"My wounds make me a better healer"	Resists personal resolution; identity tied to woundedness
The Self-Critical Martyr	Judge + Victim	Standards trigger self-sacrifice	"Still not enough, but I'm trying harder than anyone"	Exhaustion displayed as moral evidence; rejects help
The Analytical Perfectionist	Expert + Judge	Knowledge weaponized as evaluation	"Flawless or worthless"	Corrects others; never feels adequately prepared

A Note on Emerging Research

The taxonomy presented here reflects terms that have achieved sufficient cross-cohort stability to warrant inclusion as a clinical reference. Additional profile categories — including value-driven hybrid patterns, recovery integration profiles, and triangulation dynamics — are currently under active investigation. As the EJV Pattern Assessment is applied across broader populations and additional cohorts, these categories will be formalized and added to future editions of this taxonomy.

Bibliography

Adler, A. (1927). *Understanding human nature*. Greenberg.

Adler, A. (1931). *What life should mean to you*. Little, Brown.

Bar-On, R. (2006). The Bar-On model of emotional-social intelligence (ESI). *Psicothema, 18*, 13–25.

Beck, A. T. (1967). *Depression: Clinical, experimental, and theoretical aspects*. Harper & Row.

Beck, A. T. (1976). *Cognitive therapy and the emotional disorders*. International Universities Press.

Burns, D. D. (1980). *Feeling good: The new mood therapy*. William Morrow.

Buss, D. M. (1999). *Evolutionary psychology: The new science of the mind*. Allyn & Bacon.

Cosmides, L., & Tooby, J. (1997). Evolutionary psychology: A primer. Center for Evolutionary Psychology, University of California, Santa Barbara.

de Shazer, S. (1985). *Keys to solution in brief therapy*. W. W. Norton.

de Shazer, S. (1988). *Clues: Investigating solutions in brief therapy*. W. W. Norton.

Ellis, A. (1962). *Reason and emotion in psychotherapy*. Lyle Stuart.

Epstein, S. (1998). *Constructive thinking: The key to emotional intelligence*. Praeger.

Erikson, E. H. (1950). *Childhood and society*. W. W. Norton.

Frankl, V. E. (1946/1959). *Man's search for meaning*. Beacon Press.

Freud, A. (1936). *The ego and the mechanisms of defence.* International Universities Press.

Freud, S. (1894). The neuro-psychoses of defence. In J. Strachey (Ed. & Trans.), *The standard edition of the complete psychological works of Sigmund Freud* (Vol. 3, pp. 41–61). Hogarth Press.

Gardner, H. (1983). *Frames of mind: The theory of multiple intelligences*. Basic Books.

Gardner, H. (1999). *Intelligence reframed: Multiple intelligences for the 21st century*. Basic Books.

Gilbert, P. (2009). *The compassionate mind: A new approach to life's challenges*. Constable.

Glasser, W. (1998). *Choice theory: A new psychology of personal freedom*. HarperCollins.

Goleman, D. (1995). *Emotional intelligence: Why it matters more than IQ*. Bantam Books.

Hayes, S. C., Strosahl, K. D., & Wilson, K. G. (1999). *Acceptance and commitment therapy: An experiential approach to behavior change*. Guilford Press.

Heider, F. (1958). *The psychology of interpersonal relations*. Wiley.

Juran, J. M. (1951). *Quality control handbook*. McGraw-Hill.

Kelley, H. H. (1967). Attribution theory in social psychology. In D. Levine (Ed.), *Nebraska Symposium on Motivation* (Vol. 15, pp. 192–238). University of Nebraska Press.

Kernberg, O. F. (1975). *Borderline conditions and pathological narcissism*. Jason Aronson.

Linehan, M. M. (1993). *Cognitive-behavioral treatment of borderline personality disorder*. Guilford Press.

Linville, P. W. (1987). Self-complexity as a cognitive buffer against stress-related illness and depression. *Journal of Personality and Social Psychology, 52*(4), 663–676.

Low, G. R., & Hammett, R. D. (2024). *Transformative emotional intelligence: A positive career and life guide*. Emotional Intelligence Training and Research Institute.

Mayer, J. D., & Salovey, P. (1997). What is emotional intelligence? In P. Salovey & D. Sluyter (Eds.), *Emotional development and emotional intelligence: Educational implications* (pp. 3–31). Basic Books.

Meichenbaum, D. (1977). *Cognitive-behavior modification: An integrative approach*. Plenum Press.

Nelson, D. B., & Low, G. R. (2011). *Emotional intelligence: Achieving academic and career excellence in college and in life* (2nd ed.). Pearson Higher Education.

Nelson, D. B., Low, G. R., Hammett, R. D., & Sen, A. (2013). *Professional coaching: A transformative and research-based model*. Emotional Intelligence Learning Systems.

Nelson, D. B., Low, G. R., Nelson, K. W., & Hammett, R. D. (2015). *Teaching and learning excellence: Engaging self and others with emotional intelligence*. Emotional Intelligence Learning Systems.

Perls, F. (1969). *Gestalt therapy verbatim*. Real People Press.

Plutchik, R. (1979). A general psychoevolutionary theory of emotion. In R. Plutchik & H. Kellerman (Eds.), *Emotion: Theory, research, and experience* (Vol. 1, pp. 3–33). Academic Press.

Quality of Motivation Services International. (1989). *Quality of Motivation Questionnaire* [Assessment instrument]. Quality of Motivation Services International. https://www.qomsi.com

Rogers, C. R. (1961). *On becoming a person: A therapist's view of psychotherapy.* Houghton Mifflin.

Ruiz, D. M. (1997). *The four agreements: A practical guide to personal freedom.* Amber-Allen Publishing.

Ruiz, D. M., Jr. (2013). *The five levels of attachment: Toltec wisdom for the modern world.* Hierophant Publishing.

Salovey, P., & Mayer, J. D. (1990). Emotional intelligence. *Imagination, Cognition and Personality, 9*(3), 185–211.

Spranger, E. (1928). *Types of men: The psychology and ethics of personality* (P. J. W. Pigors, Trans.). Max Niemeyer Verlag. (Original work published 1914)

Target Training International. (n.d.). *TTI Success Insights TriMetrix* [Assessment instrument]. TTI Success Insights. https://www.ttisi.com

Target Training International. (2020). *TTI Success Insights Motivation Insights technical manual* (Version 1.0). TTI Success Insights.

Target Training International. (2021). *TTI Success Insights Style Insights technical manual* (Version 1.0).   TTI Success Insights.

Tolle, E. (1999). *The power of now: A guide to spiritual enlightenment*. Namaste Publishing.

Twain, M. (1894). *Pudd'nhead Wilson*. Charles L. Webster & Company.

Vaillant, G. E. (1977). *Adaptation to life*. Little, Brown.

Weiner, B. (1986). *An attributional theory of motivation and emotion*. Springer-Verlag.

About the Author

Glenn Short, LPC, is a Licensed Professional Counselor and Nationally Certified Counselor with over 25 years of experience in clinical mental health. As both a Professor of Practice at Sul Ross State University and a counselor, he has spent years exploring why intelligent people sabotage themselves despite knowing better. This has led him to develop the Ego Intelligence framework - a research-informed theory explaining how unconscious defensive patterns hijack our best capabilities.

Through Ego Intelligence, he offers counselors, students, and frustrated individuals a path to genuine transformation.

His mission is to help readers of all ages discover their authentic selves and practice intentional decision-making rooted in emotional intelligence. The hope is that we find awareness in the space between stimulus and response and fill it with Authentic Being.

Scan the QR Code to access our website or go to www.appliedalternatives.net